WOMAN AT THE DEVIL'S DOOR

WOMAN AT THE DEVIL'S DOOR

THE UNTOLD STORY OF
THE HAMPSTEAD MURDERESS

SARAH BETH HOPTON

INDIANA UNIVERSITY PRESS

This book is a publication of

Indiana University Press
Office of Scholarly Publishing
Herman B Wells Library 350
1320 East 10th Street
Bloomington, Indiana 47405 USA

iupress.indiana.edu

Woman at the Devil's Door: The Extraordinary True Story of Mary Pearcey and the Hampstead Murders, by Sarah Beth Hopton

First North American Edition, published by Indiana University Press, 2018
This edition is only for sale in North America, and was licensed from the original publisher, Mango Books, UK.

Cataloging information is available from the Library of Congress.

ISBN 978-0-253-03462-5 (paperback)
ISBN 978-0-253-03463-2 (ebook)

1 2 3 4 5 23 22 21 20 19 18

For my family, but especially Mimi,
who never tired of hearing my stories.
I sure miss telling them to you.

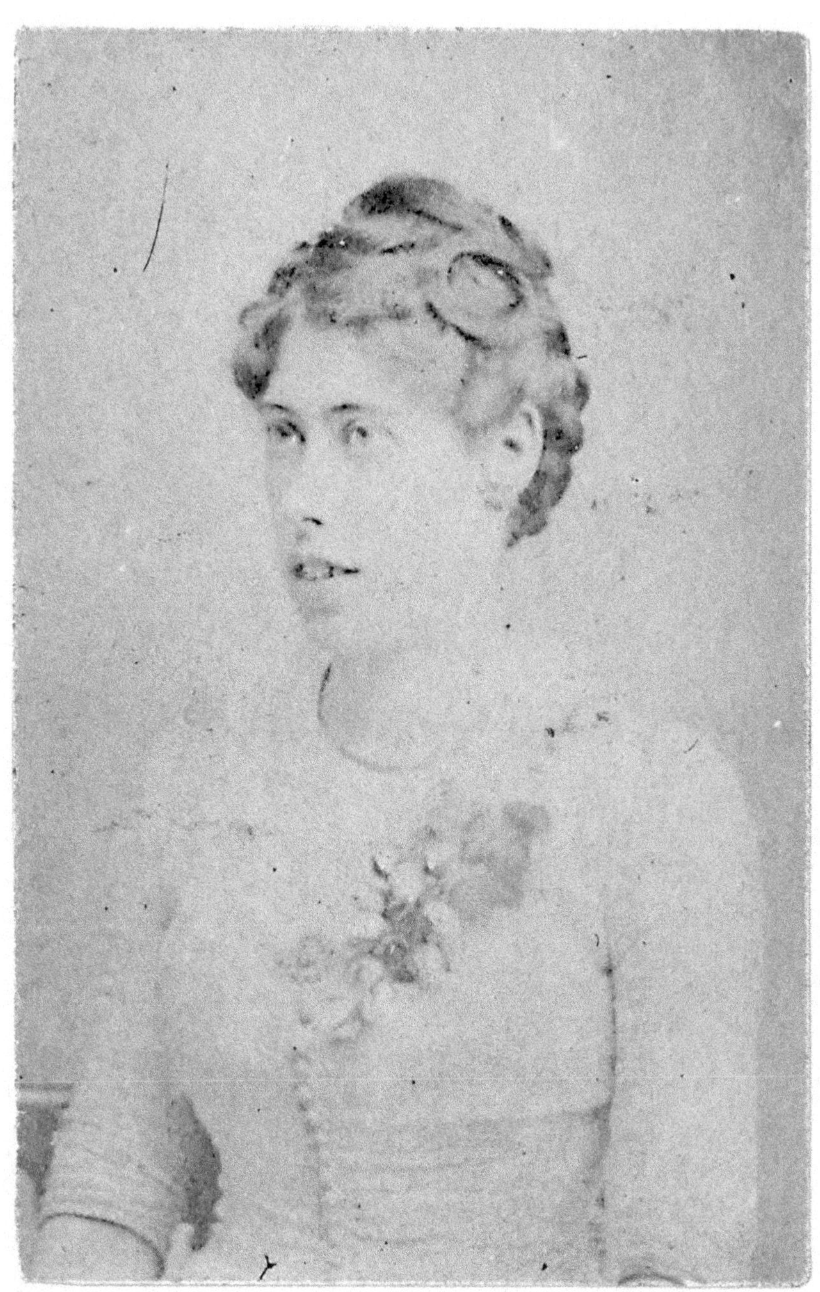

Courtesy the Mayor's Office for Policing and Crime

CONTENTS

② ACKNOWLEDGMENTS

This book took a decade to write. It went through countless revisions as it tried to figure out what it wanted to be. It was first conceived and written as fiction, then creative nonfiction, sold to a literary agency, then withdrawn, repurposed itself as something between creative nonfiction and biographical history and finally sold again. There were many people over the last decade who financially supported, edited, and counseled me off ledges, and to list you all here would require a separate book. But know that I know who you are and that your support was essential.

Having said that, there is one person who I would like to acknowledge by name. He stuck with me, this case, and the manuscript far longer than I had reason to expect, and contributed far more to its success than many know.

Thank you Mark Ripper for helping me tell the truth, well. I hope you're proud of our book.

SARAH BETH HOPTON
January 2017

WOMAN AT THE DEVIL'S DOOR

I see when men love women
They give them but a little of their lives,
But women when they love give everything.

~Oscar Wilde

THE CRIME

IT was Friday, October 24, 1890, just after seven o'clock, when 19-year-old clerk Somerled Macdonald was walking home toward 5 Belsize Park in London. He rarely took this route home - in fact, he hadn't taken this route for at least three months[1] - but he was in a hurry to go back out, and he knew of a shortcut through a middle-class suburb from Eton Avenue to Crossfield Road, where many of the houses were still under construction. The area was ill lit[2] and secluded, the nearest gas lamps several hundred yards apart, and with no moon, the night was unusually dark.[3]

When he reached the back of the late Mr McLeod's house at 28 Adamson Road,[4] he noticed a "dark object" lying at the side of the street, but couldn't tell what it was. When he walked past the figure, he recognised the outline of a woman, her face covered by what appeared to be a jacket.[5] He walked on, thinking she was probably drunk, but then he began to wonder if maybe she had fallen in a fit.[6] He circled back and then hastened to Swiss Cottage Railway Station to find a constable to help her.

He spotted Constable Arthur Gardiner walking along Upper

Avenue Road.[7] On arriving back at the body PC Gardiner checked the woman's pulse; she had none. He lit a match by which to better see, and then drew back the brown, sleeveless cardigan that covered her face, illuminating a horror beneath.[8] The woman's face was blood-smeared and her throat was cut "ear to ear."[9] Gardiner blew his whistle stridently.[10]

Somerled Macdonald went to fetch a doctor he knew in Belsize Park. At the same time, medical student Arthur Claude Fox, who lived nearby, happened upon the scene and offered to assist. Shortly thereafter, Macdonald returned with Dr Arthur Wells, an ophthalmic and aural surgeon, and Wells went right to work. He found a bare patch of skin on the woman's legs and arms and tested her temperature with his hand; her legs were still warm, and her arms not quite cold. Dr Wells believed the woman was only recently dead, perhaps not more than an hour so, but it was impossible to be more specific than that, as her clothing may have kept her body warmer longer.[11]

Constables John Stalker and Frederick Algar had heard Gardiner's distress whistle and answered, so that now there was a small crowd forming around the tree where the dead woman lay. Gardiner sent word to Inspector Wright, who was on duty at Hampstead police station, and requested he come at once with an ambulance.[12]

By 8.30pm - an hour and a half after the body was found - S Division's Inspector Thomas Wright, a veteran detective who'd joined the Metropolitan Police more than a decade previously, had arrived with officers in tow wheeling an ambulance.

Wright studied the body closely. The woman's head lay toward the road, her feet toward a hoarding which fenced a building site. As Wright later described the woman, her right leg was perfectly straight, and her left leg was drawn under her body, bent up and at an angle. Her right arm was extended, and her hand clenched; her left arm drawn up above her shoulder.[13] Wright and Gardiner rummaged through her clothes, but found little that could help. The woman was bare of most effects except a handkerchief stuffed deep into a pocket,[14] a metal brooch - missing one of its stones - and, on the collar of her jacket, a pearl stud set on a metal shaft.[15]

While Wright continued to analyse the body's unnatural position, his colleagues searched the area. Rather remarkably, Sergeant William Brown spotted blood no more than the size of a five-shilling piece on a pile of bricks.[16] This was remarkable because there was a conspicuous absence of blood altogether, and the light was very bad, making it difficult to see. Near these bricks Brown also found a small brass nut - from what he couldn't say - but it too was speckled with blood and so he pocketed the nut to study later.

By now, the press had arrived at Crossfield Road. They prowled for scoops and glimpses of the mutilated corpse to pencil in their sketchbooks, but were probably kept from seeing the body, as a sketch of the place where the body was found appeared in *Lloyd's Weekly Newspaper* two days later, but showed only the trees and the hoarding near which the victim was found, but not the victim.[17]

Rumour swirled. A cabman told the Swiss Cottage stationmaster, Mr Smith, that he was hailed around 7.00pm by a well-dressed man who told him to drive to Chalk Farm station as quickly as possible, and that he would give him double fare. The man paid as promised, his fare already in hand as they pulled to the station entrance.[18] This lead was reported in several newspapers, but nothing came of it. The earliest editions covering the crime also reported the rumour that those who saw the body thought they recognised the victim as a local prostitute,[19] yet constables who had patrolled the neighbourhood for years and were later paraded in front of the corpse said they didn't recognise her at all. Another dead end.[20]

With "great care,"[21] the victim's body was removed to the Hampstead Hill police station, and later to the Hampstead mortuary, where Dr Wells, Mr Fox and Dr Herbert Cooper, the divisional surgeon, made an external examination and found her injuries to be of a "most brutal character."[22] The woman's windpipe and spinal column had been divided, nearly separating her head from her body. She suffered a compound comminuted fracture to the skull, which meant that she'd been hit so hard with some object that shards of skull had splintered into her brain. Her hands, knuckles and body were scratched and gashed, cut with some sharp object, in some places quite deep. Doctors found a small bloodstain over her right hip and a bruise above her right ankle.

The kinds of wounds found on the victim's body suggested police should look for a "heavy, pointed"[23] murder weapon near the scene. The *Pall Mall Gazette* proposed a pickaxe.[24] Other suggested weapons included a hatchet, hammer and a razor, but the only potential weapon actually found at the scene that Friday night was a brick taken from the garden of a nearby house. It was heavy enough to have crushed the victim's skull, and appeared to have blood and hair on it, but like the story of the man who hailed the cab, the brick eventually proved to be irrelevant.

Meanwhile, two-and-a-half miles from Crossfield Road, PC 434S John Roser walked his beat in Hamilton Terrace, a firmly upper-middle-class neighbourhood of Gothic semi-detached villas. He'd been on the clock for less than an hour when, at half past 10,[25] he noticed an abandoned bassinette perambulator, or what mothers the country over called a 'pram,' standing against the garden wall of No. 35, a brown skin rug draped over the hood.

He went over to look at it, holding his lantern near. Turning up the edge of the rug, Roser discovered that the underside was lined with red cloth. He tugged the rug off the perambulator; the handle was broken. The pram looked wet, but it hadn't rained. Even though the light was dim, Roser was sure he saw blood. As S Division was abuzz with the news of the murdered woman at Crossfield Road, Roser undoubtedly heard about the crime when he came on duty that night. He probably made the connection quite quickly: this might be the vehicle in which the murdered woman's body had been conveyed. He threw the rug back over the pram and pushed it toward the police station.

Inspector John Holland was the senior officer on duty at the station that night. He saw Roser wheel in the curious object and went to look at it. In some approximation of an evidence room, away from the rowdiness of the station lobby and holding cells, the two officers studied the pram, which now could be seen to be very clearly soaked with blood. Smartly, Holland saved a "teaspoon" of it for later examination.[26] Like a Matryoshka doll, they pulled bloody objects from the pram, one more bizarre than the next: a waterproof apron, the steel part of the pram's handle, black hairs which looked human, a piece of string, and a piece of candy, still wrapped in paper, speckled with blood.[27] The brass nut Sergeant Brown pocketed at the scene earlier that night would turn out to be the very piece of evidence that definitively connected the body to the pram. Later, when he produced the nut and attempted to affix it back to the carriage, it fit exactly.[28]

Lacking any hard leads, the victim's description was telegraphed to all police stations in the district. Inspector Bannister enlisted the press's help too, hoping a family member might read the description of the woman's body or the clothes she wore and come forward to identify her.[29] The woman was described as about 30-years-old with dark hair and complexion, and blue eyes. She stood approximately 5ft 6in tall[30] and wore an imitation astrakhan jacket, black cashmere dress, red and yellow striped petticoats, blue woollen stockings with suspenders and white linen drawers - the initials 'P.H.' embroidered thereon. The collar of her dress was fastened with a metal brooch set with stones, one of which was missing, and the manner of her undergarments suggested she might have been nursing a child.[31]

In a separate interview with reporters conducted that night, Dr Wells, the first medical practitioner on the scene, described the manner of the woman's terrible death. He said the blow to her head would have been enough to kill her, which made the cut to her throat rather curious and quite unnecessary. More curious still was the cleanness of the cut; whoever killed her took his time, the doctor told reporters, as the cut appeared to have been made "very leisurely."[32]

The early edition of the *Pall Mall Gazette* reported that police were looking for a man "aged forty, nearly six feet high, with a dark moustache, and wearing a light suit and a peak cap," who had been loitering in the vicinity of the scene of the murder several nights in a row.[33] This description was strikingly similar to that given by

Thomas Ede of a suspicious-looking man he thought might have been the serial killer Jack the Ripper. Ede's man was described as 5ft 8in tall, about 35-years-old with a dark moustache and whiskers. He wore a double-peaked cap, dark brown jacket, a pair of overalls and dark trousers.[34] Regrettably, both descriptions were too generic to prove helpful to either case, but the *Pall Mall Gazette*'s description probably served to strengthen the suspicion that the woman was the latest Ripper victim.

Back at the crime scene, a pressman from *Lloyd's Weekly Newspaper* approached Inspector Thomas Bannister for a comment. Bannister, who had now taken charge of the case, stood alongside two plain-clothed officers.

"Will you kindly give me some details?" the reporter asked. "Of course I mean anything you do not mind the public knowing."[35]

"It was found about a half an hour after the body, and may form an important clue,"[36] Bannister said, speaking of the pram. Finding the pram must have bolstered Bannister's belief that they were closing in on their man, for, throughout the entire interview, the reporter noted that he smiled wryly, though reporters of the day were known to add such little details for colour and interest, even if they weren't true.

Bannister described the pram as hooded, painted dark blue and "picked out" with yellow, the wicker portion being painted dark brown. The handle was broken and had been found in the bottom of the carriage along with the brown goatskin rug lined with a scarlet-coloured cloth, which was saturated with blood. The Inspector thought that the butterscotch found in the bottom of the carriage had been recently purchased since it remained wrapped, and the presence of a sweet suggested that a child had lately occupied the pram. They'd also found a hair, Bannister said, and he felt certain it belonged to the victim discovered at Crossfield Road, as he had personally compared a strand of it to strands from the dead woman's head and they seemed to match.

"Now what is your theory?" the reporter asked.

Bannister hesitated, perhaps because he did not have enough

information to fully commit to a theory, or perhaps - as he told the reporter - because police had not yet identified the victim, and thus had not yet notified her family.

"Well I must leave for you to decide whether she was murdered in the street or not," Bannister said. If she'd been killed outside somewhere then surely she'd have a latchkey or money on her person, but none was found. He suspected she'd been killed in a nearby house, which is why he'd sent his officers to search every last one in the area. Then, Bannister concluded, the murderer conveyed the dead body in the pram to the spot where she was dumped.

"One thing is absolutely clear," Bannister said, "it would be impossible for anyone to take the body of a woman very far in such a small conveyance," but to dispose of the body in the pram would be easy enough. "For, supposing he entered the road from the Avenue. He would pass along this pathway, and in this dark spot would tip it up, the body would roll out just in the position in which it was found, and the man would continue his walk with the perambulator," he said.

"But doesn't it strike you that a man wheeling a perambulator would be noticed?" the reporter asked.

Bannister hoped so. "Yes, that is why I am telling you this, as I desire the public be made aware that we want to find out whether any man was seen wheeling one between seven and eight on Friday night," he said.

"Do you think a woman could have wheeled the body to where it was found?" the reporter asked.

"I don't think it likely," Bannister said. "If she did she could not wheel it far."

He admitted, however, that he found it strange the murderer dumped the body where he did, but then wheeled the pram elsewhere when he could have just as easily - and at far less risk - abandoned the pram with the body still inside in a darker spot on the walkway, walking off into the night unnoticed.

"Is there any feature of the case which would connect it with the so-called 'Jack the Ripper' murders?" the reporter asked.

"None," Bannister said conclusively. "Though very cleverly planned, it is quite distinct."[37]

Bannister's confidence was probably the result of a conversation with Chief Inspector Donald Swanson, the lead investigator into the Whitechapel murders, who had been to the scene already, and had decided - and probably told Inspector Bannister - this crime wasn't related to the unsolved Ripper murders. And, he was right. Everything about it was different. Still, Swanson's presence, coupled with the shocking manner in which the woman was murdered, and rumours that the victim was a prostitute, caused many papers to speculate the Ripper was at work again. In fact, most of the major dailies ran some version of the following in their early edition:

"In some points the murder seems to resemble [says the Central News] Jack the Ripper's handiwork - the terrible gash which almost beheaded the body having evidently been inflicted from behind."[38]

That the Ripper *might* be at work again brought other notable officers to the scene too. Lt. Colonel Bolton James Monsell, a chief constable with the Metropolitan Police, had been to the scene, had seen the woman's corpse, and agreed with Swanson: the murdered woman found at Crossfield was definitely *not* a Ripper victim.[39]

But it was too late. News that the Ripper might be murdering again had telegraphed through London so lightning-quick that the superintendent on duty at Scotland Yard endured an exhausting night of answering public inquiries and calming public angst.[40] To dispel the panic, Scotland Yard put all available resources into the case, sparing no one, not even Chief Constable Melville Macnaghten, who had just returned from a month's holiday the day before.

At 4.00am the police bell clanged in Macnaghten's home. He rushed downstairs knowing something "out of the common was on the carpet."[41] A constable handed him a telegram bearing the details of the horrible crime, but as nothing could be done at that early hour, or in the dark, he telegraphed back that he would meet the Inspector heading the investigation at first light.

At the same time, a Central News correspondent following the case managed to get into the "dismal little mortuary opposite the workhouse at New End,"[42] to which the victim's body had been removed. After studying the wounds, the correspondent wrote that only once before had he seen "so dreadful a sight."[43] The woman's head was only attached to her body by the skin at the back of the neck and her wounds, which were of a "fearful character," suggested the murderer had killed with an "excess of hellish rage."[44]

Superintendent Beard, Chief Inspector Cole, Inspectors Collis and Wright, and Detective Inspector Bannister "worked with energy" through the night to find the real killer and quash media speculation.[45] Every coffee house, lodging house and similar places were searched thoroughly, but at midnight police were no closer to naming the victim, or her murderer.[46] At dawn, Inspector Collis[47] and a staff of detectives continued to search the empty houses and adjoining gardens within a quarter-mile radius of the crime scene, but frustratingly turned up no new clues. As dawn turned to morning and the police went home to their beds weary, a single guard was appointed to stand over a board marking the spot where police had found the poor creature, her head nearly severed from her body.[48]

Just after 6 o'clock that Saturday morning, October 25, 1890, Frank Hogg woke alone. He was not terribly concerned by his wife's absence from their bed. They had discussed that if her father's poor health worsened she would go to Rickmansworth to be with him.[49] Frank was a 31-year-old furniture porter employed by his older brother Frederick, who owned the F.H. Hogg removal company on the border of Camden and Kentish Town.

Frank dressed, walked down the stairs of 141 Prince of Wales Road, and into the brisk morning, heading toward Priory Mews to feed and water the company's horses. At half past eight, he had finished with the horses and then stopped by his brother's house nearby.

During a conversation with his brother he casually remarked, "I have lost the missus and little one."

"What, gone away?" his brother replied.

"Yes."

"Don't you know where she has gone to?"

"I expect to Chorleywood, because her father is so ill,"[50] Frank said, and then he went home.

Frank half-expected a telegram to be waiting for him when he got back home, but there wasn't one. He saw his landlady in the kitchen, and they talked, but he did not mention his wife's absence.[51] His sister and mother came up to the kitchen soon after and he asked his sister whether she'd seen his wife, Phoebe, and their baby Phoebe Hanslope[52] Hogg,[53] nicknamed and usually called 'Tiggie'.[54] He asked his mother if his wife had sent a telegram.

"No," old Mrs Hogg said. "Can you understand it?"

Frank reasoned that Phoebe probably couldn't send word to him until the telegraph office opened at 8 o'clock.[55] His sister Clara said she had last seen her sister-in-law and the baby on the stairs around three o'clock the afternoon before. They were getting ready to go out, but she didn't know where they were going.

Reports later confirmed that Phoebe went and bought sweets at Mrs Mulcaster's shop on Great College Street, and possibly grapes at the grocer's.[56] But, it was not unusual for Phoebe Hogg to disappear in the middle of the day without telling Clara or old Mrs Hogg where she was going. She was a private - some said secretive - woman who avoided speaking to her in-laws if she could.[57] But Clara must have somewhat carefully watched Phoebe from the window because she later recalled that Phoebe was wearing her wedding ring and carried a purse.[58]

After breakfast, Frank's feeling about his wife's prolonged absence shifted from mild unease to earnest concern,[59] and the family began to make more urgent plans to confirm she was in Chorleywood. Frank grabbed his things and headed for the train station. It would take him roughly half an hour by train to get to Rickmansworth. As he left, he told his sister to go and see if Phoebe had visited a family friend named Mrs Pearcey. Mrs Pearcey had said something strange to him just a few days before about his wife secretly visiting her. He was doubtful she was there, but perhaps she knew something. Clara agreed.

The Hoggs had known Mrs Pearcey for many years, and Clara particularly considered her a friend, ever helpful in times of crisis.[60] Earlier that year, in fact, Mrs Pearcey had nursed her sister-in-law, Phoebe, back to health after what turned out to be a uterine ulcer incapacitated her for weeks.[61] According to the Hogg's landlady, Phoebe had been "dangerously ill,"[62] but after Mrs Pearcey nursed her, she was better, and Phoebe was "much attached" to the woman she affectionately called by her family nickname, Nellie.[63]

It was only six minutes' walk to 2 Priory Street[64] where Mrs Pearcey lived, and Clara arrived at her flat just after 9 o'clock in the morning.

Mrs Pearcey opened the door to her friend and probably smiled, happy to see her friend, but Clara wasted no time with formality or nicety.

"Did she come here yesterday?" Clara asked, meaning Phoebe.

"No," Mrs Pearcey replied, perhaps a bit taken aback at Clara's directness.

"Did you see anything of her?" Clara pressed anxiously.

"No."

Clara went into the hallway and then one of the bedrooms, and explained that Phoebe was gone - the baby too - and they were all quite worried. She asked a third time if Phoebe had been there at all yesterday. Clara's nervousness must have rattled Mrs Pearcey, for she quickly changed her story.

"Well as you press me I will tell you. Phoebe wished me particularly not to say anything, and that is why I said 'No.' She did come round about five o'clock. She asked me to mind the baby a little while, and I refused. She also asked me to lend her some money. I could not lend her any, as I had only 1s 1½d in my purse. She could have had the shilling if she had liked."[65]

Far from exciting suspicion, this information seemed to give Clara a little hope. Someone had seen Phoebe after she left the house, so perhaps the family's worst fears were unfounded. She asked Mrs Pearcey to come with her to the Kentish Town railway station[66] to see if Phoebe had booked a pram and bought a ticket to Chorleywood, as she often did when she travelled with the baby to see her family. Before she could say yes, Mrs Pearcey heard someone come downstairs. She left Clara and went into the hall, closing the bedroom door behind her.

Mrs Pearcey talked with a man in the passage while Clara waited inside her rooms. Later, when questioned, Clara said she didn't recognise the man's voice, nor could she hear their conversation, but learned that Mrs Pearcey was talking to her neighbour, a Mr Butler. Mrs Pearcey had heard him going out and said she caught him in the hall to ask what time he thought he saw the pram in the hallway the night before, presumably to give this information to Clara. He said it must have been about ten minutes past six o'clock, and then he went out.[67] Mrs Pearcey went back inside, grabbed her hat and handkerchief, and she and Clara left together. A few minutes later the women overtook Mr Butler on the street, and they seemed to him to be in a great hurry.[68]

As the women turned onto Prince of Wales Road, Mrs Pearcey suggested she, alone, would go on to Kentish Town station to inquire about the pram. She told Clara to go back and wait for Frank, who would surely bring Phoebe back all right from Rickmansworth.[69] The women parted and Clara saw Mrs Pearcey step onto a tram headed for the station.[70] Half an hour later, Mrs Pearcey met Clara back at Prince of Wales Road with no word of the pram or Phoebe.

Fidgety with nervous energy, Clara walked into the hall for something when Mrs Barraud, her landlady, swooped in with the news.

"What a terrible murder this is at Hampstead!" she said. "They say Jack the Ripper has been about here."

"Good God!" exclaimed Clara.[71]

From the details Mrs Barraud could remember, Clara grew concerned. Could it be Phoebe? She asked for more details from her landlady, but she'd told her all she remembered. Clara went inside and relayed the story to Mrs Pearcey, and they decided they should try to find the report Mrs Barraud referenced and read the account for themselves. Mrs Pearcey volunteered to try to find the paper from which Mrs Barraud was reading, and went out. When she returned with a paper, she and Clara scavenged the broadsheet together until they found the article Mrs Barraud had read; the dreadful details were just as the landlady had said.

Mrs Pearcey offered to buy yet another newspaper so they could compare the details in each account,[72] but when she returned the second time, she said, "You read it. I can't,"[73] and handed the papers to Clara.

Clara read. Some accounts mentioned the pram, while others didn't, but when she read that police had found the initials "P.H." embroidered on the victim's linen undergarments, there was no doubt in anyone's mind that Phoebe was the woman found at Crossfield Road. Clara wanted to go to the mortuary immediately to identify her body, but Mrs Pearcey entreated her to stay a little longer and wait for Frank to return from Rickmansworth. She was sure he would have Phoebe with him. Clara conceded, but shortly thereafter exclaimed, "I cannot wait any longer. I must go and see."[74]

After the women had left for the mortuary, Frank returned, but with no news of Phoebe. His mother said, "Don't upset yourself, but look at that paper," referring to one of any number of those the girls had left behind.

He read the account, and from it felt sure his poor wife had been murdered.[75]

It took Clara and Mrs Pearcey a little less than half an hour to walk to the Hampstead police station, which was at the end of Rosslyn Hill Road. Sergeant Edward Nursey greeted them when they reached the counter. They explained they were there to identify the body of the dead woman found at Crossfield Road the night before. He fetched Inspector Bannister at once,[76] who received the women and then accompanied them to the mortuary. It was just after 11 o'clock.

As promised, Melville Macnaghten had arrived at the Hampstead mortuary early and had been updated on the details of the case. At 37, Macnaghten was almost a decade younger than Inspector Bannister, the lead investigator on the case. He had entered the Metropolitan Police force just over a year earlier as Assistant Chief Constable of the Criminal Investigation Department, and was relatively inexperienced in murder investigations, with neither military nor political experience - in fact, very little policing experience at all. But he was tall and prepossessing, and subordinates often described him as having "a military air,"[77] which, if it didn't quite qualify him for the post, perhaps made serving him in it a little easier.

The mortuary was appropriately gloomy and damp. Inspector Bannister, presumably, introduced Macnaghten to the women and explained who they were and why they were there. Then, the four of them proceeded to where the body was, but just as Inspector Bannister opened the door to usher Mrs Pearcey, Clara, and Macnaghten inside, he stopped, turned around, and told the women to steel themselves for what they were about to see.

Dr Thomas Bond, Divisional Surgeon for Scotland Yard, had only just arrived and had not yet begun his examination of the deceased when Clara and Mrs Pearcey entered. Presumably with a nod from Bannister, Dr Bond helped the women to the hip-high stone slab, atop which lay a mutilated corpse. A sheet covered most of the victim's body. Even so, Clara recognised Phoebe's clothes. Dr Bond drew down the sheet covering Phoebe's face, which had not yet been washed, so that Mrs Pearcey and Clara could get a better look.

"Oh that is not her!" Mrs Pearcey said directly.

It must have been a revolting sight. Phoebe's face was dirty and disfigured.

"I don't recognise her features," Clara said.

Dr Bond recovered the deceased with the sheet, and Bannister steered the women back into the hallway where he drilled, "Surely, if she is a relation, and you have been living together, you can form some reliable opinion as to whether she is the person."

"I am no relation," Mrs Pearcey volunteered, "I am only a friend."

"When did you last see her?" Bannister asked.

"I have not seen her for several days," Mrs Pearcey answered, the lie slipping quickly from her lips.

"She left home yesterday afternoon at three o'clock," Clara added, truthfully.[78]

Bannister took them back inside for a second look.

The mortuary photograph of Phoebe (see illustration section) shows the extent of the injuries to her face, which resulted in a patchwork of white and yellow splotches and dark purplish-green bruises around her forehead and cheeks. Her jet-black hair was matted with blood and dirt. Her eyes are closed, but it would have been difficult to tell their colour even if open, as a gray-blue film would have already settled over them. Her mouth is slightly open, hinged in a strange way because of the terrific wound in her throat.[79]

For Clara, Phoebe's disfigurement was both horrifying and strangely hypnotic. She later described the scene at the mortuary as a "dreadful, shocking sight," but the longer she stood gazing at Phoebe's corpse, trying to make sense of the sight before her, the more agitated Mrs Pearcey became.[80]

Clara reached out her hand to touch Phoebe, but Mrs Pearcey pulled her back.

"Oh, don't touch her!" she cried.

"Don't drag me!" Clara barked.

Bannister asked Dr Bond to wash the blood and dirt from the victim's face, telling the women to turn their heads while he did so.[81] Mrs Pearcey became "hysterical" and tugged at Clara's arm, insisting the woman on the slab wasn't Phoebe,[82] but Clara stood steady. When Dr Bond finished wiping the victim's face as clean as he could get it, Inspector Bannister asked Clara to look at the woman again.

Clara turned her head. "Yes, that's her," she said.

She reached out again to tenderly touch Phoebe's exposed hand.

"Oh don't touch it!" Mary said again, trying to drag Clara away once more.

"You go out!" Clara ordered. "Don't drag me. It is her."

"Don't drag her," Bannister said, clearly annoyed. "She can bear it if you leave her alone."[83]

Once outside, Mrs Pearcey calmed down, but her reaction to the body excited suspicion among the detectives present.[84] Macnaghten would write later in his memoirs that he believed it might have been the last time he nabbed a suspect through the "ordeal by touch,"[85] though this was likely a bit of creative invention on his part. Macnaghten was an unreliable witness, later misremembering, dramatizing, and even fabricating several facts related to the Hampstead murders in his memoirs *Days of My Years*.[86]

While Mrs Pearcey's behavior may have tickled police intuition, Clara later said she hadn't an inkling that her friend may have been involved in the crime, not even after her strange reaction at the mortuary. In fact, Clara insisted she and Mrs Pearcey persevere in their own investigation. There was, after all, the matter of the baby, who had not yet been found and, amazingly, Mrs Pearcey agreed. Inspector Bannister, happy to keep the women close to the investigation so he could watch them from a distance, sent the women with Sergeant Edward Nursey to Portland Town police station to identify the pram found the night before.

Once at the station, Clara positively identified the pram; it belonged to her sister-in-law. She also confirmed that baby Tiggie enjoyed sucking on butterscotch, just like the one found unwrapped in the pram. She didn't know who the rug and apron belonged to, but they were not hers, and they were not Phoebe's. Mrs Pearcey said nothing.

While the women were at the Portland Town police station, Inspector Bannister, Superintendent Beard and Macnaghten headed for Prince of Wales Road where they intended to interview Frank Hogg and his mother, Maria Hogg. According to Macnaghten, they had only walked a few paces toward Frank's house, when a young woman approached and begged to speak with Macnaghten alone. He later wrote that he sent Bannister and Beard on to Prince of Wales Road, while he and the girl - a Miss Elizabeth Styles - ducked into a "dripping alley."[87] The girl said she suspected she knew who'd murdered her aunt,[88] and Macnaghten listened to a most interesting tale of love, betrayal and murder, as raindrops thumped against the shoulders of his wool coat.[89]

When Clara, Mrs Pearcey and their police detail arrived back at 141 Prince of Wales Road, Inspector Bannister, Macnaghten and Superintendent Beard were waiting in the parlour. Old Mrs Hogg and Frank were there too. Based on Clara's identification of the body and the pram, the police could now confirm and tell the Hoggs what all had come to suspect: the woman found butchered at Crossfield Road was Phoebe Hogg. As the news sunk in, Bannister organised a search of the house. He took the kitchen, leaving Macnaghten and Beard to watch and talk with a stunned Frank Hogg and the others.

As the search wore on, Superintendent Beard struck up a conversation with Old Mrs Hogg to pass the time. She was apparently "cheery and chatty,"[90] despite the gravity of the officers' visit. The Chief Constable addressed her as "Mother,"[91] presumably to build rapport with her, which delighted her so much that she offered to share some of her port wine with him as they talked.

"I made it a rule in India," Macnaghten said, "never to drink until the sun had set."

Old Mrs Hogg obliged, and, according to Macnaghten anyway, the bottle of "fine old fruity" stayed corked.[92]

What they talked about wasn't recorded, which means it probably didn't amount to much. Neither did the search. In fact, the inspectors who searched 141 Prince of Wales Road ultimately found nothing that would lead them to suspect that anyone there - the Hoggs, that is - had anything to do with Phoebe Hogg's death.[93] As a last measure, however, and driven largely by protocol, Inspector Bannister asked to search Frank Hogg's person. Hogg stood as the inspector patted him down. Bannister found a key and asked to whom it belonged. It was the latchkey to 2 Priory Street, Hogg reluctantly admitted, where Mrs Pearcey lived. Bannister must have wondered, and possibly even asked, why Frank Hogg would have a private latchkey to another woman's house? Old Mrs Hogg and Clara must have wondered the same.

If they weren't suspects before, both Frank and Mrs Pearcey

certainly were now, and Inspector Bannister wished to question Frank, Clara and Mrs Pearcey at the station at once.

Back at the mortuary, Dr Thomas Bond continued with his examination of Phoebe's body. Bond was a renowned surgeon who had been involved in several infamous cases, most recently the Thames Torso Murders.[94] In 1873 he won a post at Westminster Hospital, and over the course of his career developed a reputation as an enthusiastic lecturer on forensic medicine.

Though the Thames Torso Murders were his most recent case of acclaim, Bond had also conducted or assisted in the autopsies of Mary Jane Kelly, Rose Mylett and Alice McKenzie, all of whom were connected - even if only peripherally - to the Ripper murders.[95] From clinical work conducted in the post-mortem room and a good deal of paperwork sifted through at his office, Bond opined that the Ripper - whomever he was - lacked the scientific and anatomical knowledge of a surgeon or a butcher, contradicting a prevalent and persistent theory about the Ripper's occupation. Bond's initial report was lost to the public for many years, however, and his views on the anatomical knowledge of the killer were therefore unknown and had little appreciable impact on popular opinions or alternative theories about the Ripper's identity and occupation for some time. But eventually his conclusions were made public in 1988, and he was thereafter referred to as the father of modern profiling.[96]

In addition to being experienced, Bond was well liked, especially among the press, who wrote that his evidence was always clear.[97] The press and general public were increasingly interested in such clear details too, since forensic science and psychology were popular and novel subjects. As a medical man, Bond was lucky to work at the time and in the place he did. He worked in a nascent field during the age of wonder, when advances in science, medicine, and criminology stirred the imagination and excited the Victorian penchant of playing amateur scientist, doctor, or sleuth.

In 1813, Mathieu Orfila published a study that launched the field of toxicology. By 1835, Ludwig Teichmann, a Polish scientist, had developed a microscopic crystal test for haemoglobin that enabled surgeons to determine the presence of blood in dried stains. One year later, the eminent Scottish chemist James Marsh developed a test for arsenic, which was used for the first time in the celebrated LaFarge poisoning case of 1840. And by the 1880s Major Llewellyn William Atcherley had developed the idea of 'modus operandi', or method of operation, wherein information from different crime scenes was used to establish a pattern of behavior in the committal of a crime.[98] By and large, however, Victorian forensics played little actual role in solving most cases, even though formal training in forensic medicine existed at the time.

It wasn't that forensics was unimportant to criminology, but that scientific practice simply hadn't caught up to the theory or popular dramatizations of it. For example, the biggest breakthrough in crime detection - fingerprinting - was, in 1890, still two years away from development, and more than ten years away from becoming standard police procedure. Still, medical jurists were an important part of investigations, though "the many-sided subject" of forensic medicine had no single starting point, and thus was a rather difficult endeavour, even among the best of medical jurists like Bond.[99] As the Director of Criminal Investigation for Scotland Yard, Sir Howard Vincent said of this kind of work, "It is often very easy to find out the author of an offence, but it is quite another matter to be able to prove the legal guilt of the delinquent by legal means."[100]

Forensic techniques were popularised by writers such as Dickens and Sir Arthur Conan Doyle, who created the best-known alienist-detective in his beloved stories of Sherlock Holmes. Doyle's skills of detection may not have been as sharp in real life as his alter ego's, but he proposed an interesting theory about the most famous crime of his day. Doyle offered that Jack the Ripper may have disguised himself as a woman, or may have actually been a woman. This would have made it easier to access and gain the trust of the women murdered, he supposed.[101]

Though Dr Bond surely had heard the rumours that Jack the

Ripper was again at work, it's impossible to know whether he began the autopsy with the Ripper in mind. His duty that day was not to propose potential murderers, but to determine if the victim had, in fact, been murdered. Bond's responsibility was to observe and record the condition of the body before the post-mortem examination, to see if her corpse could offer clues about the crimes committed against it. It was not, as the stories of Sherlock Holmes would suggest, 'elementary'. On the contrary, the real-life practice of such dark arts was difficult and depressing,[102] and the truth was that the insights Bond tendered the police were no more or less available to him than other doctors. Nevertheless, Bond began his examination of Phoebe's body on Saturday afternoon, less than twenty-four hours after she had been found.

Dr Bond delicately tipped Phoebe's head back to measure the depth of the wound at her throat. The cut to her neck divided the spinal column such that her head held on by but a few muscles and some skin; it appeared to him that someone had tried to sever her head entirely but lost strength, or heart. Bond was also of the opinion that the neck was cut while she was still alive or only minutes dead, as the skin and muscles around the vertebral column were retracted from the cut, which only happened when a body was still warm from circulating blood.

According to Dr Bond, Phoebe suffered a blow to her head that broke the scalp open and fractured her skull in several places. Some of her skull had splintered into her brain. He suspected that she was struck with an oblong weapon which came down on her skull with "considerable violence." He found pooled blood under the scalp, and there the wound had bled so profusely that Phoebe's black hair was tangled and matted in clumps, through which it was nearly impossible to pull a comb. Her forearm was also cut, and from the depth and raggedness of the cut, Bond suspected it had been made by glass. Clearly, the wounds Phoebe Hogg suffered were too traumatic to have been self-inflicted. It didn't take a Sherlock Holmes to deduce Phoebe Hogg had indeed been murdered.

Back at the police station, Inspector Bannister questioned Clara,

Frank and Mrs Pearcey in a sequence of interviews carried out in individual rooms, which dragged into an already protracted afternoon. During the interviews more details surfaced, such as what Phoebe Hogg carried the day before her death, and how baby Tiggie had been dressed, and these were reported in the following day's newspapers. Since Clara was the only person who said she saw Phoebe and Tiggie leave the house on Friday afternoon, the information presumably came from her. Clara said that when Phoebe left on Friday she wore a "nearly new" 18-carat gold wedding band and carried a latchkey in an old Russian-leather expandable purse. As the clasp was broken, she held it together with an "india rubber band."[103] She carried in her purse 2 shillings and probably an address card, Clara said. How Clara knew what was in the purse suggests either she had a habit of riffling through Phoebe's things, or Phoebe kept these items in her purse as a matter of standard practice.

Bannister then went to another room to interview Mrs Pearcey. As the interview with Mrs Pearcey concluded, Inspector Bannister said, "I think it desirable to search your lodging. I suppose you have no objection?"

"Oh no, not the slightest," Mrs Pearcey replied, handing him her set of keys.

Bannister's decision to search her rooms could have been in consequence of his suspicion of her, piqued by her unusual behaviour at the mortuary, or it could have been because of what Phoebe's niece Lizzie Styles had told him in a separate interview, as she had been called to the station by this point too. His decision might have as well been simply a matter of procedure, for police hadn't found the crime scene yet despite having searched all the houses along Crossfield Road, both occupied and vacant. And, since Inspector Bannister had searched Frank Hogg's house, he should probably search the houses of those closest to the family too. Though he didn't know the exact relationship between Frank Hogg and Mrs Pearcey yet, clearly, they were close enough that Frank held a key to her rooms.

Bannister called Police Sergeant Edward Nursey and Detective Sergeant Edward Parsons into the interrogation room, gave them instructions, and handed them the keys to Mrs Pearcey's flat. As he did so, Mrs Pearcey jumped up, saying, "I should like to go with them because I don't think they'll be able to get in."[104]

"I was going to suggest to you that you could go if you liked," Bannister replied coolly.

About half an hour later, at roughly 3 o'clock on Saturday, October 25, Nursey, Parsons and Mrs Pearcey arrived at 2 Priory Street. Mrs Pearcey opened the street door with one of her keys and saw the two policemen into the front parlour as unconcernedly as if she had invited them to tea. Sergeant Nursey gave a cursory look about the place, but found nothing immediately out of order.

The rooms at 2 Priory Street were decorated in typical Victorian style. The walls of the parlour were covered with flower-patterned wallpaper. There was a sewing machine against one wall and an upright piano against another. Nursey went to the adjoining room, which was used as a bedroom. Mrs Pearcey unlocked the door and let him inside. There was a bed, a dresser, and a dress cabinet. The room was tidy, and nothing suggested he should look harder, so he asked to be let into the kitchen.

The kitchen was dark, a green shade pulled down over the window. Nursey walked over to the window and pulled the blind to one side in order to let some light into the room, noticing that two panes of glass were shattered, with glass shards on the ground outside.

"I was trying to catch some mice," Mrs Pearcey said, "and broke them."[105]

Mrs Pearcey went back into the parlour and sat down.

Nursey stayed in the kitchen. He let go of the blind and tugged at the cord, hoping to get a better look with the blind fully raised and more light in the room, but the cord was broken, and the blind jammed. In the streaming, filtered light of late afternoon however, he could see what looked like droplets of blood on the glass. His eyes now adjusted to the light, he looked around; blood everywhere. There were splashes and splatters and trails of blood on the ceiling and walls, the broken window, and the hearthrug was saturated with paraffin, a commonly prescribed chemical to lift heavy stains.

Nursey walked back into the parlour.

"I believe you saw her yesterday," he said.

"I know," she said, "I should have told you before this. She called about six o'clock and asked me to take care of the child, and wanted some money, but she did not come inside. I told Clara about it, and she said I had better not say anything about it, as it would seem a disgrace to ask for money."[106]

Nursey didn't answer. But, if what Clara said was true - that Phoebe left with at least two shillings in her purse the day she died - then why would she need to borrow more money?

Nursey left Mrs Pearcey with Detective Sergeant Parsons in the parlour, and went to telegraph Inspector Bannister. Alone in Parsons' presence, Mrs Pearcey nattered on about "poor dear dead Phoebe," whom she loved so much, and the dear baby who was just beginning to "prattle, oh, so prettily."[107] Then she sat down to the piano and began to play popular tunes, rather well, the constable later told a reporter for the *Sheffield Evening Telegraph*.[108]

She stopped and turned to Parsons, "I have not told a lie," she said, referencing Nursey's accusation that he thought she had seen Phoebe the day before. She told Parsons the same weakly constructed tale: that Phoebe had come by around 6.00pm and asked to borrow money. "I told her I could not lend her the money, as I had none, and could not mind the child, as I was going out. I told Clara of this, but she advised me to say nothing about it, as it would be such a disgrace if people thought Frank kept her short of money."[109]

Later, she volunteered to further explain the blood in the kitchen. "I do not enjoy very good health. On Thursday night when I came home my nose bled violently."[110]

Nursey returned at last, with Inspector Bannister only a few minutes behind him, having received the telegram to come to Priory Street at once. When Bannister arrived, Mrs Pearcey was sitting in an armchair. Inspector Bannister walked through the house and straight into the kitchen.

The kitchen was small, but adequate. There was a fireplace, and to the left a built-in cabinet filled with tableware. A dress stand was near the fireplace. There was a table and two chairs. Above the fireplace, on a ledge, were a teapot, a vase and several other kitchen utensils. A large cabinet was filled with cutlery. Bannister took in the room; he saw the broken glass, the ceiling and walls "bespattered" with blood, the paraffin-stained rug, and the two shattered windowpanes. He moved toward the fireplace and picked up a poker. The end of it was oblong. By now, Dr Bond would have shared with Inspector Bannister his initial thoughts about the murder weapon and manner of death. The poker surely triggered Bannister's memory of Bond telling him the murder weapon would be something that could strike a considerable blow, the end of which would have an oblong shape to it.

Bannister patrolled the kitchen thinking about the poker. Surely such a poker could have shattered the window if drawn back in a fight; could have streaked the walls and spotted the ceiling when plucked from a bloody wound and then plunged down into a limp body. Indeed, when he looked closely into the crevices of the poker, he found blood at the join where the handle affixed; tiny hairs sprouted from the fissures. Bannister thoroughly searched the kitchen, looking inside every drawer and behind every object. He pulled out two large carving knives from a drawer in the kitchen dresser, one stained with blood.

When he had seen what he needed to in the kitchen, he moved to the bedroom. He pulled open the wardrobe, and fished out bonnet boxes from underneath the bed. He opened boxes and in one he found a card-case with a single card in it, the words "S.H. Hogg" printed thereon. Over the course of several searches, Inspector Bannister would find many strange and incriminating artifacts, including an unloaded revolver, bullets that fit the revolver, copies of love letters sent to Frank Hogg, burned pages of novelettes, buttons in the fire grate, and sharp knives tucked behind a tea tray.

Bannister went back to search the kitchen again. On his second pass, he found a black skirt and an apron; both appeared to be bloodstained, and both seemed to have been washed, as if to get the bloodstains out. He went back into the front parlour wielding the bloodstained knives and poker. Mrs Pearcey was still sitting in the armchair. She looked at the knives and poker and began to whistle to herself. Bannister turned the items over to one of his sergeants and rummaged through Mrs Pearcey's purse. In it, he found ten shillings in silver, sixpence-halfpenny in bronze, and a duplicate receipt from a pawnshop with the name 'Ann Pearcey' scribbled on it. Though it was not uncommon for pawnbrokers to put any Christian name on it, 'Ann' happened to be her mother's middle name. Regardless of how she came into the money, she appeared to have far more than she claimed to have had when Phoebe asked to borrow some.

Bannister left Nursey and Parsons guarding Mrs Pearcey and mounted the stairs to interview her neighbours. It was now dusk, and most of the inhabitants of the house were home from work. Sarah Butler and her husband, in fact, were waiting for the detective on the second floor. Bannister also spoke with Elizabeth Crowhurst and her son, who lived on the third floor. They all told strange tales of Mrs Pearcey's comings and goings, of those who visited her, and of the unsettling events of the previous days and the night prior. When Bannister finished his interviews, he returned to the parlour downstairs. Mrs Pearcey was still whistling.

"I am going to arrest you for the wilful murder of Mrs Hogg last night," he said, "and also on suspicion of the wilful murder of the female child of Mrs Hogg."

Mrs Pearcey jumped out of the armchair.

"You can arrest me if you like," she said, somewhat dramatically. "I am quite willing to go with you, [but] I think you have made a great mistake."[111]

Despite Mrs Pearcey's bravado, Bannister was quite confident he had *not* made a mistake; the evidence in Mrs Pearcey's kitchen all but proved that to him. Though he didn't yet know if she was the architect or the assistant, he was certain she was involved in the murder of Phoebe Hogg. A cab was called to ferry them all back to the police station. Undoubtedly, the police presence would have stirred neighbourhood curiosity, and Mrs Pearcey was probably walked from her flat to the cab in front of gaping neighbours who, if they weren't in the street to watch, peered from behind their curtains.

Once inside the cab Mrs Pearcey asked, "Why do you charge me with this crime?"

"On account of the evidence," Bannister said, confidently.

"Well," she went on, "I would not do such a dreadful thing - I would not hurt anyone."[112]

It must have indeed struck Bannister as somewhat unbelievable that this pretty woman who sat in front of him in the cab, as it bumped and shouldered against street traffic, was capable of doing to another person what the injuries Phoebe Hogg endured indicated were done to her. The strength it would have taken to cut through a human vertebral column and then hoist 140 pounds of dead weight into a pram, and then push that pram *miles* across uneven cobblestone streets required a physicality Bannister doubted Mrs Pearcey had, even though others later described her as "strikingly muscular."[113] Bannister must have also wondered if the pram, which was not built to take the weight of a grown adult, could survive such a journey. As he studied her in the cab, the more logical deduction he must have arrived at was that Mrs Pearcey didn't act alone.[114]

The gaslights inside the Kentish Town police station hissed and the booking room glowed orange that Saturday night. Bannister followed standard police procedure as he read aloud the charge of "wilful murder of Phoebe Hogg and her child, Phoebe Hanslope Hogg." He remanded Mrs Pearcey into the care of Sarah Sawtell, a 36-year-old female police searcher and constable's wife, and told Mrs Pearcey to take off her gloves. When she did, Inspector Bannister noticed her hands were "very much scratched and torn about."[115]

Mrs Sawtell, who was several months pregnant, led Mrs Pearcey into a single, private cell measuring 10ft x 5ft 6in. There was a barred window large enough to let light in, but it was pitch black outside with little moonlight, so the light was very poor and the cell dim. The windowpane was shut tight, and the walls sweated from hot water circulating through pipes within them, as it was late autumn and already the weather had turned cold. With the cell door slightly ajar and unguarded, Sarah told Mrs Pearcey to undress and turn over her garments. She was given dowdy workhouse clothes in exchange.

Mrs Pearcey complied, unpinning her long brown hair. On inspection, Sarah saw nothing extraordinary on Mrs Pearcey's body or her undergarments, though the press reported the dress she wore was "saturated" with "fresh blood,"[116] a colorful exaggeration at best.[117] As Mrs Pearcey redressed in the workhouse clothes provided, she volunteered unexpectedly, "I met Mrs Hogg accidentally in the Kentish Town Road on the Wednesday afternoon. She passed me by and took no notice of me. On the Thursday I wrote a note to her, and gave it to a boy, who was to wait for an answer; it was to invite Mrs Hogg to tea on the Friday afternoon."

Sarah folded Mrs Pearcey's clothes and put them in a paper bag.

"Did she come on the Friday afternoon?" Sarah asked.

"Yes, between four and a quarter past, and as we were having tea Mrs Hogg made some remark, which I did not like; one word brought up another—" She stopped abruptly.

"Perhaps I had better say no more."[118]

Mrs Sawtell took Mrs Pearcey's old clothes to Inspector Bannister's office, as instructed, but she did not mention the conversation to him. In fact, as she was quite rushed, she handed over the clothes and left, and did not actually see Bannister again until the following week. Even then, she didn't mention Mrs Pearcey's quasi-confession.

The astonishing news that a *woman* had been arrested for the ghastly murder in Hampstead telegraphed through press offices around Britain and beyond, and the public clamoured for details. Many reporters covering the case wondered what Bannister himself considered: whether Mrs Pearcey had acted alone.[119] Even with the blood evidence in her kitchen and her scratched hands and fingers, it was almost too much to believe. In fact, the immediate belief in an accomplice to the crime was so strong, the *Daily News* reported that a man in Kentish Town had actually been arrested in connection with the murder. When proven false, the newspaper quickly retracted its story, but the thought had already lodged in the public mind.

As any armchair sleuth who read *Holmes* knew, the most likely accomplices to murder were those closest to the murdered, and the press was immediate in its distrust and suspicion of Phoebe's husband, Frank Hogg. In a case already so "full of surprises," the press felt it was only a matter of time before his role in the crime would be revealed. Still, only Mrs Pearcey was taken into custody that Saturday night, exactly twenty-four hours after the body of Phoebe Hogg had been found.

At 10.15pm there was a knock on the door at 141 Prince of Wales Road. Maria Hogg, Frank and Clara's mother, was the only one at home. She had most likely already been barraged by media, who continued to loiter outside the house waiting for Clara and Frank, who had not yet returned from the police station. Old Mrs Hogg answered the knock and took receipt of a telegram addressed, strangely, to Mrs Pearcey. Mrs Pearcey had never received any correspondence at the Hogg house before, so it was odd that she should do so now. If that wasn't peculiar enough, the contents of the telegram, which bore no return receipt or name, made the delivery even stranger. The telegram, postmarked from Gravesend, read:

"Office surrounded Gravesend. Get protection. Telegraph at once."

Old Mrs Hogg summoned the police immediately, and in consequence of the telegram one Inspector Miller started for Gravesend that very night.[120]

At approximately 1.00am, after signing sworn statements that satisfied Inspector Bannister that neither was involved in the crime, Frank and Clara Hogg were free to go home. Despite being weary from the ordeal, Frank and Clara were either followed from the police station by reporters or met by those dogged enough to stay put outside their home, but, either way, they were both grilled for details about what had happened throughout the day.

Before Clara left the police station, she had been told that her friend Mrs Pearcey was detained and charged with the murder of her sister-in-law Phoebe. Perhaps thinking it would provoke new information, she was also told about the overwhelming evidence found in Pearcey's kitchen. Clara knew about the knives, the bloodstained hearthrug and the poker with hairs stuck to it, which seemingly matched Phoebe's.[121] And yet, despite hearing such crushing evidence, Clara told a *Lloyd's* reporter who had hounded her that night she couldn't understand why Mrs Pearcey had been detained.

"As to the body having been wheeled from there in the perambulator to the place where it was found, I cannot think that Mrs Pearcey ever could have done it," she said.[122]

The same question was put to Maria Hogg, Frank and Clara's mother. What possible motive, the reporter asked, would someone have to murder her daughter-in-law? None she could think of, she answered. "With the exception of a few 'tiffs' now and again," old Mrs Hogg said, "her son and his wife lived on good terms." And she would know because Frank, Phoebe and the baby lived on the first floor just below them.[123]

Understandably, old Mrs Hogg's answer betrayed her wish to maintain the appearance of that uniquely Victorian social code of respectability. The Hoggs had lived in Camden Town for over three decades, and her husband, who had died in January 1880, had owned a local grocery store that many of the neighbours frequented. Even in her old age - she was then 70 - Maria Hogg was well known and respected, and ties to a ghastly crime would have been quite embarrassing.

The landlady, Mrs Barraud, confirmed that the Hoggs were good people. She said she could not have wished for quieter or more respectable lodgers, in fact. As for the victim specifically, Mrs Phoebe Hogg was a "fine, strong, handsome woman, of sober character, proud of her home, which she kept in excellent order, and very proud of her baby."[124]

Even so, Maria Hogg's description of her son's marriage wasn't entirely accurate. There were quarrels, the landlady added when she was interviewed, at the centre of which seemed to be visits from a Miss Elizabeth Styles, Phoebe's niece. "Words would ensue" between Frank Hogg and Elizabeth Styles, Mrs Barraud told a reporter, and one particularly "serious row" resulted in Frank forbidding Elizabeth from ever visiting the house again. Frank went so far as to stipulate that if Elizabeth should come while he was working, and Mrs Barraud or her husband answered the door to her, they should deny her entry. She would "scarcely like to do that," Mrs Baurraud added as an aside.[125]

While she didn't remember Phoebe leaving after a row on the Friday of her death, she couldn't be sure that she had even seen Frank that day, or evening. She wasn't sure he came home because his hall marker wasn't flipped to "in." A panel with a series of "in" and "out" markers which residents were encouraged to use, would indicate when everyone was in for the night, so that the hall light could be turned out, saving everyone lighting costs. The hall lamp was left burning all night and so Mrs Barraud presumed it was because Hogg stayed out all night.

The landlady also thought it was strange, she told the reporter, that although she'd seen Frank washing himself in the kitchen the morning after his wife disappeared, he hadn't asked if she had seen Phoebe. Mrs Barraud thought that were he really worried about his wife, he would have asked everyone in the house whether they'd seen her. Perhaps it was as Frank claimed though. He wasn't concerned over Phoebe's absence because he thought she had gone to see her ailing father, William Styles, who was, if census records are accurate, 76-years-old and near death.[126]

At some point, reporters were entreated to leave the Hoggs alone. It had been a very long two days, and everyone needed the relief of sleep.

Sunday, October 26, 1890 broke crisp and cool. In just 24 hours, it was reported that Priory Street was "more or less crowded with people" viewing No. 2.[127] Public interest in the case was intense and immediate, and a front-page feature in the *Illustrated Police News* a month later showed a thick crowd still outside 2 Priory Street, which had to be guarded by a policeman.[128]

The press branded Phoebe and Tiggie Hogg's double-murder "The Hampstead Tragedy", even though the baby's body had not yet been found. In an effort to assist police in that endeavour, the press circulated descriptions of the baby, as they had her mother, hoping someone had seen the infant and would come forward:

> Also missing, Phoebe Hogg, aged 18 months. Has very blue eyes; very little hair; small brown birthmark on one shin. Dress: Brown pelisse and cape; plush bonnet, with a blue bow in front; with a blue frock.[129]

The inked broadsheets describing baby Tiggie were barely dried when, at half past six in the morning, a hawker named Oliver Smith found her. He was walking inside the hedge of a vacant lot on one side of Finchley Road when his eyes fixed on something out of place in the landscape, something lying under a clump of nettles. As he drew closer, he realised that he was looking at the body of a baby girl. She was lying face down. She was fully clothed and well dressed, missing only a boot and sock.[130]

It took Smith nearly an hour to track down a constable at that early hour, but at last he encountered James Dickerson, a reserve constable with S Division, and led him back to the Cock and Hoop field where he'd found the baby.[131] In turn, Dickerson fetched a nearby general practitioner, Dr John Maundy Biggs.

When Dr Biggs arrived at the scene, he rolled the girl flat on her back and took her temperature, holding his fingers to the baby's forehead. Her body was stiff and cold.[132] He found small abrasions on her left ear and cheek, and mucous and small drops of blood oozing from her nostrils, but otherwise she looked perfectly normal, save her tiny hands, which were clenched, the nails on the left hand already turning black.[133] At first when interviewed, Dr Biggs said he held little doubt that Phoebe Hanslope Hogg died from exposure,[134] though *The Times* reported the weather the night before as singularly mild. Later, however, he said the evidence suggested to him that she'd suffocated to death.[135]

Biggs and Dickerson waited together until the ambulance arrived to convey the infant to the Hampstead mortuary. It was just after 8 o'clock on Sunday morning.

The official autopsy of Phoebe and 'Tiggie' Hogg began in earnest that very afternoon.

Dr Thomas Bond and S Division Surgeon Herbert Cooper attended, while Dr Joseph Augustus Pepper of St. Mary's Hospital performed the autopsy, aided by an assistant.[136]

Though newspapers specifically mention that Phoebe and Tiggie's bodies were taken to and autopsied at the Hampstead mortuary opposite New End Hospital, it's difficult to say with certainty that this was true, though they were certainly taken to a mortuary. It is equally impossible to detail the condition of the mortuary. Dr Edmund Gwynn, the Medical Officer of Health, contributed to an 1891 report that suggests the Hampstead mortuary was a compact and well-arranged building with rooms for both infectious and noninfectious cases. It stood directly opposite the New End Hospital, and was linked via a tunnel.[137] Dr Gwynn also notes this building - or updates to the building - was erected (or completed) in 1891, the year *after* the murders of Phoebe and 'Tiggie' Hogg. Other records suggest it was completed in 1890.[138]

Though the building may or may not have been new, Dr Pepper would have enjoyed the same basic necessities with which every mortuary was outfitted: hot and cold water, a star gaslight, the requisite systems of hoses and sinks to wash out intestines and skull cavities, and a series of knives, scalpels, curved bistouries, razors, chains, scissors, mallets, forceps and magnifying glasses.[139] A police photographer was also on hand to take photographs, a relatively new tool used in detective work, though how those photographs were used, or where they were catalogued remains unknown.[140]

Pepper had conducted dozens of autopsies during his 14-year

career, which began auspiciously as a student at University College Hospital in London, where he graduated with gold medals in medicine, surgery and forensic medicine. Professionally, he was a man of ambition: by the time he was 40, Pepper had built a bustling private consulting practice, published the book *Surgical Pathology*, and was appointed pathologist to the Home Office. Privately, however, he was "modest and retiring," at least according to his three servants. He lived alone at 13 Wimpole Street, and seemed to prefer the quiet rewards of gardening to the glittering pleasures afforded a metropolitan medical man.[141]

As a surgeon, Pepper was exacting, and missed little. This attention to detail would serve him well in his later career when he was called to testify at the infamous 1910 murder trial of Dr Hawley Harvey Crippen. In fact, it was his meticulous study, alongside that of his colleague and fellow pathologist Bernard Spilsbury, of a seven-by-six-inch piece of abdominal skin that would crack the Crippen case.[142]

Pepper began the autopsy by noting Phoebe's sex - female, and estimating her age - 32. His assistant that day wrote down her date of death: October 24, 1890; the date of the examination - October 26, 1890; and then her height and weight: 5ft 7in; 118 pounds.[143] Though a complete record of the autopsy procedure is lost to time, it's likely that Pepper would have followed a course of inspection similar to the standards introduced by Rudolf Ludwig Karl Virchow in 1874. These techniques were further updated and systematised in a more famous manual published by J.D. Mann later in 1893.[144]

They included measuring the circumference of the victim's shoulders and skull; the amount of adipose tissue; and noting whether the body was emaciated or well nourished. Pepper would have checked muscular development, and the shape and appearance of the head, thorax and abdomen. He was looking for abrasions, eruptions, scars, and other wounds, and noting size, appearance, and colour. He would have studied each body part and organ in detail: her eyelids, the appearance of the corners of the eyes and the size of her pupils, in example.[145]

Pepper distinguished the specific nature, size and angle of Phoebe's wounds. On the left side of her head at the back, he found she had suffered two lacerations close together, each about two inches long. Beneath them, the skull was smashed in; here, fragments of bone had penetrated the brain. Two inches in front of that set of wounds was a smaller scalp-wound that had also broken the bone underneath, but there the brain was uninjured. On the right side of her head, towards her face, was a fourth scalp wound much like the others. Again, the skull was not broken.

None of the injuries indicated an order in which the blows were delivered, suggesting it was likely that the murderer and victim moved in response to one another, leading to injuries all over and in multiple directions on the head and body. One wound, however, suggested that whoever bludgeoned Phoebe did so standing a little behind and to the side of her. She had a large bruise over her left eyebrow, and several small wounds on her face. Her hands and wrists were severely bruised and she had a jagged incised wound on her front left forearm, most likely a defence wound. The cut to her neck was made left to right and from below, and could have only been made with an exceedingly sharp instrument.

After studying her wounds, Dr Pepper decided that any one of them, but particularly the blow to the back of her head, would have rendered Phoebe unconscious, but not necessarily dead. When the bone splintered into her brain, she probably would have dropped to the floor and possibly convulsed into unconsciousness. It was a small mercy in an otherwise horrific and painful death, made more so by the fact that Pepper believed Phoebe was still alive when her throat was cut, as there was very little blood left in her heart and organs upon examination.

After he finished studying her chest and head wounds, Dr Pepper investigated her stomach and uterus, looking for evidence of injury. He found nothing of note. Recording the size and thickness of the uterine wall, Pepper speculated she had delivered at least one child. He examined her pelvic floor and there found a "very large abscess" behind the womb. He guessed it had formed over several months and speculated it might have made Phoebe rather weak, perhaps even easily overcome. He later amended this finding, saying that though she may have been weaker than normal, she was clearly strong enough to push a two-year-old in a heavy pram.[146]

The autopsy of Phoebe Hogg took a little over four hours to complete.

After a short break, Pepper turned his attention to Phoebe's child. He removed her dress, white stockings and remaining boot. He examined the body and the contents of her stomach carefully, looking for traces of poison, a natural assumption given she seemed otherwise unharmed. She was scrupulously clean, not a drop of blood or dirt on her, except a small smudge on her face, perhaps incurred while trying to roll over. The contents of her stomach contained some substance like a berry with a skin on it, but the child's exterior body was unremarkable except that it was dead.[147]

Ultimately, Dr Pepper couldn't determine whether the baby died from smothering or from exposure to the cold, as there were signs that suggested either explanation was plausible. Her lips were pale blue, for example - a sign of cyanosis - which could have been caused by a lack of oxygen in the blood due to death from exposure, or death from asphyxiation; he just couldn't be sure.[148]

After the autopsies were completed, Drs Pepper, Bond and Cooper met Inspector Bannister at the police station to examine the evidence collected over the past two days from what was, by now, most certainly determined to be the crime scene: 2 Priory Street. Presumably, Dr Pepper also relayed to detectives his initital autopsy findings.

At the police station, Dr Pepper analysed the bassinette. Dark clumps of hair and fur were trapped in the now congealed and clotted blood on the seat. He compared the hair to that on Phoebe's head and they matched as nearly as he could tell, but as he was not in a laboratory or mortuary, he hadn't a microscope with which to examine them, so he could not be certain they were hers or, for that matter, even human.

The pram was literally "covered with blood," and the hairs, which were at least the same length and colour as those on Phoebe's head, suggested that while Phoebe had most certainly been conveyed in the pram, her daughter had not. If Tiggie were conveyed to the field where she was found by pram, then she must have been wrapped tightly in some kind of waterproofed cloth, as there was "not a spot of blood" on the child's clothing, Pepper later testified.[149]

Police Sergeant William Brown later brought Dr Pepper a number of sealed bags of evidence collected from the crime scene for his review. In fact, over the course of two weeks, Dr Pepper would analyse a total of 35 objects or articles related to the case. He started with the most valuable item first: the poker.

Inspector Bannister believed this was the murder weapon, so he was undoubtedly disappointed that Pepper found just "a trace" of blood in the crevice of the handle and the lower part of the shaft. More disappointing yet, Dr Pepper could not say whose blood it was, or even whether the blood was human. It was quite possible - probable even - that in attempting to clean up the crime scene, the murderer wiped the poker clean.[150]

A black cloth jacket confiscated from Mrs Pearcey when she was remanded was in a second parcel delivered to Dr Pepper. There were small blood spots just above the left pocket and on the left sleeve, which Pepper cut out for microscopic analysis, but this too proved unhelpful. All he could say about the blood was that it was mammalian. It could have been hers, or Phoebe's, or mouse blood. Mrs Pearcey had, apparently, told Clara that she scratched her hands the day of the murder killing mice, which "ran about the kitchen in thousands." There was no blood on the brown petticoat examined, but there were bloodstains on the red flannel petticoat, which he thought were naturally caused, meaning menstrual blood. There were no stains on the black-and-white striped petticoat.[151]

On the body of the dark striped dress, however, Pepper found four bloodstained places that looked like they'd been washed or wiped, indicating that someone had tried to remove the blood. He obtained blood crystals from the fabric. There was also a stain on the white cotton bodice; none on the white chemise, but on the light grey skirt there was "a quantity of blood" across numerous spots and stains. Pepper cut the greater part of these stains out for analysis, but there were stains and patches of dried blood on the right and left side of the skirt, and on its flounce. He also found bloodstains on the dark striped skirt.[152]

The rug lined with red cloth was saturated with blood, and the apron was covered in clotted blood. The black striped apron and alpaca dustcoat - both bloodstained - had been taken from Mrs Pearcey's kitchen. All told, Pepper found 28 articles with blood on them. Pepper was quickly mounting an overwhelming, if circumstantial, forensic case against Mary Eleanor Pearcey.[153]

Later that Sunday afternoon, a carpenter named John Charles Pearcey appeared at Kentish Town police station. He had information about the woman arrested for the murder of Phoebe Hogg. In fact, they had been living together as husband and wife for a few years, and he felt he ought to tell somebody what he knew about her.

News of the murder had not yet reached the Styles family in Rickmansworth,[154] so when one of Phoebe's brothers decided to surprise his sister with a visit on Sunday afternoon, he was met at the door with the terrible news of the double murder. Those who had to tell him recalled that upon hearing how his sister and niece met their terrible end, he was "entirely unmanned."[155]

THE INQUEST

ON Monday, October 27, Mrs Pearcey took her second breakfast as a prisoner, now at Holloway gaol, and waited for a warder to escort her to the prison van, which would ferry her to the Marylebone Police Court for the first of many hearings.

The police court was a regal, two-storied Italianate building, made of white brick and Portland stone, but compared to the more ceremonious courts, like the Old Bailey, the police courts were relatively modest buildings known more for efficiently processing volumes of legal business than for their architectural grandeur.[1] The police courts acted like a court of summary jurisdiction wherein the job of the magistrate was to determine if enough evidence existed to move a case to the Central Criminal Court.

The Black Maria stopped in front of the police court, dividing an eager crowd that had formed along the pavement and overflowed into the streets, hoping to catch a glimpse of the supposed murderess. Inside, the courtroom and hallway of the court were crowded and loud.[2] Mrs Pearcey was drawn from the van and hurried through the jostling crowd. It was the first time the press and general public had laid eyes on her, and, perhaps unsurprisingly, she was not on her best form. One reporter, who must have been close to her, noted that her eyes were "bloodshot." He suspected her two nights in jail had left her "dejected."[3] The crowd pushed into the courtroom, eager to get a better look at Mrs Pearcey, but she was quickly hidden away in an anteroom to await her solicitor.

The reading public devoured news of what had been reported as "the Hampstead Tragedy" and had, in a matter of days, cultivated the "deepest interest" in the case. News of the double murder and the pretty, young killer was wired as far away as North Carolina and Mexico.[4] *The New York Times* and *Washington Post* eagerly covered the case for its readers too, as did papers in Ireland, Spain and throughout Europe. Female murderers were rare, and those who killed someone other than a child or husband rarer still, which was, no doubt, part of the allure of the crime.[5] But the case also fascinated because the public strongly believed all had not yet been revealed. Like a good Dickensian serial, police had not yet caught the real criminal mastermind. The papers bolstered such speculative sensation by writing for some time that police were always but a hair's-breadth from capturing Mrs Pearcey's accomplice, such as this comment in the *Sheffield Evening Telegraph*:

> Since Saturday by a well devised system of observation the police have discovered that a second person was implicated with the suspected woman Pearcey, and the clue thus found is being so closely followed that an arrest may be expected.[6]

Though the spectacle attracted a crowd from all classes and both sexes, women watched the case with particular fascination. One writer for the *Evening News and Post*, especially disgusted by the turnout of women, for whom he thought the proceedings too vulgar, wrote, "We would gladly publish the name of every woman who disgraced her sex by rushing to that wretched sight as if it were the finest kind of raree show."[7]

In response to such disciplining, the *Women's Penny Paper* cuttingly replied: "An eye-witness has seen fit to write to the daily press objecting to the presence of women in the court...Is it not time that men learned... that where women cannot go unharmed is no right place for themselves, and since a woman is in the dock it is not women but men who ought to be excluded?"[8]

The Hampstead murders were not the first case to draw such attention from the 'gentler sex'. The trial of Adelaide Bartlett, which took place four years earlier in April 1886, generated female interest and male approbation in equal measure.

At 11 o'clock, Frederick Freke Palmer stepped out of his office at 122 Seymour Place and headed north toward the Marylebone Police Court just a few minutes' walk away. When he arrived, he too had to fight his way through the jostling crowd, cutting the quickest path to the anteroom where his client awaited him.

Freke Palmer was the 28-year-old solicitor who took Pearcey's case. He was but four years older than his client, and had only been in practice for six years. Though he was on his way to establishing himself as a brilliant advocate, and establishing one of the largest criminal practices in the world,[9] he had represented just one other client in a capital case before Pearcey. Though he may have been inexperienced, those who knew him said he was scrupulously fair and dealt honestly with all his clients. Already, he had an impressive knowledge of the finer points of law and administration, and later, was quite successful in negotiating reduced sentences or commutations.[10]

At this point in his career, however, he had about as much experience in defending murderesses as Mrs Pearcey had money to pay for her defence.[11] Of course, what Mrs Pearcey lacked in financial resources, she would more than make up for in notoriety. Perhaps this was why Palmer took her case. Though neither could have known it then, the Hampstead murders would become a *cause célèbre*, which would prove of great value to Palmer's practice and public persona. Indeed, the Hampstead Tragedy would become a gothic sensation to rival the Kent, Maybrick and Crippen cases, talked and written about for more than one hundred and twenty years, and catalogued as one of England's most bizarre and notable crimes.[12]

As all solicitor-client conversation was privileged, there is no record of what transpired between Palmer and Pearcey that Monday morning in the anteroom of the police court, but surely, after the customary introductions, Palmer would have explained to his client as directly as possible the charges against her and the seriousness of those charges. Whatever courage she had, she would need to gather up, for the most personal details of her life were about to be scrutinised by strangers, published in newspapers, and gossiped about around the world. Before leaving the anteroom, Freke Palmer surely asked his client, as he would countless times in the coming weeks, whether she wished to confess to the crime, to which she replied - as she would at every further occasion in some variation - "I know nothing about it."[13]

When asked, at the end of his career, why he'd never written his memoirs, Palmer quipped that if he'd written a "tenth of what I know, London would no longer come with its secrets."[14] Palmer may have become London's great secret-keeper, but Pearcey never trusted him with the secrets of her case, a fact he must have realised early on would make his defence of her a Sisyphean task.

At half-past one in the afternoon, the magistrate, Mr William Major Cooke, took his seat on the Bench and asked the usher to bring the prisoner into the courtroom. According to sketches in the *Illustrated Police News*, Cooke was a severe-looking man. Balding on top and old, he had a fleshy face and lips that naturally settled into a grimace. He peered at those paraded in front of him over small wire spectacles.

The woman led from the anteroom to the dock defied easy categorisation. A reporter for the *Manchester Guardian* wrote that she "stood the gaze of a score of newspaper artists"[15] rather indifferently, as they sketched her looking "beggarly" in police-issued clothes. She wore a "very old dress and a shabby shawl,"[16] and many early illustrations of her portray her as gaunt and haggard. Even poorly dressed, she must have had her charms, and if not classic beauty, the assets of youth: smooth, fair skin, bright eyes, and lovely russet-coloured hair. Most reporters described her as a fairly good-looking woman, tall and slim, though not skinny. She had "thinly pencilled eyebrows," which framed remarkable "bright blue eyes," wrote one reporter, but her jaw receded slightly so that, when in repose, two misshapen teeth were just visible pressing upon her plump bottom lip. To some of the reporters who sketched her that day, she appeared "nervous" and "fragile,"[17] but to others she seemed unmoved by her terrible predicament.[18]

According to a female correspondent who later wrote a letter to the *Lloyd's Weekly Newspaper* to set the record straight, these descriptions of her were inaccurate. Men, who were clearly incapable of the job, the correspondent complained, had let desire guide their pens. By her description, Mrs Pearcey was five feet six inches tall, neither slight nor stout, with delicate colouring and small, shapely hands, but not a "single good feature" in her face.[19] Her eyes were dark and bright, but too small, her mouth was large and badly-formed owing to the set of crooked teeth which were hidden by her lips, and she had a weak, receding chin.

Despite this disagreement about her physical attributes, most reporters and commentators agreed that Mrs Pearcey did not betray even a glimpse of the "vicious character" with which police endowed her.[20] Indeed, there was "nothing of the murderess in her appearance."[21] But then, what *did* a murderess look like?

The first witness called to testify at the hearing was Frank Samuel Hogg. As Frank talked, Mrs Pearcey's gaze altered between him and Magistrate Cooke, and only once or twice wandered to others in the courtroom. Whether standing or sitting (toward the end of the proceedings she asked to sit), she was still and passive, except when she occasionally bent forward to whisper to her solicitor, Freke Palmer.[22]

Frank delivered much of his testimony amid sobs "so heavy that his words were almost choked in the utterance,"[23] but some later argued that his public wailing was too exaggerated, and provoked suspicion, not sympathy. Throughout Frank's testimony, Mrs Pearcey stared straight in front of her, her hands clasped so tightly that no one could see the scratches on them from the fight she purportedly had with her victim the Friday before.[24]

After Mr Cooke excused Frank from the box, he then called Inspector Bannister. Bannister described Mrs Pearcey's strange behaviour at the mortuary, and her "perfect indifference" when they searched her house.[25] He described the bloodstains on the ceiling, floors and walls; the broken windowpane glass, the hearthrug stained with blood, the many items that looked like someone had attempted to wash them with paraffin, and the scratches on Mrs Pearcey's hands. He also added that though she represented herself as married, she was not. She had been living with a man named John Charles Pearcey, who had voluntarily come forward just the day before. Mrs Pearcey had likely adopted John Pearcey's last name for the sake of respectability, but they were not legally married.[26] Her real name was, he announced, Mary Eleanor Wheeler.

Freke Palmer asked clarifying questions of the two witnesses, but reserved his defence.

Upon conclusion of the hearing, Inspector Bannister asked Mr Cooke for a remand. He had taken statements from neighbours who would testify they saw Mrs Pearcey wheeling the pram away from the murder scene on the night in question, he said. Cooke granted a week's remand, and the inquest was scheduled for the following day, to be held at the Hampstead Drill Hall.

In the last moments before adjournment, Freke Palmer asked the magistrate whether the workhouse clothing his client wore might be exchanged for some of her own, or at least clothing more befitting a woman of her station. Palmer was undoubtedly aware of the way that rank and class - or the *perception* of class - could tip the scales of justice.

Mr Cooke granted his request.

At half past nine in the morning on October 28, 1890, a jury of

12 men were sworn and conducted to the mortuary to view the corpses of Phoebe and Tiggie Hogg. It was, without question, a short but haunting visit. Once this ordeal was over, the jury was whisked back to the Drill Hall and seated by 10 o'clock, so that Mr Danford Thomas could begin his inquest into their deaths punctually.[27]

The Hall was packed, but the crowd comfortably accommodated, thanks to the good work of the court clerk, Mr Walter Schröder, who masterfully orchestrated all who had business before the court to a comfortable seat from which they could take in the day's evidence.[28] As the court convened, Phoebe and Tiggie's bodies were removed from the mortuary to William Clatworthy's funeral parlour on the High Street.[29]

The purpose of the Coroner's court was to ascertain the identity of the victims and what caused their deaths. If any laws had been broken, as in the case of murder, the jury had an opportunity to name the killer, presuming sufficient evidence existed for them to do so, and depending on the verdict, the case moved to the Central Criminal Court.

The coroner, Mr George Danford Thomas, was both medical doctor and barrister. His medical explanations and the organisation of his summation were impressive and exhaustive, and often led juries, which tended to be composed largely of uneducated men, to "obvious" conclusions even when the evidence was technical, complicated, or, in Mary Pearcey's case, circumstantial and incomplete.

On the coroner's right sat the jury, and beyond them, at a special table, the police, represented by Detective Inspector Bannister, Superintendent Beard and Sergeant Huntley, along with Inspectors Collis, Wright and Warner (who had prepared "excellent plans" showing where the bodies of both victims were found and how they were positioned). A chair was placed in front of the coroner's table for witnesses, who were allowed to testify seated.

As at the magistrate's hearing, Frank Hogg was the first witness. He repeated much of the same evidence he'd given the day before, about where he lived and worked, and his relationship to the accused, but with one significant and strategic difference: the truth of his affair with Mrs Pearcey.

"I am going to speak the truth, sir," he said. "It's the best. I confess I was intimate with Mrs Pearcey. I don't think my wife knew anything about it."

This 'confession' was most likely in response to hard questions put to him about the nature of his relationship with Mrs Pearcey the day before. When asked whether he had called round to 2 Priory Street on the night of the murders, Frank said he was at the house at a few minutes past ten. He had stopped by right after he got off from work. Finding Mrs Pearcey out, he scribbled a note for her and left. Frank had told the magistrate that he had last seen Mrs Pearcey on Wednesday afternoon, but even then, only for a minute, as he was busy with other things.[30] When pressed for details about how it was that he let himself in to 2 Priory Street, Frank had been forced to admit that he had his own latchkey. At this point he no doubt realised that the affair was obvious, and further omissions would only make him look guilty.

Frank told Mr Danford Thomas that he had last seen his wife alive at 9 o'clock on the morning of her death. She and the child were then at home, and in perfect health. He'd gone to work and not returned until 10 o'clock that evening. He spied the note on the table his wife had left him.[31]

"Did you inquire from the people in the house when you came home about your wife?" the coroner asked.

"No. I made no inquiry because I thought it was all right," Frank said.

"What did you do next?"

"I did nothing because I thought perhaps my wife had met her sister Emma at the Kentish Town railway station."[32]

Though there was a perfectly logical explanation for her absence, Frank said he was uneasy, and slept badly the rest of the night. In fact, he said, he was so worried about his wife that he'd slept with all his clothes on.[33] He then got up around six and went to his brother's place at 70 Castle Road. It was around 6.20am when he got there. He worked in the stables for a while and then stopped by his brother's house. He recounted their conversation and then said he went home.

"Who is Mrs Pearcey," the coroner asked, "We don't know anything about her. Is she a friend of yours? A neighbour?"

"She was a friend," Frank said.

"Did you know Mr Pearcey?"

"No. I have seen a person called Mr Pearcey, whom I believe to be her husband."

Frank then told the coroner what he did to try and find his wife and baby. He said he'd gone to Chorleywood but returned with no news about her. Before he left, he sent Clara to see if Mrs Pearcey knew anything about Phoebe. He said that upon reading the newspaper his mother gave him, he knew, almost immediately, that the murdered woman found at Crossfield Road was his wife.

"And you saw in it an account of the death?" the coroner asked.

"Yes."

"What did you do then?"

"I hardly know," Frank said.

"Did you have any dispute with Mrs Pearcey?"

Accidentally, Frank proceeded to describe a dispute he'd had with his wife about letters.

"She was always writing letters when I came home," Frank said, "and would not let me see them, and I insisted that I ought to see them. Then one day she was reading a letter when I came home, and would not let me see it, and I said I ought to see it. That led to our separation for one night," Frank said.

"How were you separated?" the coroner asked.

"She went away for one night," Frank said.

"Well, well; don't call that a separation," the coroner said.

"The quarrel was made up, and we were all right again."

"May I take it that since then you and your wife have lived happily and comfortably together?" asked the coroner.

"Perfectly," Frank answered.

"Do you know that she [Phoebe] had been in the habit of visiting her [Mrs Pearcey] during the last eight months? Has she, to your knowledge, been visiting Mrs Pearcey?"

"No; never to my knowledge, and never since the time of the dispute between me and my wife."

"Is there anything else that you would wish to tell us about this matter? Was she fond of her child?"

"Oh," Frank answered, sobbing, "yes."

"In your relations with Mrs Pearcey has your wife been the subject of conversation with Mrs Pearcey?"

"She has very often asked after her."

"Did Mrs Pearcey manifest any enmity towards your wife?"

"She always spoke very kindly of her."

"Did you think your wife discovered that you were intimate with Mrs Pearcey?"

"I do not think she did."[34]

The pram was then rolled into court. At the sight of it, Frank dramatically fell on one knee, leaned over the side of the carriage and sobbed, "Oh my poor child!" He seemed about to bury his head in the pram when a coroner's officer pulled him off it.[35] Two officers helped him to another seat.[36]

When he had recovered, Freke Palmer questioned Frank Hogg.

"When I went to Mrs Pearcey she was not at home. Previous to this Mrs Pearcey led me to believe that my wife might have been there; but as far as I am concerned my wife never manifested any suspicion as to my relationship with Mrs Pearcey," Frank said.

"You saw Mrs Pearcey before you knew of the death of your wife?" Palmer asked.

"Yes. I merely asked if the 'pram' was up there."

"Had you forbidden your wife to visit Mrs Pearcey?"

"No."

Palmer asked whether Frank quarrelled with his wife about Mrs Pearcey.

"No."

"You had no thought that your wife suspected your visits to Mrs Pearcey?"

"No, I had not. She went to my brother's last February or March at the wish of her friends."

"Do you know why they wished her to go away?"

"No."

"Was it because they objected to Mrs Pearcey being her nurse?"

"No; certainly not. After my wife went away she soon got well again."

"Did your wife send for Mrs Pearcey?"

"No," Frank said. "She came quite unexpectedly."[37]

The coroner moved the line of questioning on to the suspicious objects found at the house. In response, Frank reiterated what he'd already told detectives: the ring, which the police had confiscated from Mrs Pearcey, was not his wife's missing wedding ring. He was sure of this because he specifically recalled seeing it stamped 18 carat when he bought it in Camden Town, and the ring in police possession was only 9 carats.[38] Furthermore, he had never seen or worn the cardigan found draped across his wife's chest and head, though he said he had owned one similar several years before.

At last, Frank stepped down.

Somerled Macdonald and then Constable Gardiner testified to finding Phoebe and to seeing the "terrible gash" in Phoebe's throat.[39]

Dr Wells then enthralled those in the room by elaborating on that wound. Phoebe's throat had been cut so severely, he said, that her head was "merely hanging by a piece of skin."[40] He described some of her injuries to the jury, and said that those to her head alone were sufficient to have caused death, making the need to nearly decapitate Phoebe Hogg either practical, or deeply personal.

Dr Pepper testified next.

"Do you think the wounds were inflicted during life or after death?" the coroner asked.

"Undoubtedly during life; not necessarily during consciousness," Dr Pepper answered.

The wound to her neck divided everything except the skin and some muscles at the back, a wound so grave it could only have been made with a "very sharp" knife. One of the knives the police produced was a white-handled carving knife; it was in good condition and not much used. The jury examined the knife carefully, but Dr Pepper did not believe either of the two knives produced were sufficiently sharp to do the job.[41]

"There were several bruises about both hands and wrists of the deceased woman," Pepper continued, "and on the left arm a large bruise, as if the deceased had put up her arm to defend herself."

Internally, the organs were generally healthy, except for the large abscess he found, which had been forming for some months and from which she likely suffered "a good deal." It had nothing to do whatever with her death, except that it would have made her weak, he added.[42]

"What was the immediate cause of death?" the coroner asked.

"The immediate cause of death I take to have been syncope from loss of blood, following from a compound fracture of the skull, injury to the brain, and an incised wound on the neck," Dr Pepper replied.

He thought that a rolling pin or a poker could have caused the wound to her head and the bruises on her body, but whatever instrument the murderer used, it was used with great force. The doctor was shown the poker recovered from Mrs Pearcey's house, and agreed that it was quite capable of doing the job.

As for the child, she was "very fine" and "exceedingly well nourished," Pepper said.[43] She bore small abrasions on her forehead, nose and upper lip, the kind that might be produced when a child, running too fast, fell, face first, to the ground. She was probably alive when her face was marked up, he said, because blood had trickled from the abrasions at some point, but these small cuts and bruises had nothing to do with her death.

There were two "furrows" in her neck caused by clothes that were tightly fitted,[44] and food in her stomach. Her mouth and throat were free of any foreign objects, but her windpipe was slightly congested, as were her lungs and other organs, especially her brain. Dr Pepper said smothering could cause such injuries, though exposure was still a possibility. There were no marks of strangulation, but he suspected if she had been smothered, it was with some object like a cushion being "overlaid" on top of her chest, which caused her to stop breathing.[45] Hence, no strangulation marks. There was a tiny amount of blood on the hood and bib of her outfit, but these looked like droplets of blood from a small wound - perhaps from the scuffmarks on her head.[46]

Other witnesses were called: Oliver Smith, the hawker who found Tiggie, and Dr Biggs of Child's Hill, who confirmed Dr Pepper's autopsy findings on the baby. Detective Inspector Bannister repeated the evidence he'd given at the police court on Monday.[47]

Dr Thomas Bond was next called, and corroborated the results of Pepper's post-mortem examination and causes of death for both Phoebe and the child. He was with Inspector Bannister at 2 Priory Street on October 31, he said, and saw the blood in the kitchen, on the windowpanes, walls, ceiling and different articles of furniture. Though he had not yet finished his examination of some of the articles, he confirmed that though there were several small "woolly" hairs on the poker, they were not human. The hair and knives Bond found in the pram and kitchen were problematic too. Of the three hairs found in the pram, only one was human and, when looked at closely under the microscope, it did not match those taken for comparison from Phoebe Hogg. One of the knives produced could not have produced the injury to Phoebe's throat because the blade was rusted. In fact, neither of the knives produced at the inquest was sharp enough to cut through windpipe and bone. Bond could not confirm how Mrs Pearcey got the scratches on her knuckles and hands, and could only say they were recent.

John Charles Pearcey then took the chair at the front of the room. He was a carpenter and joiner living in Camden High Street, he told the court. He was single now, but had known the prisoner as Mary Eleanor Wheeler since 1885, when she was 18. They had lived together as husband and wife.

If he remembered correctly, they'd met while she was living on Fleet Street,[48] and while she worked at a sealskin factory.[49] In 1888 they separated, and she moved out. He hadn't visited her rooms at 2 Priory Street, but he knew where she lived. In fact, they had run into each other frequently on the street and still talked, though the relationship had been strained.

He knew about Frank Hogg, and he knew that Frank was married to Phoebe. To his knowledge, Mrs Pearcey considered Phoebe a "kind friend" and spoke of her often, and sweetly.[50] He thought he recalled Mrs Pearcey saying such things about their friendship before Phoebe and Frank married, some three or four years ago, but he could have been mistaken. He was not mistaken however, about the cardigan found across Phoebe's body; he recognised it as his. The sleeves had been cut out of it and he'd left it at the flat he shared with Mrs Pearcey on Bayham Street some years back. He knew it because of a distinct burn mark on the left pocket made from a box of matches he kept in that same pocket, used to light stoves[51] at work.[52]

The last John Pearcey had seen of his common-law wife was on Thursday, October 23, when he'd stopped to talk with her at the gate to 2 Priory Street.[53] They hadn't talked much lately, and when they did talk, he had not spoken to her "very kindly," for he was still wounded over the end of their relationship.[54] Anyway, he stopped on his way to the farrier's shop, and asked why her blinds were drawn.[55] She said her 14-year-old brother had died and that the funeral was planned for Tuesday.[56]

John Pearcey settled two more mysteries for the jury: he identified a gentleman caller he said visited Mrs Pearcey regularly, and confirmed that the two rings she wore were *both* hers. In fact, he thought the gentleman had given her the expensive gold one.[57] It was likely one of the many gifts he gave her during his weekly visits, which John said took place on Fridays.

At this revelation Mrs Pearcey's solicitor, Freke Palmer, paused proceedings to suggest the details of this other man should be reported to the police at once, as there had been suspicion of an accomplice. The coroner agreed. If someone would like to come forward, the coroner said, he would be "very happy to hear him."[58]

In fact, there was someone who needed to come forward, and Charles Crichton, called by police, made his way to the head table to give his evidence.

Crichton was a gentleman of independent means living in

Northfleet, Kent.[59] He had known Mrs Pearcey for about three years, he said, and had seen her last on Monday, October 20 at her house on Priory Street. He'd been ill all week, and hadn't been to London during the week of the murders. In fact, he'd scarcely been out of his house since coming down with sickness. His brother, who he'd brought as a character witness, could attest to his illness and whereabouts.

Eager to extricate himself from the proceedings, as the press still had not dropped the theory of a male accomplice,[60] Crichton said he knew nothing whatsoever of Mr and Mrs Hogg, except for a photograph he'd once seen of the couple which Mrs Pearcey kept in a book she read.[61] Mrs Pearcey had told him they were friends of hers. Detective Miller, who'd gone searching for Mr Crichton based on the mysterious telegram delivered to the Hogg house, handed the coroner the telegraph. The coroner read it to himself.

"This is simply a letter personal to yourself," the coroner said, "There is nothing in it."

"It is simply one of many such," Crichton answered.

As there were no additional clues contained in the letter or telegram relevant to the case, and since Charles Crichton could account for his whereabouts on the 24th, he was excused from the proceedings almost as quickly as he was called into them. While the telegram Crichton sent didn't prove particularly illuminating, the next witness, Martha Styles, was ready to tell of another note far more scintillating.

Martha Styles was a 28-year-old dressmaker[62] who lived in Egham, Surrey; she was also Phoebe Hogg's younger sister. The *Illustrated Police News* depicted Martha wearing a straw boater hat[63] with a mid-length mourning veil covering her face, her hair wrapped in a tight, low bun. She said that she last saw Phoebe alive at ten minutes past six on Thursday, October 23, the same day that John Pearcey said he questioned why Mrs Pearcey's blinds were drawn.[64]

Martha said that she and Phoebe were at Finchley Road station on the North London Railway, taking trains back to their respective homes having visited their niece, Lizzie Styles, to whom they were both close. Phoebe had the baby in the pram. While they waited, Phoebe told Martha about a note she'd received from Mrs Pearcey. She said the note was written on white paper and had been delivered by a boy. Martha recalled the note from memory. She said the words written were, "Dearest, Come round this afternoon and bring our little darling. Do not fail."[65] The note was unsigned, but Phoebe said she was sure of its author. She had received others like it and knew the handwriting to be Mrs Pearcey's.

Martha then told the court an even stranger tale. About three weeks before the murders, she said, Phoebe had received another unsigned note by messenger boy, asking her to meet at a public house. When she arrived she saw Mrs Pearcey, whom she presumed to have written the note. Mrs Pearcey then invited her on an excursion to look over an empty house in Southend. Mrs Pearcey tried to convince Phoebe that it would only be a day-long outing, and Phoebe could even borrow Mrs Pearcey's nurse (though she never mentioned the nurse's name) who would happily mind Tiggie so they could go, just the two of them. Phoebe must have said she would think it over and then left.

Later, she went to 2 Priory Street to decline the offer.

"Well, I must go," Phoebe purportedly said, after belying some nervousness, "or Frank will be home."

"Oh no," Mrs Pearcey replied venomously, clearly upset by the slight. "He won't be home before eight o'clock."[66]

An infuriated Phoebe later retold the story to her sister. She ordered Martha to throw the note into the fire and said defiantly, "If she waits for me to go she will wait a very long time."[67]

When Martha concluded her testimony the courtroom erupted in whispers.[68]

The coroner took Martha's testimony to mean that Phoebe harbored suspicion of Mrs Pearcey. He asked if there was any cause for such suspicion. Martha said that Phoebe had indeed grown suspicious of Mrs Pearcey, a suspicion first sparked when she unexpectedly came to nurse her sister during an illness the February before. The Hoggs, Martha said, insisted Phoebe suffered a miscarriage, which would explain her symptoms, but Phoebe's family believed Frank was starving her to death, which would also explain her symptoms. The Styles' eventually wondered whether Phoebe might have even been poisoned, Martha said, for she had suffered "great pain" after she took the medicine Frank gave her.[69]

"Of course, her husband was away all day at business," the coroner said, "and the only person left was Mrs Pearcey?"

"No," Martha corrected, "he was not at work all the time. He was lounging about home part of the time."

"Did she quite recover?" the coroner asked.

"She [Phoebe] has never been so well since her illness last February," Martha said.[70]

Lizzie Styles, Phoebe's niece, was next called. She wore a more ornate mourning hat than her aunt with no veil. A reporter for *Lloyd's Weekly Newspaper* later described her as a "tall, graceful girl, beyond the usual height, intelligent, and well educated, and a very good sample of the best class of domestic servant."[71]

"I am a nursemaid living at Albion Road, London, but my home is at Folkestone. The deceased, Mrs Hogg, was my aunt, and I was very intimate with her," she said.

Elizabeth Styles was born in May 1860, and was only seven years younger than her aunt. Their closeness in age accounted, in part, for their attachment to each other. They had both been domestic servants who lived and worked near each other before Phoebe's marriage to Frank, and grew especially close after Lizzie's mother died a decade earlier. Lizzie confirmed that Phoebe had indeed nursed a growing suspicion of Mrs Pearcey,[72] but added little to her Aunt's shocking testimony.

John Pearcey was then recalled and cross-examined. Freke Palmer pressed him to confirm that the cardigan thrown across Phoebe's face was indeed his. After all, it had been several years since he'd last seen it; could he really be sure? Palmer also attempted to portray Pearcey as the embittered and scorned lover with vengeful motivations in coming forward. By his own admission he had not spoken kindly to Mrs Pearcey in the two years since their separation for a "simple"[73] reason; presumably, his feelings were still hurt over her affair with Frank.

Mr and Mrs Butler, who lived on the second floor at 2 Priory Street next gave evidence.

Both said that they saw the pram in the passage of the house on the day of the murders. It was evening, just after work; around 6.00pm. The Butlers remembered the time because as they came in - first Sarah and then Walter - Mrs Pearcey cautioned them not to bump into the pram. The hallway was unusually dark, which was also memorable, Sarah said, because Mrs Pearcey almost always kept it lit.[74]

Though eyewitness accounts were notoriously unreliable, Mrs Butler said she knew the pram, as she'd seen it at the house at least twice before. She had also seen the baby and Mrs Hogg, although she understood Frank to be Mrs Pearcey's husband and Phoebe her sister-in-law, since that is what Mrs Pearcey had told her.[75] Sarah testified to finding a pile of burnt paper and ash against the back of the kitchen door, and to seeing broken glass shattered outside the kitchen. She had also found the scullery waterlogged when she came downstairs for breakfast on the morning after the murders. She said she found it peculiar that some of the things in the zinc bath,[76] including the kitchen curtains, appeared to have blood on them, which had to be recent because the curtains were put up clean only the week before.[77]

Mr Butler had had strange encounters with Mrs Pearcey of his own. He told the inquest that when he was going out on Saturday last, she had stopped him in the hallway. She closed the door behind her as they talked in the hall so that he couldn't see who was in her rooms, but he knew someone was in there. She asked him whether he could remember what time it was that he had seen the pram in the hall the night before, to which he replied that he believed it was between six o'clock and ten past. Then he left. Shortly afterwards he saw Mrs Pearcey and Clara Hogg walking stridently, so much so that they overtook him on the pavement. He swore he saw Mrs Pearcey carrying a bundle in her arms, but Clara later "emphatically" denied that Mrs Pearcey left her house carrying anything except a pocket-handkerchief.[78]

As Inspector Bannister had promised at the conclusion of the hearing the previous day, several other witnesses had been found who could link Mrs Pearcey to the victims, and also the pram. These were now called to give evidence.

Elizabeth Rodgers, who lived at 7 Priory Place, just around the corner from Priory Street, said she saw Mrs Pearcey wheeling "a heavily laden bassinette perambulator" a few minutes past 6 the Friday last.[79] She said the pram was long and seemed to be very full. It was "very high at the front, but lower towards the handles." Mrs Pearcey struggled to push its weight, her head bent over the handle of the pram.[80] She knew it was Mrs Pearcey because it was odd to see her wheeling a pram and the image stuck out in her mind. She didn't think much of it at the time because people about the neighbourhood were in the habit of wheeling "work" - meaning laundry - to the station to send to the City. But, it was odd because Mrs Pearcey usually paid others - herself included - to do her mangling.

Mrs Rodgers was in the middle of the road and Mrs Pearcey was on the path. As she was some distance away and it was dusk, Mrs Rodgers couldn't really see what was in the pram, but she could see that whatever it was, was covered with "some black stuff ". She remembered that Mrs Pearcey was wearing a long grey ulster and a small black satin hat with three feathers in it. She watched Mrs Pearcey turn left toward Kentish Town Road, and assumed she was heading to the train station. Why else would she choose such a "dismal" and empty thoroughfare through which to push a heavily-laden pram?

At noon, the inquest recessed for lunch. During the hour-long break large crowds gathered in and about the court.[81]

In the afternoon session Elizabeth Andrews, the maid who first found the pram leaning against 34 Hamilton Terrace, testified, as did Constable Roser who made the find of the child's butterscotch stuck to the pram's bloodied seat. Police had tracked down the butterscotch purveyor, Mrs Mulcaster of 62 Haverstock Hill,[82] who would later clarify that in fact it wasn't butterscotch at all, but an Everton toffee, made at her own shop and sold in lumps.[83]

Police Sergeant Brown was then called. He was the officer who had recovered the brass nut near Phoebe Hogg's head, which he now surmised popped off when the pram was turned on its side and Phoebe was "tumbled out."[84]

Next, Mrs Piddington, Mrs Pearcey's young neighbour, recounted her terror at hearing glass shattering next door and a baby crying out.[85] She said she called out to Mrs Pearcey several times, but there was never any answer in return.

Inspector Holland and Police Sergeant Nursey also gave evidence, and, as the last witness of the day, Clara Hogg was called forward.

Clara's testimony lacked the drama of the divisional surgeons, who spoke of blood spatter and sharp knives, or of policemen who wheeled the blood-encrusted pram into view, or even of those who retold the horror of finding the bodies, or hearing the baby scream, but she knew Mrs Pearcey well, and had been with her the whole of that terrible day after the crime,[86] and her testimony was thus compelling.

Clara explained that she went to Mrs Pearcey on Saturday morning and asked if she had seen or heard anything of Phoebe the day before. At first, Clara said, she said no, but when pressed she said that Phoebe had been at the house around 5.00pm and asked her to mind the baby for a while, which she refused to do. She asked to borrow money and Mrs Pearcey said she could have a shilling if she liked. While Clara hadn't any idea that Mrs Pearcey and her brother were having an affair, she never advised, or had reason to advise Mrs Pearcey to lie to police about when or why Phoebe came round the day of her death.

Mr Danford Thomas then asked Inspector Bannister whether he could produce any additional material evidence if the case were adjourned. Bannister said he could not.

"You think you have sifted the case to the bottom, except the fact of anyone seeing the crime actually committed?" the coroner asked.

"Yes," Bannister said.[87]

Mr Danford Thomas then summed up the case, dwelling on Phoebe's unhappy life with the Hoggs and Frank and Mrs Pearcey's affair, which he thought, constituted motive. There was no doubt a struggle ensued in the kitchen, the coroner said, though just what precipitated the struggle remained unclear. So far as the chain of evidence was concerned, Phoebe Hogg's body was then removed from 2 Priory Street in the perambulator and dumped at Crossfield Road. Mr Danford Thomas gave no opinion as to how he thought the baby was conveyed, but he had no doubt that whoever wheeled the pram to Crossfield Road also murdered the child. If the jury had no reasonable doubt that Mrs Pearcey was the murderer, then they should return a verdict accordingly. The evidence, he said, clearly pointed to the guilt of one party and one party only.[88]

The jury, who consulted for one minute,[89] agreed, deciding it was unnecessary to adjourn the inquiry for further evidence, and returned a verdict of "wilful murder" against Mary Eleanor Wheeler, otherwise known as Mrs Pearcey.

Before Frank Hogg left the inquest, Inspector Bannister requested permission to make a cast of Phoebe's head. Frank agreed. Coroner Danford Thomas passed along jury compliments about the intelligence and vigilance of his men,[90] and the room went silent as the last of those who attended shuffled outside and Mr Walter Schröder, the court clerk, closed the doors to the hall behind him.

It was surely chaotic as the Hoggs retreated from the inquest and Mrs Pearcey was escorted from the hall and ferried back to Holloway Gaol. Though the press was not allowed to interview Mrs Pearcey directly, the Hoggs were fair game, and the press swarmed around 141 Prince of Wales Road, eager for statements.

The press wanted to know many things, but primarily whether certain statements made at the inquest were true. Frank, Clara,

Edwin (Frank's older brother), Mrs Edwin Hogg and even old Mrs Hogg were unequivocal: much of what was said at the inquest was patently false, especially where it concerned Frank and Phoebe's marriage.[91]

"For the past six months," Edwin told the reporter, "my brother and his wife have lived upon the most amicable terms. Several times my wife and myself have spoken to her and asked, 'Phoebe, are you perfectly happy?' and she has replied, 'Yes, perfectly happy.'"

It was true that Phoebe had been ill, and it was true she and Frank had separated in February, but they didn't separate over her illness, her marriage, or her husband's infidelity, but over the letters Phoebe sent and received, but hid from her husband. In consequence of arguments over the letters - not her health - Phoebe had fled to her family's house in Mill Hill. The argument, such as it was, was really much about nothing. Edwin and Frank arrived the very next morning and persuaded Phoebe to come back home. Edwin, who helped facilitate the reconciliation personally, recounted the story to the reporter.

"Phoebe," he had said, "do you wish to see your husband?"

"Does Frank want to see me?" Phoebe had asked.

"That is not the question," Edwin said. "Have you thought of what you are doing by leaving him? You have only been away from him a day, but you must know the longer you are away from him the more difficult will be a reconciliation. I have come to ask you whether you wish to see him and return to him."[92]

Phoebe relented, put her head on Edwin's shoulder and burst into sobs, and then agreed to return home. Edwin called his younger brother into the room, and the pair were immediately reconciled. At least, that was Edwin's account of events.

Phoebe may have indeed wished to return to her husband, but not to Prince of Wales Road. Edwin attributed this resistance to shame; she couldn't bear others knowing she'd left over such a trivial matter, he said. But she had hardly been gone for twenty-four hours before their reconciliation. Phoebe wrote to Frank a few days after she agreed to return to him, but before she'd come home, and asked whether he had successfully found a new apartment for them. She desperately wanted to avoid judgment - real or imagined - from those who knew she had "been away." Phoebe stayed on at her sister's house while Frank, presumably, looked for new accommodation, but he never found suitable rooms, he said, and with no recourse, Phoebe returned to Prince of Wales Road several days later.[93]

The reporter asked Edwin whether there was another, perhaps secret, reason why Phoebe didn't want to return to Prince of Wales Road, but Edwin rejected any explanation except the one he had given. She was embarrassed that she had left her husband over something so "trivial," Edwin reiterated, especially since Phoebe later told Edwin there had been no letters from anyone except her niece, Lizzie Styles.[94] She had "acted so foolishly and childishly," Edwin said, and didn't want anyone to know about it.

Here Frank interjected.

"Her brother-in-law [Edwin] quite agreed with me that it was only my right that I should insist that my wife's letters should be shown to me," he said, petulantly.[95]

In later testimony, perhaps to seem less sulky and peevish, Frank made up a story that he wanted to read the letters because he thought Phoebe was having an affair.[96] When Lizzie heard this, she dismissed the theory entirely, telling a reporter that her aunt would never have an affair; she was too demure and circumspect for that - the kind of woman who wouldn't even speak to people on the street.[97] Perhaps it was a bit of projection on Frank's part. Despite his insistence in court that his wife never knew of his affair with Mrs Pearcey, Lizzie was fairly certain Phoebe knew all but chose to stay quiet. Even so, "no woman likes her husband to be away from her visiting another woman," Lizzie said.[98]

Though the Hoggs did their best to portray the marriage as a happy one, and their treatment of Phoebe as good, Lizzie, Martha and Phoebe's older brother knew her to be "unhappy."[99] In fact, Phoebe's life was described as a "perfect misery" once she entered her husband's house by one report.[100]

Though Frank consistently downplayed the quarrel over the

letters, Lizzie intimated that the argument was far more serious, and was not simply about privacy, but also about money and Mrs Pearcey.

The letters, as it transpired, were all written to, or received by, members of the Styles family with whom Phoebe kept up correspondence. These letters were deeply important to Phoebe, and when Frank put a stop to them her first impulse was defiance. "I will have these letters," Phoebe said. "I will have them sent to Lizzie,"[101] meaning, she would use her niece to secret the letters and replies. Though she didn't say it during the inquest, Lizzie later told a reporter that Frank's paranoia about the letters was not entirely unfounded. Phoebe wouldn't show the letters to Frank because from time to time they contained "expressions not favourable to him or his family."[102]

Lizzie admitted to the reporter that relatives on both sides of families - the Hoggs and Styles - interfered with Phoebe and Frank's marriage,[103] which may have contributed to Phoebe's unhappiness so that, to limit family interference, she eventually agreed to stop sending and receiving the letters. She also conceded that friends or family could not visit without formal invitation. This request seemed directed specifically at Lizzie, whom Frank felt was a troublemaker and a liar. In return, Phoebe demanded that Frank's friends could no longer visit either - specifically Mrs Pearcey - though she stopped short of demanding he stop visiting her. Perhaps she didn't ask it of him because she took it on faith that he would, as he said he would, look for a different place for them to live. Had Frank moved Phoebe and the baby, Lizzie reflected, "they would have been happier."[104] And, presumably, still alive.

Though the letters have been lost to history, it's likely that Phoebe talked about their financial troubles and her concern for the baby. When they married in November 1888, Frank was then working regularly for his brother at the F.H. Hogg removing company, but for unknown reasons, he left his brother's employ and went to work at Shoolbred's. He worked irregularly, though not because there wasn't enough work, rather, because he didn't really want to work, according to Lizzie. Frank "worked at jobs when he wanted," she told a reporter.[105]

An offhand comment Mrs Pearcey made to a neighbour, Mrs Piddington, in an unrelated conversation supports Lizzie's assertion that Frank was in and out of work and that the family fell on harder financial times. Mrs Pearcey told Mrs Piddington that after Frank left the family business he "had not so much money as he used to have."[106]

Phoebe described her family's diminished financial situation as "very narrow straights," which were particularly difficult to bear, since she had lived so many years in "good service."[107] Being short of money wasn't about lacking material comforts either, Lizzie qualified, but providing basic needs. According to Lizzie, her aunt had to, on occasion, "deprive herself of food in order to supply necessaries for her child."[108]

Predictably, the Hoggs denied this.

"What do you say to the evidence of the sister and niece that Mrs Hogg, during her illness, did not have sufficient nourishment?" a reporter asked during an interview post inquest.

"I can, and wish to, absolutely deny it," Edwin Hogg said.

"During the illness my wife sent down everything that could be needed - wine, eggs, and every necessary nourishment," he said.[109]

"Besides," Mrs Sarah Hogg, Edwin's wife interjected, "she could not have wanted for food because she knew her husband's table was always open to her."[110]

"As to the nature of her illness," Edwin continued, "she would not acknowledge that it was a miscarriage, and the only other explanation she could make of her weakness to her sister was, I suppose, that she was not well and properly fed."[111]

When Phoebe became sick in February, the illness defied diagnosis. She was weak and pale, and the Hoggs decided she had miscarried, even though Phoebe unswervingly denied having been pregnant. Miscarriage or not, the Hoggs maintained that she wasn't deliberately starved, and if she was hungry and thin it was because she had nursed an overgrown suspicion of her husband and refused to eat properly. On one occasion, Sarah Hogg remembered, Phoebe had refused to touch some custard that she had taken to her, fearing someone had tampered with it.[112] She was also irrationally fearful of doctors, and refused to visit one until it was critically necessary. If they were poisoning her, Sarah Hogg argued, then why would they pay for her doctor's visits and medicine? It made no sense.

But, little about the relationship between Phoebe, Frank, and Mrs Pearcey made sense. For example, in almost every account Frank appears consistently perplexed about Phoebe's secret visits and exchanges with Mrs Pearcey. When a reporter asked if he had any idea about the unsigned letters which Mrs Pearcey sent to Phoebe, or that Phoebe had met her at a pub, he answered bewilderedly, "not the slightest." Perhaps it was possible that one invitation could slip past him, but multiple? Even he doubted it. "Don't you think it would be a singular thing for those letters to be coming here without my hearing something about them? And, moreover, I never was aware of her visiting Mrs Pearcey or that they were on terms of great intimacy?" he claimed.[113] And yet, it was to Mrs Pearcey's house that Frank directed Clara the day after the murders. When asked why he sent Clara to 2 Priory Street, he said he was confused and wanted to explore every possibility in order to find his wife.

Furthermore, Edwin said that he and his wife had tea with Phoebe only five weeks before her murder and inquired how she was doing. Phoebe said she was quite happy. "If she had had that letter from Mrs Pearcey, is it not strange she did not mention it to my wife? I also think it peculiar that the sister should not have spoken about it to some one at the time."[114]

Perhaps neither Phoebe nor Martha said anything to anyone because while she didn't trust Mrs Pearcey, she also didn't fear her, underestimating the lengths she would go when provoked. Frank certainly suggested such a theory, as he repeatedly said he never saw any signs of such fear.

"She [Phoebe] was certainly very reticent, but at the same time if she had received those peculiar letters I think she would have shown them to me. As to the statement about Mrs Pearcey's nurse, I have never heard of such a person, and I don't believe there is such a woman."[115]

Reporters couldn't get enough of the story and spent much time after the inquest tracking down leads and verifying - as best they could - the accusations and statements made during the inquest. One reporter for *The Times* tracked down Dr Louis Bennett Claremont, who lived at 31 Malden Crescent, off Prince of Wales Road, whose assistant, Dr G.W. Collins, had written a prescription for Phoebe during her illness in January, 1890. It was easy enough to reconstruct Phoebe's case through the notes Collins left before he moved to Wanstead, and based on those prescriptions, Dr Claremont confirmed that Phoebe had not miscarried.

On January 28, Phoebe was given belladonna, glycerin and an unnamed lotion. Belladonna, a rather toxic perennial plant native to Europe sometimes known as 'deadly nightshade', was commonly used to treat gastrointestinal disorders, though its medicinal effects were dubious.[116] The glycerin prescribed may have been an element of her treatment, as it was a typical medical additive used as a lubricant and humectant, but it may also have been prescribed alone, as glycerin was occasionally used as a laxative too. Phoebe's symptoms, which were later found to be the result of a uterine abscess, may have been mistakenly attributed to gastrointestinal disruption.

On January 30, Dr Collins gave her a tonic and a "simple medicine" to take home with her.[117] Frank administered them. Though Dr Claremont didn't see Phoebe Hogg that day, he knew her, he said, and characterised her as generally a rather "weak, anemic woman."[118]

Phoebe did not get better, even after taking the medicine. In fact, as Martha testified at the inquest, Phoebe got worse, and though she recovered, she was never as well as she was before January. Contradicting Martha's observation, Frank maintained that Phoebe had become "quite well" under his lover's care.[119] At the time, neither Martha nor Phoebe suspected Frank of tampering with her medicine, but later, Martha would come to believe her brother-in-law and the woman who "quite unexpectedly" showed up to nurse her sister,[120] Mrs Pearcey, had tried to poison Phoebe.[121]

On October 29, the day after the inquest, Frank, Clara and other witnesses engaged in the case filed in and out of the Treasury all morning, submitting depositions. Police were told that a pawnbroker at Streatham had realised that a ring recently pledged matched the description of Phoebe Hogg's missing wedding band. Frank sustained that neither ring taken from Mrs Pearcey belonged to Phoebe, but Clara had, at first, insisted the gold ring taken from Mrs Pearcey *was* her sister-in-law's. Lizzie Styles said "it's exactly like it," but after Frank said it wasn't his wife's ring Clara then doubted it was too.[122] For his part, Inspector Bannister remained unconvinced since he had slid the gold ring on Phoebe's finger and said it covered the sun mark exactly.[123]

After Frank signed his deposition, he accompanied one of the detectives to the pawnbroker's shop, hoping to positively identify the ring, while Clara returned home. Clara and old Mrs Hogg waited the rest of the afternoon and into the evening for Frank, but he did not return until after nine o'clock in the evening, and when he did he was, according to friends who had seen him, "quite mad" with grief.[124] Apparently, as he and a detective were walking back through Camden Town, Frank realised they were near the undertaker's, and insisted they stop.

Numbers of people had been to the undertaker's already, offering various sums of money - as much as 2s 6d[125] - for a glimpse of Phoebe and Tiggie's remains. Some of the crowd had made their way to the premises of one undertaker, Mr E. Richards on Great College Street, erroneously believing that he had been commissioned to service the Hoggs' funerary needs.[126] But enough knew it was actually William Alpen Clatworthy, of Clatworthy & Co, who had been instructed, and he had spent an exhausting day refusing mobs of morbid gawkers. He was probably a little surprised, then, to open the shop door that night to Frank Hogg.

Frank asked in a "strange and sharp manner" if he could see his wife and child, Mr Clatworthy later told a reporter.[127] He reluctantly agreed, and escorted Frank to the back room where his wife and daughter's polished elm coffin rested on trestles. Frank grew distressed at the sight, but regained his composure, bent down and kissed the faces of his wife and child, and then immediately left.

Witnesses told a reporter that when he got home he grieved and lamented, exclaiming that his wife and child were in their rooms above and he wanted to see them. He was inconsolable and "would not take rest," and his brothers were sent for in case he had to be restrained. Those who saw the episode swore that his appearance, manner and shrieks of grief, were evidence that his "mind had given way to the strain of circumstances," though stories of his temporary insanity were later said to have been greatly exaggerated.[128]

A newsman went to Clatworthy's shop on Camden High Street soon after the rumour of Frank's madness spread. He knocked; Clatworthy answered. A "knot of women" pushed and shoved against the door, and Clatworthy had a difficult time allowing only the reporter inside before slamming it shut on the macabre horde. The reporter saw Phoebe and Tiggie Hogg - child atop the breast of her mother - and reported that Phoebe looked "peaceful," although her face, forehead, hands and arms bore the shocking evidence of the dreadful struggle that preceded her death.[129]

The ring found at the Streatham pawnshop turned out to be another dead end, but police did find the boy who delivered the note written by Mrs Pearcey which invited Phoebe Hogg to tea that Friday. Willie Holmes told police, in a voluntary statement, that around 11am on Friday morning, while he was on errands for his mother, Mrs Pearcey gave him a letter and a penny, and instructed him to deliver the letter to Mrs Hogg. He dashed home first, then ran across the street and delivered the note to the woman who opened the door.[130] Whether it was Mrs Hogg to whom he gave the note he couldn't be sure, although when he saw Phoebe's body at the mortuary later, he said she was *not* the woman to whom he'd given the note.

As Willie was going over to deliver the letter, his mother, Elizabeth Ann Holmes, stepped out to see her son skittering across the street. She then noticed a woman waiting about, and remembered her because when the lady saw she was being observed she put a handkerchief in front of her face.[131] Elizabeth Holmes didn't recognise the woman then, but would later identify her as Mrs Pearcey.

Though the contents of the letter inviting Phoebe to Southend-on-Sea and the note delivered by Willie Holmes are more or less known, the letter which Mrs Pearcey sent to Phoebe on Friday remained a complete mystery.

"She [Phoebe] never liked Mrs Pearcey, and I never did," Lizzie told a reporter. "I know my aunt was afraid of her, for when she spoke to us about the Southend affair she said, 'No fear of me going to Southend. Why, I might be thrown over the cliffs, and none of you would know anything about it here.'"[132]

But if Phoebe feared Mrs Pearcey so much, how was it that Mrs Pearcey induced her to visit her, the reporter logically asked.

"That I cannot tell," Lizzie said, "there must have been some very strong inducement in the letter which she received on Friday morning."[133]

Back at the Hoggs' rooms, Frank and Clara were presumably spending much of the time arranging the funeral with the undertaker and parish ministers. When they were not otherwise occupied with these details, they were helping police. Clara and Frank accompanied detectives to Albany Street police station to identify retrieved clothing which police thought might be related to the case, but neither of them recognised any of the articles produced.[134]

On Thursday, November 30, at a meeting of the Hampstead Vestry, members decided to erect additional gas lamps along Crossfield Road, the dark thoroughfare where Phoebe Hogg's mutilated body was found the Friday before.[135]

As the case worked its way through the system and was increasingly reported in the press, additional eyewitnesses came forward with information connected to the crime. Mrs Crowhurst, the widow who lived on the first floor of 2 Priory Street, reported seeing a light move through Mrs Pearcey's bedroom late at night. At quarter past ten, she told a reporter, she heard the front door to 2 Priory Street open "very quietly."[136] Then she heard someone moving about. She went and looked over the banisters and saw the reflection of a light being carried about, but could not make out what or who it was, so she went back to her room and went to bed. As Frank testified, he had visited Mrs Pearcey on the night of the murders just after 10.00pm, but, finding her not at home, left her a note on an envelope, set it on the mantel, and went home.

Elizabeth Rodgers gave several interviews in the days following the inquest, elaborating on her involvement in the case. In fact, she became something of a local celebrity now that the neighbourhood was blitzed by "small knots of people," which loitered outside 2 Priory Street discussing the tragedy.[137] So persistent and numerous were these visits that one of the detectives had to plug the keyholes of the main door to keep people from spying inside.[138]

"I could not mistake her," Rodgers told a reporter for the *Daily News*, because "I used to do mangling for her."[139]

Rodgers said she'd been reading *Lloyd's* around noon on Sunday and saw there had been a murder at Hampstead. As she read further, she saw that Mrs Pearcey had been named as the prime suspect, and on reading that police suspected that the body had been transported in a pram, Mrs Rodgers exclaimed to her mother, "Why, mother, I saw her just under the railway arch, going along with a loaded bassinette."[140]

Apparently Mrs Pearcey came to have Mrs Rodgers mangle her laundry with some regularity, though she had no work for her during the week of the murders. Whenever they met, it was generally on the street, and Mrs Pearcey was always alone. So far as Mrs Rodgers knew, Mrs Pearcey was a "quiet woman" who generally kept herself "respectable."[141]

Detective Inspector Bannister worked himself as hard as he worked his team of detectives, revisiting 2 Priory Street several times to shore up the police theory of what happened that fateful Friday afternoon. It did not escape notice that while there were supposed to be five identical buttons on Phoebe's dress, four were missing. On one of the visits to Mrs Pearcey's rooms, Bannister found one of those missing buttons, along with a button of a different style, in the fire grate at 2 Priory Street,[142] establishing that Phoebe was indeed at 2 Priory Street at *some* point recently, and suggesting that the buttons were burned because they were incriminating, identifying evidence.[143]

Bannister also conducted an experiment, getting into the pram and wheeling about, which he said proved the pram could bear the weight of a full-grown human body.[144]

Detective's found a woman's skirt, dirty and drenched with rainwater, about 200 yards from where baby Tiggie was discovered. The press speculated that it might have been used to wrap the baby and keep her clean of her mother's blood as she made the trek to her final resting spot underneath the nettle bush, but it was never proved to be related to the case.[145]

Mrs Pearcey's solicitor Freke Palmer asked Bannister to organise a visit to the scene so he could examine it for himself as he mounted her defence. Bannister obliged, as he was particularly keen to check over the grate again to determine whether any evidence of Phoebe's missing hat or purse remained. It was during this visit to the crime scene that a quantity of letters was discovered, among them a rather large amount of correspondence with an unnamed someone in America.[146]

In the drawer of a dresser in the kitchen a revolver was discovered, and in the parlour, behind a tea-tray on the sideboard, a tin box containing pin-fire cartridges which matched.[147]

As the detectives combed over the flat again, Palmer made interesting observations of his own. The front and back rooms were small, he noticed; the kitchen and hallway cramped. The hallway where the pram was wedged measured only 37 inches wide, but it was big enough to just pass through. Even so, the rooms were nicely appointed; neither expensive nor cheap.

The houses along Priory Street ranged in rent from £35 to a little over £40 a year and were occupied by mostly a "superior class" of tradesman and mechanics.[148]

Palmer's client had first lived in the upper rooms at No. 2 and at some point, for reasons unknown, moved downstairs. Neighbourly descriptions of Mrs Pearcey were largely positive. Often she was described as a woman "very well conducted."[149] Neighbours in Kentish Town later told a *Lloyd's* reporter that she was perceived as having a generally kind disposition. She took great pride in cultivating the garden at the back of the shared house, and seemed pleased when she had salad to share with others.[150]

This kindness extended beyond her neighbours too.

One story was told to a reporter about a beggar who knocked at one of the doors and was turned away abruptly. The beggar said, "Well, thank God they are not all hardhearted people, for the lady next door at No. 2 had got some feeling." According to the neighbour's story, Mrs Pearcey had given the beggar 3d and some bread and butter.[151]

Though she may have been kind, she wasn't without her detractors. Mrs Crowhurst, worried about the "goings on" at 2 Priory Street, and felt that there was "a great deal" not right with Mrs Pearcey.[152] Even so, the ghastly murder didn't reconcile with what most of her neighbours knew of her. Some said they would not have made the connection that the murderer was their neighbour Mrs Pearcey had the papers not named her and listed her address explicitly. Those living at 2 Priory Street were, understandably, shocked that a crime so ghastly had been perpetrated under their very roof without a single person seeing or hearing it. Later, Palmer would make this a central argument in his appeal for her life.

Mrs Crowhurst, the widow who lived with her son on the first floor, said she was thankful she was out when the murders were committed, but that she must have just come in "directly afterwards, when all was quiet, and the poor creatures' lives were gone."[153] Friday was the first night she'd slept in her rooms for some time, as she had been away caring for her pregnant daughter. She was scheduled to have been home at four o'clock, but had missed her train and didn't get home until five.

"They all tell me that perhaps it was very providential I did not come in just at the time, for if I had perhaps, rather than have let me live to tell the tale, those who committed the murder might have killed me, too," she told a reporter.[154]

When she arrived home that Friday, Mrs Crowhurst said all was quiet and nothing seemed amiss, so she went upstairs, lit the fire, and got her tea. Mrs Butler came in after her and, as she came into the hallway, Mrs Crowhurst heard Mrs Pearcey say, "Mind, Mrs Butler. There is something in the passage." Mrs Pearcey came out of her room and deftly led Mrs Butler by the pram so that she didn't accidentally "rip her dress."[155]

In retrospect, Mrs Crowhurst said, "I suppose really she was afraid that she might have put her hand on the body, and have perhaps smeared her hand and clothes with the blood."[156]

Later, the Butlers went out for the night, and around 8.00pm Mrs Crowhurst's son came home for tea. He then went out to the back garden, which meant he passed Mrs Pearcey's rear kitchen window and the scullery. When he came back inside, he asked his mother how Mrs Pearcey's kitchen windows came to be smashed and the blind pulled down, and the oilcloth all wet and lying about in the yard.

She attributed the smashed glass to a row Mrs Pearcey must have had with her husband or one of her "gentlemen." "I do not like the looks of some that come and I hardly think it is safe to be here," she said. Her son agreed, and they made a pact to find new housing as soon as possible.[157]

Which of Mrs Pearcey's callers Mrs Crowhurst didn't like the look of is unknown, but she knew Mr Crichton and Mr Hogg. She had opened the door to Mr Crichton a few times, as he came to visit Mary nearly every week, usually on Mondays.[158] She also knew Hogg, whom Mrs Pearcey always represented as her husband. Hogg would often take his dinner and tea at Mrs Pearcey's, sometimes two or three times a week, and on those days she would make a great fuss saying, "Well, I must go and get my husband's dinner ready. He will be in directly." On the occasions when Frank did not show up, Mrs Pearcey was uneasy and said things like, "I wonder where he is that he does not come."[159]

Mrs Piddington, the young married woman who lived at No. 3, also had more to say on the matter. Her husband, a railway man who alternated night and day duty, was off duty, in bed and fast asleep on the afternoon of the murders. She had been clearing up her rooms on Friday afternoon when she saw the dressmaker's wicker stand which she'd borrowed from Mrs Pearcey and, deciding it was time to give it back, walked downstairs with it at about half past four. While she was passing the landing window she heard banging and then crashing coming quite distinctly from Mrs Pearcey's back kitchen, she said. She froze and listened for a minute, and then heard a window shatter. She ran down the stairs, out into her own back garden and called over the fence. She heard a little baby screaming and crying.

"It was terrible to hear it," she said.

Then, another thud. She called out to Mrs Pearcey five or six times, but Mrs Pearcey didn't answer. Nervous and terribly frightened, she didn't know what to do, so she put the wicker dress stand over the wall into Mrs Pearcey's garden and, alarmed that the baby was screaming "so dreadfully," called out to her again and then waited.[160]

She thought perhaps Mrs Pearcey and her husband (she mistakenly thought Hogg was Mr Pearcey) were quarrelling, and, not wanting to get involved, waited only a moment more before going back into the house and shutting the door, the baby still screaming "fearfully."[161]

After a time, all went quiet and still, and the baby cried no more.

Later, when she was not so scared, Mrs Piddington went back down and looked over the wall. The wicker dress stand was gone. Mrs Pearcey, or someone else, had fetched it inside. She saw the broken glass of the kitchen window. When she went to the Treasury to give her statement, Mrs Piddington was particularly aghast at being told that the prosecution suspected as she was calling out to check on Mrs Pearcey, the murderer was trying to cut off Phoebe's head, which caused the baby to cry.

"My calling out no doubt frightened them," Mrs Piddington said. "They say what a pity it is that I did not see who fetched the wicker dress stand in; for then I should have seen who the real murderer was, for whoever fetched it in, their hands must have been reeking with blood, as there are the blood marks on the dress-stand where they took hold of it and carried it in."[162]

Others who claimed to see Mrs Pearcey at different points in her long journey that night came forward. *Lloyd's* reported the story of a young woman regularly employed by a well-known business in the West End, but who wished to remain anonymous, who said she knew Mrs Pearcey well.

Shortly after 8.00pm on Friday, the young woman said she stepped outside her workplace to meet a friend of hers. They met, walked down Great Portland Street, and there ran into Mrs Pearcey standing in the street. The woman was struck by how dishevelled Mrs Pearcey looked. She had never before seen her "so untidy and dejected" in public. She wore her hat, but her hair was messy. She wore no gloves and her hands looked "stained."[163] She appeared to be greatly agitated too, turning her head this way and that, her eyes darting back and forth, as if looking to see if she were being watched.

The young lady observed Mrs Pearcey for a few minutes and then decided to see if she was all right, but reconsidered. Instead, she and a friend walked away, but the woman was as certain of seeing Mrs Pearcey as she was of telling the reporter about it at that moment, and offered to take the reporter to the dark flagstone where she stood that night as proof.[164]

Whether this eyewitness was credible or not is difficult to tell, but probably not. She could have been mistaken or lying, or simply wanted to inject herself into an increasingly high-profile trial, without getting too involved. Police never tracked down the anonymous source or her friend, so they never testified in court.

The theory of an accomplice, or accomplices, was again revived when Mr Charles Stockwell, a file cutter who lived at 1 Priory Street, stated he was sure the noise that came from Mrs Pearcey's flat that afternoon and all night could not have been made by just one person.

"I was at work finishing some files in my back kitchen when I and my wife were suddenly startled by a great noise. It was like 'crash, crash, crash, and bang, bang, bang, bang, bang!' I said to my wife, 'Whatever is that? Is it something coming down, or is it in Mrs Pearcey's?'"[165]

Realising that a wall had not in fact come down, they ran into the garden to call out to Mrs Pearcey to make sure she was alright. When their calls went unanswered they thought they'd just overheard a row and went back inside, not wanting to interfere between "a man and his wife."[166] The noise stopped for some time, and all was quiet until later that night when it sounded like people "walking about and clearing up."[167] The noise lasted through the night, Stockwell said, and it sounded like multiple people were going in and out, in and out. The next morning, it was obvious to Stockwell that the front steps and stones had been carefully washed. While it was certainly possible Mrs Pearcey enlisted help to clean up that night, Mr Stockwell's statement was given after the inquest, at a time when much about the crime, its culprit and her efforts to evade detection had been widely reported.[168]

All through the weekend, the excitement concerning the murders showed little signs of abating, and extended well beyond the neighbourhoods of Kentish and Camden towns.

"The dreadful affair has made a very painful impression in the locality of Rickmansworth being almost the sole topic of conversation during the week," wrote the *Herts Advertiser*, mindful of Phoebe's link to that locale.[169]

Inspector Bannister and Superintendent Beard met with Commissioner Sir Edward Bradford at Scotland Yard to go over the forensic evidence against Mrs Pearcey, which was now overwhelming. Bannister probably told Bradford of a particularly interesting bloodstain on the window frame of one of the broken glass panes. It was a set of bloody fingerprints, as if imprinted with three fingers of each hand. Though fingerprinting was still a decade away from being standard police practice, one wonders if the same experimental instinct that put Bannister in the pram also compelled him to think about comparing the size and shape of the prints to his suspected murderess. In addition, splashes of blood on the other panes had been discovered, which had clearly been smeared while wet with a cloth, as one would when trying to clean up.[170]

After interviewing Bannister about his last search of Mrs Pearcey's rooms, the *Pall Mall Gazette* retracted their supposition that she had an accomplice.

Inspector Bannister and his team of detectives stayed close to all involved in the case, and were well aware of the dangerous antipathy growing toward Frank Hogg. As the funeral of Phoebe and Tiggie Hogg approached, the Hogg family devised a misinformation campaign about the date and time of the internment, hoping to avoid an increasingly curious but angry crowd.[171] In any event, the police agreed to arrange a significant presence to guard the procession, and keep Frank Hogg from being "roughly handled" by the mob.[172]

Freke Palmer had visited his client at Holloway Gaol after the inquest, during which time Mrs Pearcey spoke freely with him about the prison authorities' kind and fair treatment of her, though she seemed rather put out that they had kept her in workhouse clothes too long. She was quite happy when they were finally exchanged for others more suitable to her social position,[173] and she maintained her innocence of the crime, claiming again that her memory of what happened the week before was still "a perfect blank."[174]

Now that there was, as the *Pall Mall Gazette* reported at last, "practically no doubt that only one person was concerned in the crime,"[175] the press and public wanted to know more about the Hampstead murderess. The police were equally interested in Mrs Pearcey's early life, and began making inquiries to locate friends and family who may have information that could help contextualise the crime.

A reporter for *Lloyd's* found a man that frequented the same pub as Mary Wheeler and John Pearcey, who said the people in their neighbourhood used to tease John Pearcey about how it was that he'd nabbed such a "nice girl."[176] This man also remembered Mrs Pearcey frequently sitting at the open front parlour window of their apartments on Bayham Street. She was always smiling, he said, and had a kind word for the people she knew as they passed by. No one ever saw anything "fast" about her, and everyone always took her to be John Pearcey's legitimate wife.[177] How this well-read, pretty woman of 24 achieved a place in the "front rank of murderesses" was a present mystery that perhaps only her past could explain.[178]

THE MURDERESS, THE LOVER AND THE WIFE

MRS Pearcey was born Mary Eleanor Wheeler in Ightham, Kent on Monday, March 26, 1866,[1] and baptised on April 28 of the same year.[2] The weather on the day of her birth was reported favourable, "breezy and dry."[3] It was the kind of country day worthy of a Wordsworth poem.

A Mrs Taylor, who said she nursed Mary's mother Charlotte Ann Wheeler during the delivery, remembered the day Mary was born. She later described the baby to a reporter as "pretty" with "light hair and large blue eyes."[4]

"We had such a good home too," Charlotte later said, "and we never had a misword in our lives," referring to her relationship to her husband.[5] In retrospect, and certainly as compared to the draughty, near-empty room from which she gave the interview decades later,[6] Charlotte idealised the family's time in Ightham as postcard-perfect.[7]

But memory softens and sweetens the bitterness and boredom of reality, and the reality was that Charlotte suffered "a terrible grief" at the time her daughter was born.[8] The grief resulted from disappointing her family, who had disowned her when she didn't marry the man they'd chosen for her. She worried this grief would contaminate her baby, and she worried about the consequences of carrying a child when she was prone to fits.[9]

It was the combination of this toxic grief and bad genes, Charlotte later said, that made Nellie - Mary's family nickname - too sympathetic and susceptible to other people's grief,[10] which, perhaps, caused her to behave in unpredictable ways.

The toxicity of emotions was not an uncommon idea. Many expectant mothers of the era worried that, through some mystical mechanism or chance encounter with a beast, they would imprint the bad psychic energy or physical characteristics of the beast onto their children. The belief was called "maternal impression."[11] Joseph Merrick, given the show name "The Elephant Man" by his manager Tom Norman in order to drum up a crowd, used this theory to partly explain his own, rare medical condition. Merrick explained his illness this way: his mother was knocked over and frightened by an elephant while she was pregnant. This encounter resulted in the thick lesions that covered his body. In truth, Merrick probably suffered from a combination of Neurofibromatosis Type I and Proteus Syndrome, both years from diagnosis or treatment.

While Charlotte hadn't been knocked over by an elephant, she worried her daughter had met with a different sort of beast, albeit an invisible one: depression. Though scientifically dubious, maternal impression presaged genetic transference, which was still a century away from widespread understanding. In other words, the mechanism was wrong, but Charlotte's maternal instinct was not, and she indeed had cause to worry that she might have passed on a genetic predisposition to epilepsy and mental illness.

Charlotte Kelly was born in Gillingham. She had spent her youth at Rainham and Rochester, and was a Sunday school teacher at St. John's church. At church she met her first love, an architect and surveyor by profession (his name has been lost to history). Her father, Michael Kelly, accepted their courtship and the boy's proposal. In fact, the marriage would have been a source of family pride, for while most of Charlotte's friends and family were in service to Her Majesty's

Army or Navy, her architect belonged to a higher class. Had they been successfully married she would have undoubtedly been well provided for since he and his friends were well-to-do.

The marriage didn't happen however, because soon after it was arranged, Charlotte went to visit her brother and, while boarding his boat, met James Wheeler, who immediately fell in love with her and courted her aggressively.

As Charlotte later retold the tale of their courtship, when she was leaving the ship James said, "There goes my wife. Either that girl or nobody for me." She said that it could never be, for someone else had claim to her heart and would have something to say about it, but James was undeterred. "It will be the case of the best man winning," he quipped.[12]

James Whitford Wheeler was born on October 8, 1829 in Birmingham. Not only was he a low-ranking seaman who would never be able to provide for Charlotte as her architect could have, he had also been married before, to a Miss Elizabeth Wilson.[13]

Nonetheless, on February 14, 1865[14] - almost certainly not a coincidence - the romantic Charlotte married her rascal sailor, in secret, while in Kent. It seems she went to some lengths to conceal her identity because the marriage registration notes her name as Charlotte Ann Kennedy, a 'widow', whose father's name was William Kelly (deceased), when, of course, neither were true. Charming, "fine, handsome, and cheerful looking,"[15] James would prove to be the "kindest of husbands."[16]

According to Mr James Dunn, a resident of Ightham who knew the Wheelers, they lived in a quaint, old-fashioned cottage. Mr Dunn described Mr Wheeler as a "tall, thin man with dark hair and a dark complexion," and Mrs Wheeler as a "tall, slender woman, with very fair hair." They were nice, quiet, respectable people, he said, with whom he often spoke. James Wheeler joined the Kent constabulary and was appointed the village policeman, a sad irony given his daughter's eventual fate. When he was off duty, James was remembered wearing a blue jersey and playing with the children, who he let chase after him. When on duty however, he was a "different sort of man," Mr Dunn said, and the children dared not speak to him.[17]

Mr Dunn remembered Mary Eleanor's birth as an occasion with much "rejoicing going on afterwards."

The Wheelers didn't stay long in Ightham though. A few months after Mary was born, they left for the neighbouring village of Wrotham. Again, James served as a policeman, according to Mr Dunn. After that Mr Dunn didn't see or know much of James or his family.[18]

Nellie was a kind child, but painfully sensitive, Charlotte remembered. She would give up nearly everything she had to other children, she said, and she could never bear to see a child beaten.

"If any of them had done wrong at any time," Charlotte said, "she would try to hide them and then go to their father or their mother, and say, 'You won't beat them, will you?' and she would often cry till they promised not to do so."[19]

Her mother thought her daughter "kind and good natured" - the sort to give the last penny out of her pocket if she thought others were in distress.[20] That said, when she was denied anything she wanted, she took it to heart and could be impressively self-destructive.

By the mid nineteenth century, Victorian England was a country and culture of radical change. Railway lines criss-crossed the countryside, connecting rural villages to the metropolis. Steamships regularly crossed the Atlantic in a matter of days. The first commercially successful bicycle caught on in Europe, and the Penny Post, developed by Sir Rowland Hill, afforded even the poorest villager a cheap, efficient means of communication. It was an exciting time full of technocratic optimism and about two years after Nellie was born, the Wheelers traded the "pretty districts of Kent" for the whirl and wonder of the capital.

According to Charlotte, James Wheeler had been invalided out of the Royal Marines, and though he'd tried his hand at the constabulary, he wanted steadier work. Fortuitously, he found employment almost immediately as a delivery foreman at the Hermitage Steam Wharf in Wapping - a giant, industrial warehouse on the Thames. His wages were enough to afford rooms at No. 36 Gloster Street.[21] He must have been a good, hard worker, for he stayed at the Wharf for 14 years.

Their tenement at Gloster Street was a mansion in Kensington compared to the workhouse. Although not yet a byword for "ghetto," the East End of London in the 1860s and 70s looked much like it would 20 years later when the Whitechapel murders launched the district into infamy. Overcrowded, diseased and destitute, the East End in the late 1860s was a hotchpotch of working-class and unemployed families, many of them immigrants, trying to make their way in a city that could not deliver on all the promises of prosperity it made.

Since the time of Queen Elizabeth I, English society dealt with the destitute through a haphazard system of laws - mainly financed by a series of taxes and rates assessing citizens who owned or rented houses of a certain value. In 1834, the government passed the Poor Law Amendment Act, which centralised the system and encouraged the use of large-scale, morbid-looking buildings called workhouses.[22] The old and disabled could apply for money and food, and stay in their own homes if they had other family to take care of them. Those without family, who were neither old nor infirm, entered the workhouse, where they worked for food and a coffin-like bed in which to sleep.

Writing about the wards of the Wapping workhouse, Charles Dickens said the building was degenerate and behind the times, "a mere series of garrets or lofts with every inconvenient and objectionable circumstance in their construction, and only accessible by steep and narrow staircases, infamously ill-adapted for the passage up-stairs of the sick or down-stairs of the dead."[23] Most early and mid-century workhouse infirmaries were little more than holding cells and took on many prison-like aspects. "A bed in the miserable rooms, here on bedsteads, there (for a charge, as I understood it) on the floor, were women in every stage of distress and disease," wrote Dickens.[24]

Families went to great lengths to avoid workhouses - colloquially called a 'spike' - if they could, but sickness was a routine cause of poverty, and one of the fastest routes into the workhouse.[25]

The Metropolitan Poor Law Amendment Act, which separated Poor Law infirmaries from the London workhouses, was passed in 1867. A resident medical superintendent, who led mostly trained nursing staff, managed the new infirmaries, unlike the old system, which largely used 'pauper' nurses to tend to the sickest among them. After 1860, roughly one-third of Poor Law infirmary entrants were non-paupers, but because of the affiliation with poor relief, a stay in hospital was a considerable source of embarrassment, to be avoided if it could.[26]

Avoiding the workhouse and poor law infirmaries would prove impossible for Charlotte and Nellie, as both suffered fits, which may or may not have been epileptic in nature. In fact, sadly, Charlotte would live out her last days and die in the Stepney Union in Mile End, Old Town.[27] What medical records exist are unclear whether Charlotte's fits were life-long, but Nellie's fits seem to have been caused, triggered, or exacerbated after an incident in a garden when she was only two-years-old, and dogged her until her death.

In her deposition, Charlotte said that Nellie fell out of a nurse's arms onto stones in the garden as a toddler.[28] A few weeks later she began touching her head where she'd hit it, crying incessantly. When she was old enough to speak, she complained that her head hurt. Perhaps it was the intensity of this brain-on-fire that once caused Nellie to try and drown herself in the River Lea. She was rescued, according to a reporter from *Lloyd's*, by a nearby resident who heard the splash. Whether Nellie actually attempted suicide or just threatened it is unclear from the account.[29]

It is equally unclear the kinds of seizures Nellie suffered, or the type of epilepsy she had. In the 1860s, medicine had not yet advanced to the point where it could prove scarring of the brain resulted in headaches, temperament changes and seizures, or what would be called today temporal lobe epilepsy.[30]

In cases of temporal lobe epilepsy, the cells in or around a lesion formed on the brain are so damaged they don't behave as healthy cells might. The brain misfires, shooting off bursts of electricity that can cause excruciating headaches and various types of seizures. Some seizures cause the person to fall down and convulse, but others are subtler and simply cause the person to act strangely, or to appear to stare into the distance.[31] Lesions have numerous causes, but are most commonly the result of head trauma, as when a toddler is dropped headfirst on a hard surface.

John Hughlings Jackson, one of the first and most eminent doctors of the Victorian era to study epilepsy in detail, described the epileptic brain cells as the "mad part" of the brain that makes nearby "sane cells... act madly."[32] It was an unfortunate analogy, describing psychologically what was largely neuroelectrical, but Jackson was merely adding to the existing historic and literary record, which had long since equated epilepsy with madness or possession.

In Roman and Greek mythology, for example, the Gods were responsible for epileptic fits, but it was considered a "sacred disease", a form of divine madness. In fact the term itself originated from the Greek word *epilepsia*, meaning seizure, as in a god seizing control of a mortal's body.[33] In Middle Age and Renaissance cultures, however, European Christians held that epilepsy was the outward expression of the inward battle for the soul, a fight between Satan and the Holy Ghost, and as far back as 650 BC, seizures were attributed to the Devil.[34] In fact, the Hindus of India dedicated a special demon - Grahi - to explain epilepsy within their culture, and it was no coincidence that Grahi was a feminine deity, as the fiercest Hindu gods were almost always female.

Though strides in understanding the science of epilepsy, and treating epileptics with compassion, were made during the fin de siècle, Victorians were generally afraid of epileptics. Despite evolving understanding of the etiology of the disease, epilepsy remained largely a socially constructed affliction, shaped by a Smilesian[35] ethic that valued hard work, good order, diligence and temperance. Epileptics contradicted notions of social responsibility and respectability, and as a consequence, they were often socially marginalized, stigmatized, and increasingly confined to lunatic asylums or epileptic colonies, having violated "the laws of nature."[36] As a socially constructed affliction, it was no surprise then that the treatment of epilepsy varied by class. Epilepsy could be a private misfortune among the bourgeoisie, but was often characterised as a dangerous - even criminal - character flaw among the working poor.

Mid and late nineteenth century Victorians equated epilepsy with a kind of moral insanity - an inability to maintain control over one's faculties. The prominent Italian criminologist Cesare Lombroso described the violent thrashing sometimes associated with epilepsy as "furor epilepticus,"or epileptic fury, which helped fuse the ideas between epilepsy and violence.[37] Though his major theories were largely discredited by the Edwardian era, Lombroso's atavistic theories of crime were wildly popular in the last decades of Victoria's reign. And, Stevenson's *The Strange Case of Dr Jekyll and Mr Hyde* served as the perfect metaphor for the unspoken anxieties surrounding epileptics. Epilepsy was an affliction that could transform otherwise sane men and women into criminal beasts. Such assumptions about the disease enabled doctors to treat patients in unscientific, and sometimes inhuman, ways, and so there was great impetus to resist designations of 'epileptic' or 'lunatic' and it was generally advisable to avoid the asylum with the same vigour one avoided the workhouse.[38]

In 1868 Charlotte and James had a second daughter, Amelia Elizabeth Wheeler, and a third daughter, Charlotte Amy Whitford Wheeler, was born in 1871. Both were baptised at the Anglican St. Philip's church in Stepney.[39] In the 1871 census, the family was living at 2 William Street South in Mile End Old Town.[40] Six months later, on August 31, Amelia died of pneumonia. Three more children - all boys - joined the family: James John Henry Wheeler was born on December 4, 1872 and baptised at St. George-in-the-East the following April. Charles Thomas William Wheeler was born March 21, 1875, and also baptised at St. George-in-the-East, and John

Wheeler was born sometime around 1879.[41]

The family moved at least twice between the birth of the sons - to 60 Great Hermitage Street[42] and then, to 62 St. George Street[43] - but stayed in the Stepney parish.

James Wheeler loved all his children, Charlotte said, but he was particularly tender toward Mary.

"Oh how fond he used to be of that child," and she of him. At seeing her father returning from the wharf, Mary would run to meet him, and all the children would cling round him. "It was all love and happiness at home when he was with us," Charlotte said wistfully.[44]

Five children was certainly a demand on the Wheelers' financial resources, but they were better off than many of the working poor. "We had such a good home," Charlotte said, "for he was in a capital position,"[45] meaning, he did well enough at the wharf to provide what Charlotte thought was a decent standard of living.

Mary was educated first at Wapping, and then at a school on Cannon Street Road.[46] By the time she achieved Standard VI, she would have been able to read poetry, write paragraphs and perform basic mathematics. It seems she favoured language though and was a voracious reader, though whether her reading was to stave off boredom or was for pleasure, no one knows. Still, she was fond of or familiar enough with the poet Longfellow to quote him in a love letter she would write years later.

"She was always full of life and spirits," Charlotte told a reporter, "and they were her really happy days."[47]

The happy days were not to last, however. Mary left school in her late teens and went to work for her uncle, John H. Kelly, at his newsagent's shop in Stepney. His shop was close to where he lived at 150 Whitehorse Street and not far from a German family, the Prümmers,[48] who, in 1881 were living at 105 Whitehorse Street.[49] Her uncle later said of Mary that she was his favourite niece, and was known for having a "kind and gentle disposition."[50] At some point she stopped selling newspapers for her uncle and went to work for the Prümmers as a nurse to their newborn son, George William Cristoph Prümmer. By Mrs Prümmer's account, Mary was "a great favourite" in their house, owing to her "kind and affectionate nature" and her "gentle ways."[51]

Mary worked hard, but she never outgrew the "growing pains," as her mother called them, that plagued her youth. She constantly suffered debilitating headaches and fits, and never knew what caused them, which seemed to be a source of great anxiety for her later in life. "Mother," she would say, "I can't tell what is the matter with my head."[52] The "storm within" is how painter Vincent van Gogh explained the headaches, paranoia, and personality changes that preceded his own temporal lobe epileptic fits,[53] and Mary described similar symptoms and outcomes.

Mary's fits grew rather worse as she got older, and during one particularly severe seizure Mr Prümmer had to hold her down. When she came round, Mrs Prümmer said she stared vacantly about and seemed quite dazed. She was so ill thereafter that she was unable to work, and eventually went to the infirmary seeking whatever treatment she could afford.[54] The sick asylum doctor may have prescribed potassium bromide - one of the few antiepileptic drugs available - or laudanum to relieve the pain of the preceding headaches.[55]

With a young child to consider, the Prümmers dismissed Mary from service sometime in July of 1882.[56] The dismissal was understandable, but painful.

Just a little over a month later, she suffered another significant emotional shock. On or near August 15, 1882, men arrived at the Wheeler house on 16 Maroon Street in Mile End, where the family had moved the previous year. They were carrying James Wheeler, her father, on a gurney; he was unable to move. There had been an accident at work, and his injuries were severe. He died forty-eight hours later.[57]

James' death launched the Wheeler family into a spiral of grief, illness, and poverty from which they never recovered. Charlotte did the best she could, taking on needlework and laundry and "what we could get to do," but only two months later, in September 1882, she was grievously ill, and spent four months in the sick asylum, no doubt as much aggrieved by the loss of her "good husband," as the other physical maladies that troubled her. Charlotte's brother-in-law, a tradesman in the East End, later said of James' accidental death that it was a "terrible blow to the family." Mary took it especially hard, the uncle said, "It was a great misfortune for her."[58]

A few months after her father's death, Mary tried to hang herself. She'd tied a rope around her neck and hooked it on a nail, then kicked out a laundry basket from beneath her feet and was dangling - already black in the face from oxygen deprivation - when a neighbour-friend, Mrs Buckley, helped Charlotte lift the girl down. They only just saved her life.[59] "In another minute, if we had not seen her," Charlotte later told a reporter, "she would have been dead."[60]

In looking back on the event, Charlotte felt her husband's death marked the beginning of the end for her daughter. "But there, if he had been alive, poor man," she said ruefully, "it [the murders] would not have happened at all."[61]

Sometime around October 10, Charlotte realised she was too ill to care for her family anymore. She applied to the workhouse to be admitted with at least one of her children, no doubt hoping to reduce the number of children left at home for Mary to look after in her absence. In the event, only son Charles was admitted.

While her mother was away, Mary used what remained of her father's £10 life insurance policy to keep her brothers and sisters fed and clothed, but they were forced to let go the better part of their flat, and eventually took in short-term lodgers to avoid sending the younger children - Charlotte Amy, John, and James - into the workhouse.[62] Taking in lodgers was a risky business, and the pressure on Mary must have been immense. Though she probably received limited support from relatives and friends, some of who were listed in the Stepney Union records in 1889, the majority of the work fell onto teenaged Mary,[63] and the entire family came to depend on her.

She took whatever work was available to her. She had, at that time, spent considerable time with the neighbourhood Jewesses through whom she'd heard of a rich old gentleman who needed a maid somewhere near Leman Street.[64] She went to clean for the old man, who liked Mary immediately, and perhaps too ardently. When Charlotte found out that her daughter was there alone with the old man, she forbade her to go back. The old man was reportedly so bereft over losing Mary's company that he showed up at the Wheeler flat to beg Charlotte for her daughter's return. Charlotte refused. It was during this time, Charlotte later recalled, that things got "rather worse."[65]

One of the lodgers the Wheelers accepted was a Mrs West and her 23 or 24-year-old son. Mrs West was a machinist, and her son a shunter.[66] Mother and son occupied the top rooms of the Wheeler house, and Mrs West took to Mary immediately, or perhaps Mary took to her son. Either way, Mrs West persistently - and over Charlotte's objections - invited Mary upstairs to teach her to sew. Charlotte forbade her daughter from visiting the Wests, though why is unclear. Mary went anyway, and developed a close relationship with Mrs West, and her son.[67] Presumably, this was easy to do since her mother was in and out of hospital.

According to his sworn testimony, John Lawrence Bosley, a dispenser at the Stepney Union, said he remembered that on September 6, 1882, Mary came to the Union to get medicine for her mother, and while waiting she suffered an epileptic fit and fell to the ground. Bosley picked her up, and after she came to put her in a conveyance and sent her home.[68]

Mary had another violent seizure on October 3, 1882, according to her cousin Augustine Cotterill, and was picked up off Commercial Road and admitted to the Q Ward of Stepney infirmary.[69] According to the Admission and Discharge Register, she was "fetched out by her young man" on October 5. Who, exactly, the young man was, is uncertain, but the Stepney Union records report that Mary had married a man by the last name of West, who was a shunter, just like the upstairs lodger's son.

The chronology of events from this point forward is imprecise at best, a web of misquotes, misremembering and half-truths that is difficult to untangle. If the marriage happened at all - and there are no records to suggest it did - then it could have happened while the Wests were still living in the Wheeler flat and Charlotte was sick, or after they fell into arrears, were evicted, and convinced Mary to come with them. It seems all of this happened sometime between October 1882 and July 1883. Recounting that terrible year to a reporter, Charlotte later said, "I always looked upon that as the cause of my daughter's downfall."[70]

By July 1883, Mary was no longer living with her family. "I never knew where she took her to," Charlotte told a reporter, referring to Mrs West, "and I could not find her."[71]

It was a year or more before Charlotte saw her daughter again. Charlotte heard she was working for a woman in the fur trade, and eventually that she was staying in Cannon Street Road in Shadwell. She believed that Mrs West had "poisoned the girl's mind," and tried to coax Mary back home, but Mary refused, saying she was most comfortable.[72] Charlotte relented, reluctantly leaving her daughter.[73]

Mary then unexpectedly turned up again at her mother's house with a "slim young lady, dressed in black, who wore gold spectacles."[74] She said she and her friend were going abroad; they'd been engaged in service and were both going to work for the same family. As they were going quite far away - Australia - Mary wanted to come and say goodbye. She told her mother the name of the ship on which she was to sail, and then wished her family farewell. She never mentioned Mrs West, or her "husband," the shunter.

Some time later, Charlotte read an announcement that the ship was lost mid-ocean; all passengers drowned.[75] "We then mourned for her loss and expected to hear no more of her, and that was the reason we then made no more inquiries," Charlotte later told a reporter.[76]

Records show that Charlotte Wheeler applied for medical relief in 1884 and 1885, but in 1886 her health improved, and she did not apply for relief again until 1887, and then only for temporary medical relief, twice. On September 6, 1888, according to sick asylum records, "a woman" requested medical relief for Charlotte, saying she was at home. The woman was unnamed, but was probably her younger daughter Charlotte Amy, or perhaps another relative.

It seems Charlotte had sent son James to live with his godmother, and the youngest boy John - who was often as sick as his mother - stayed home. Charlotte minded a neighbour's baby and took in laundry to make ends meet, but then broke her mangle and had to rely on medical relief for 13 weeks to get the family by.

It must have seemed miraculous then when, five years after Mary presumably drowned at sea, she arrived at Charlotte's door, resurrected. If Charlotte's account of the story is true, her daughter "came among them again" on Easter Sunday,[77] about the same time that her brother James joined the Marines, which fell, not in May as Charlotte had misremembered, but on April 21, 1889.

Mary came inside the house and kissed her brothers, sisters and cousins affectionately, as if nothing at all was strange about her sudden appearance, or her complete absence over the past five years. She then sat down to regale them with a most unbelievable story.[78] She had changed her mind about Australia at the last minute - and good thing too, considering the ship sank - and instead, she had accepted a different proposal and was "taken on" to the Continent. She'd been to Norway, Mary said, and "all the chief places of Europe." When she returned to London, having "enjoyed herself in Norway," she married a Mr Charles Pearcey and they now lived together at 2 Priory Street.[79]

There are no travel records to support Mary's assertion that she visited the Continent, or Norway, with a gentleman friend or alone, which isn't to say it didn't happen, for she might have travelled under another name. But, more likely, this was an example of a pattern she would come to perfect wherein she cast herself in the role she wanted but couldn't have in the realities of others with whom she was close, but not close enough. These composite histories usually served a particular end - to appear more respectable than she was, to deflect nosiness, or simply to entertain. But for all their detail, Mary's stories were never very convincing.

"I know nothing of who it was that took her on to the Continent, or who she went to Norway with," Charlotte later said. "I cannot even say whether it is true that she went on a tour over the Continent or not."[80]

Mary invited her mother to visit and to meet her new husband, and Charlotte accepted, visiting 2 Priory Street twice. But on both occasions, she said that Charles was away. His absence struck Charlotte as odd. What was truly odd was that Mary invited her mother to meet him at all, since she and John Pearcey had already separated at this point.

Pearcey said he met Mary Wheeler when she was 18 or 19 near Fleet Street.[81] He was, by any definition, a good-looking man. The illustrations of him in court indicate that he had a strong jawline and a small nose, and sported a trim, fashionable moustache. His fair hair was thick and combed up and back, and he was described, in 1890 anyway, as a broad-shouldered, smart looking man; the "lady-killing" type.[82]

If Mary married the West boy, or anyone else for that matter, she promoted herself as an available woman when she met John Pearcey, and later when she met Frank Hogg. At some point, Mary and John Pearcey moved in together to 5 Manor Place, Walworth Road, in south London. John was a carpenter and made no more than £30 a year, not nearly enough to fund grand trips to the Continent. So if Mary's travel tales were true, they were not afforded by John Pearcey.

It wasn't long before the relationship between John and Mary began to fracture. One evening, John "spoke sharply" to Mary. In response, she grabbed a bottle of poison and impulsively poured it down her throat. Fearful she'd die, John forced salted water into her stomach until she vomited. The ordeal exhausted and terrified Mary, and she cried bitterly and then fell asleep. John waited for her to wake up so he could squabble with her for scaring him so, but when she awoke she complained of a pain in her head, and claimed to have no recollection of what had happened before. Flabbergasted, John pointed to where she'd vomited.[83]

About three months later, it happened again. John spoke to her "very strongly," and Mary dashed upstairs. Knowing what to expect this time, he followed her and was just in time to prevent her from swallowing the contents of a bottle marked 'poison'. Again with "great difficulty" he made her vomit by drinking a concoction of salt and water.[84]

Mary seized. She collapsed, and John later recalled that her hands were clenched into fists so tight that her fingernails pierced her palms, causing them to bleed. When she was fully conscious again and saw the blood on her palms, she fell into another fit. Then, according to John, she flew around the room crying and laughing, and again complained of violent pains in her head. When Mary finally recovered, John said she remembered "nothing of what had occurred, nor of her attempt to poison herself."[85]

The episodes became more constant, more violent, and less predictable. In one of her fits Mary fell on the floor, driving a hairpin into her head. Other fits caused her to fall off her chair and were followed by unsettling attacks of inappropriate "laughing" and "weeping." On other occasions still, she would tear into an "uncontrollable paroxysm of rage, dance with anger, and immediately afterwards fall into a fit." On recovering, she sometimes sang and cried. Other times that she seized, her body became so rigid that John had to use force to prise open her hands and jaw, presumably to stick something in her mouth so she wouldn't bite off her own tongue.[86]

Though sometimes her "fits" followed a typical epileptic seizure profile, other parts of her behaviour did not, and seemed to suggest any number of mental illnesses. Whether biological or psychological, coping with an illness as intense as hers must have exhausted John, but all evidence points to his faithfulness to her. Though he may not have understood her, he pitied her, describing her in his affidavit as a "continual sufferer" of poor health.[87]

As her behaviour became more erratic, Mary began to obsess with what triggered her fits. She was particularly concerned with a soft, pulpy spot on top of her head - ostensibly the fontanels - that she claimed had never quite closed and was the cause of all her anguish. She had explained to friends, including Charles Crichton, that the spot, about the size of a half-crown, was the reason she seized. John confirmed that if he touched that spot exactly, she'd faint.[88]

Despite a growing sense of helplessness, John continued to care for Mary, for she was "a very tender-hearted, kind and affectionate girl, most generous, and good natured." He later deposed that he was of the opinion that Mary was "incapable of any act of violence or of causing any hurt or pain to a fellow creature."[89]

All told, the couple lived together for three years, moving from Manor Place, Walworth Road to Old Kent Road, and finally to Bayham Street in Camden Town.[90] Mary had become despondant, sick and miserable, and according to John, she began seeing other men.[91] Though he cared for her deeply, he had limits and they decided to part company.

One of the men she started seeing was Charles Crichton, whom she may have seen on and off again for years already, and who provided her a small allowance. The other man was the son of a grocer on 87 King Street, Mr Frank Hogg.

Frank Samuel Hogg was born to Maria and James Hogg in the autumn of 1859 in St. Pancras.[92] Frank's father was born in Bury St Edmunds, Suffolk, and his mother in nearby Thurston. He had three older brothers - Frederick, Edwin and James - and an older sister named Clara.

As an adult he was described as an "unprepossessing" man, "not strongly motivated to work,"[93] who attended the Polytechnic, but later dropped out.[94] Even his lover described him as somewhat petulant, writing in a letter that he should avoid reacting melodramatically every time things didn't go his own way.[95] Despite such unflattering descriptions, which may or may not have been fair since they were constructed, in part, by the testimony of those with motive to portray him as an unfit husband, Frank Hogg must have had his charms.

Mary Pearcey did not withhold her common-law marital status

from Frank, telling him early in their friendship that she was married. This didn't seem to matter to him, perhaps because in the beginning their friendship was platonic. The emotional part of their affair began with letters, which Mary meticulously copied, keeping one copy and leaving the other for Frank at his family's store.[96]

When questioned about the romance at the inquest, Frank said he had known Mary for five years, but claimed they were only the "merest acquaintances" until his marriage in 1888.[97] The ardour expressed in Mary's letters to him suggest otherwise. In one letter Mary wrote, "the time has been so long today; every minute seemed an hour waiting for you."[98]

Whether their love affair was physical or not in the beginning, they were not discreet in their affection for one another. Even John Pearcey saw things between the two that gave him "suspicions." When Mary and John were still a couple they were out walking one day when they saw Phoebe, to whom Frank was betrothed. Mary said to John, "That is the lady who is going to marry Mr Hogg."[99] Why was his common-law wife keeping such close tabs on another man, he must have wondered? Mary told John that she and Phoebe had been friends "for a long time," although Frank always claimed the two met at Christmas, 1889.[100]

In a letter dated October 25, 1888, Mary told Frank she was hesitant to come by the shop as she "might make mischief." If she decided to visit, she would be careful, she wrote, especially if "an inquisitive lady should come in - you know who I mean."[101] The inquisitive lady was never identified, neither in the letter nor in court when Frank was directly asked. It was as plausible that the lady was Clara, old Mrs Hogg, or any number of neighbourhood shoppers, as it was Phoebe Styles, Frank's fiancée, though in court Frank flatly denied this.

Secrecy became a defining feature of their relationship, so much so that Mary asked Frank to return every letter she sent after reading, presumably so she could burn them.[102] Mary was keenly aware of the social codes that restrained her life. "In this false world we do not always know who are our friends, and who our enemies," she wrote in a letter to Frank, slightly misquoting Longfellow.[103]

When Frank's father James died in 1880,[104] Maria Hogg continued to manage the store at 87 King Street[105] with the help of family members until she could no longer work because of some disease that left her invalided.[106] She was 61 at the time of her husband's death, and both Frank (21) and Clara (24) still lived with her. In the 1881 census, Frank was listed as an assistant grocer and his older brother, Frederick, who was by then married with three children, was also listed as a grocer.[107] The family continued to run the grocery store at King Street for another eight years, but in 1888, after 40 years in the grocery business, the Hoggs left the store and moved into the furniture removing business.[108]

That Maria Hogg turned over the new venture to her older and presumably more enterprising son Frederick may have been one reason Frank went to work at Shoolbred's, a competing furniture and textile supplier on Tottenham Court Road.[109] But he would eventually come back to work for his eldest brother, who had moved the company to his home at 37 Hadley Street in Kentish Town.[110] Hadley Street was only a few minutes' walk to Prince of Wales Road, where Frank, Phoebe, Clara and old Mrs Hogg eventually settled.

As the Hoggs were moving into new business territory, Mrs Pearcey was making transitions of her own in the autumn of 1888. She decided to leave her common-law husband, John Pearcey, and to move into private rooms. Whether Mary left John or vice versa is hard to say, though in court, John said he was fed up with seeing her in Frank's company and wanted to part. When he questioned Mary about how she would manage after their split, she told him she was "supported by the gifts of a gentleman," presumably Charles Crichton.[111] Perhaps she pointed to the fine gold ring she wore as proof of just how well-off this gentleman was.

But it was not her older gentleman she turned to for help moving her things. For that, she turned to Frank Hogg and within a day or two of her separation from John, she'd packed her things and moved out.[112] She moved into an ordinary-looking flat on a "short, quiet street" with "delightful trees" not more than ten minutes' walk from where the Hoggs would settle on Prince of Wales Road.[113]

The autumn of 1888 was important in other ways too; it was the season in which Jack the Ripper launched his reign of terror, beginning with the murder of Mary Ann Nichols, whose mutilated body was found lying in Buck's Row (now Durward Street) in Whitechapel. The "canonical five," as they would become known - Mary Ann Nichols, Annie Chapman, Elizabeth Stride, Catherine Eddowes and Mary Jane Kelly - were all murdered between August and November.

No. 2 Priory Street, however, was in Kentish Town, several miles from the madness in the East End, and while not immune to the generalised anxiety the so-called Autumn of Terror provoked, it was a quiet area famous for the banal: floor cloth, false teeth and pianos.[114]

Kentish Town Road was a typical Victorian shopping street, with small shops let to an assortment of butchers, grocers, toymakers and others. By the early 1880s, Kentish Town had a library, elementary schools, new Anglican churches and a horse tramway, as well as its own killjoys who complained that modernity had cost the boomtown its charm and the good air of its pastoral past.[115]

Rail expansion touched the last remaining large green spaces in the area with the building of the Hampstead Junction Railway and the Kentish Town station in Prince of Wales Road, which opened in 1868. The sound of its puffing engine and hissing steam whistle became background noise in Mary Pearcey's life, as the track ran on a high arch that crossed Priory Street - the same dark archway through which Mrs Rodgers claimed to have seen Mrs Pearcey pushing a heavily laden pram on October 24th.

Priory Street was much like other streets in the area, consisting of houses built on either side of Yorkstone-paved streets. Number 2 was the second house from the right of a long row of flat-faced Georgian-style semi-detached houses. Each house was almost an exact replica of its neighbour, as they were originally envisioned as low-wage workers' quarters. Though gentler than some of the meaner streets of Whitechapel, Priory Street was largely a working-class street. On Booth's Poverty map, Priory Street was considered a 'mixed' street, with some residents comfortable and others poor.

A wrought-iron fence surrounded a small front garden at 2 Priory Street. The main door was at street level, where guests and tenants for all floors of the house entered. A narrow hallway adjoined the first-floor rooms and parlour, which Mrs Pearcey occupied in the fall of 1890.[116] There was a single, shared kitchen, a scullery and, to the right of the hallway, a staircase that led to the second and third floors. Beyond the scullery, there was a small garden, in which Mrs Pearcey purportedly grew lettuce, which she liked to give away to her neighbours.[117]

Mrs Pearcey's rooms were decorated with her personal treasures: plants, fire canopies, a tri-paneled dressing screen adorned with paper cherub cutouts, a terrarium, assorted knick-knacks made of china and glass and a rather expensive asset - an upright piano on which she often played one of her favourite songs, 'When there's love at home'.[118]

By 1890, when Mrs Pearcey was living in the ground floor rooms, she had neighbours upstairs and alongside and would have to explain the traffic of men in and out of her rooms, or else face neighbourhood gossip or, worse yet, police attention. In the narrative she constructed from bits of fact and bits of fiction, Charles Crichton became her father or sometimes friend or brother, and Frank Hogg became her husband.

Though Crichton knew of Frank Hogg, it is unclear whether Frank knew of Crichton. In court, Frank said he didn't know that another man visited her, and thought she supported herself through a "small income," which, apparently, he never considered could come from another man.[119]

Charles sometimes used the post or sent telegrams to schedule time with Mary, but according to Mrs Crowhurst, there was a standing arrangement and he came nearly every week, usually on a Monday, though sometimes more often than that.[120] Whether to discourage the two men from meeting or simply to communicate with Frank that she was out, Mary devised a special code to signal if she could receive him. When the light in the back bedroom was on, Frank explained to a reporter, then he should come around another time because she was out and might be late or, presumably, had company.[121]

The depth of Crichton's relationship with Mrs Pearcey was never thoroughly investigated and didn't seem to be well understood by anyone, even her neighbours.[122] It appears that Crichton was another lover, one who "kept" Mrs Pearcey. And while Crichton was no secret to those who lived at 2 Priory Street, his exact relationship to Mrs Pearcey was mysterious. Mrs Pearcey presented him in turn as both friend and brother,[123] though the press reported a two-year "intimacy" - a euphemism for a sexual affair – between them. In his affidavit,[124] Crichton never actually stated that they had sex, and though unlikely, it's possible his visits and financial assistance was motivated by some impulse other than lust. The length of their relationship is as difficult to peg as its foundation, but probably took place over the three years they had known each other, possibly longer.[125] Whatever tenderness he may have felt toward his young mistress, Charles Crichton was quick to drop her at the first signs of real trouble.

On Thursday, October 23, the day before the murders, Mrs Pearcey sent Crichton a letter addressed to a post office box in another district some three or four miles from his home in Gravesend. In the letter, which began "Dearest Charles," Mrs Pearcey wrote that when she had finished writing she was going to Prince of Wales Road. Her letter didn't reach Crichton until the following day, however, and the news of the double murders broke that night.

Having read of the crime, Crichton dashed off two identical telegrams - to be sure Mrs Pearcey got them, he later explained to police - addressing one to 2 Priory Street, and the other to the Hoggs' residence, whose address he'd gleaned from newspaper coverage.

The telegrams made for curious reading: "Office surrounded Gravesend. Get protection. Telegraph at once," and were signed with just an initial, bearing no other identifying information except a postmark from Gravesend.

He later explained his instruction to "get protection" was innocent enough. He meant that Mrs Pearcey should seek police protection, which was reasonable advice, he thought, given a close friend of hers had just been brutally murdered and the murderer was still at large. He never explained what he meant by "office surrounded" - nor did he explain why he didn't sign the telegram, or why Mrs Pearcey sent him letters to a post office box so far from his home, and once he made his hasty appearance at the inquest he was never heard from again, extricating himself entirely from the proceedings, except to complete a short affidavit about his relationship to Mary for her appeal months later.

Perhaps Mary felt some level of comfort that the predictability of Charles' visiting schedule and the bedroom signal would keep her two men from meeting, or maybe she no longer cared because her relationship to Charles was indeed platonic, but regardless, she gave Frank his own latchkey about a year after she moved to Priory Street so he could stop by whenever he liked. She would often leave him letters on the kitchen table if she had to go out.[126]

The content of the letters Mary wrote to Frank varied. In some, Mary was effusive, imploring him to visit. In others, she was singsong and chatty. And in others still, she betrayed a growing obsession with him. In one rather portentous letter, she wrote, "Frank Dear - You said 'if you thought I loved you' - what did you mean by that? Don't you know that I do? How can I prove to you that I do love you dearly? If there is anything I can do to prove it, I promise you it shall be done. You have more power over me than anyone on earth."[127]

In late September or early October 1888, Frank went to visit his lover at 2 Priory Street. He was distraught and anxious, and confessed that he'd made a terrible mistake. He had accidentally got Phoebe, his fiancée of two years, pregnant, and would have to marry her soon, implying he might not have married her otherwise. Melodramatically, Frank told Mary that as he saw it he had but three choices: he could flee the country, kill himself, or relent, and marry a woman he didn't love. Mary was ready to accept a marriage, but a distant move or suicide was unthinkable. In a letter dated October 2, she wrote:

> My Dear F,
>
> Do not think of going away, for my heart will break if you do; don't go dear. I won't ask you too much, only to see you for 5 minutes when you can get away; but if you go quite away, how do you think I can live? I would see you married 50 times over - yes - I could bear that far better than parting with you for ever and that is what it would be if you went out of England. My dear loving F, you was so down-hearted today that your words give me much pain, for I have only one true friend I can trust to, and that is yourself. Don't take that from me. What good would your friendship be then, with you so far away? No, no, you must not go away. My heart throbs with pain only thinking about it. What would it be if you went? I should die - And if you love me as you say you do, you will stay. Write or come soon, dear. Have I asked too much?
>
> From your loving
> M.E.
>
> P.S. I hope you got home quite safe, and things are all right and you are well."[128]

A few days before his wedding Frank was still conflicted and apparently still contemplating - or at least threatening - suicide. Mary wrote to him on the November 18:

> Dearest Frank,
>
> I cannot sleep, so am going to write you a long letter. When you read this I hope your head will be much better dear. I can't bear to see you like you were this evening. Try not to give way. Try to be brave, dear, for things will come right in the end. I know things look dark now, but it is always the darkest hour before the dawn. You said this evening, "I don't know what I ask?" But I do know. Why should you want to take your life because you want to have everything your own way? So you think you will take that which you cannot give - you will not if you love me as you say you do. Oh! Frank, I should not like to think I was the cause of all your troubles, and yet you make me think so. What can I do? I love you with all my heart, and I will love her because she will belong to you. Yes I will come and see you both if you wish it. So dear, try and be strong, as strong as me, for a

> man should be stronger than a woman. Shall I see you on Wednesday, about 2 o'clock? Try and get away too, on Friday, as I want to know if you are off on Sunday until 7 o'clock. Write me a little note in answer to this. I shall be down on Monday or Tuesday in the morning about 9 a.m.
>
> So believe me to remain your most loving
> M.E.[129]

Three days after Mary sent the letter Frank married Phoebe Styles, the maid from Rickmansworth, who was three months pregnant at the time, in a small ceremony at his parish church of St. Pancras[130] on November 21, 1888.[131] Their child, Phoebe[132] Hanslope Hogg, was born in May, 1889 and baptised on July 7 at the Haverstock Hill Holy Trinity Church.[133]

When pressed at the inquest, Frank said that the relationship between himself and Mary turned physical a month or two after he married Phoebe,[134] and he maintained this despite counsel's persistent incredulity. If true, then Frank and Mary carried on their secret physical affair for only a year, though their emotional relationship was, by then, well established.

If his mistress met his wife during this time, and for the first time, it was only briefly when Mary stopped by their new house on Prince of Wales Road. While Frank made it sound as if Mary was one of many customers who stopped by to wish the Hoggs well after their move from Camden,[135] it's possible that Frank asked her to come. "Yes I will come and see you both if you wish it," she had written him just before his wedding.[136] But the opportunity for friendship between the women didn't develop until the following Christmas when Mrs Pearcey asked her lover if he, his wife and their child would stay with her for the holiday. Frank agreed.

Though Frank maintained his wife never knew about his affair, it is difficult to imagine there wasn't a knowing glance or comment made over the two-day visit that betrayed their deep familiarity. The effrontery of Frank's decision to include his wife in such a charade was astounding. It was one of the many indications that he either thought Phoebe too dim to discover the truth about his relationship with Mary Pearcey, or didn't care if she did. It also illustrated why the public came to feel so contemptuous of Frank Hogg: had he not forced a relationship to develop between his wife and his lover, his wife and child might have lived. Frank may not have been the Devil, but he led Phoebe and Tiggie to the Devil's door.

After Christmas and Boxing Day, Mrs Pearcey visited Phoebe from time to time and looked in on the baby, who was just beginning to prattle sweetly. Then, in late January, a curious opportunity presented itself. Phoebe was ill and very weak, and could not manage her household and the baby. Mrs Pearcey suddenly showed up and volunteered to play nursemaid.[137] Though Frank reported his wife and his lover had been on "fairly intimate" terms with one another, he believed they hadn't visited each other since Christmas, after which time Phoebe hadn't uttered Mrs Pearcey's name.[138] This made her unexpected arrival, at least to Frank, rather strange, though not strange enough that he turned her gesture down. And so, Mrs Pearcey stayed with the Hoggs the first few nights she nursed Phoebe,[139] and then walked back and forth from Priory Street to Prince of Wales Road every day thereafter, caring for Phoebe for at least two weeks, and paying her patient every attention.[140]

When Phoebe's sister Martha and niece Lizzie heard that Phoebe was sick, they came to visit at once, despite Frank's insistence that her friends and family must be invited before calling. Neither Lizzie nor Martha said anything about Mrs Pearcey attending their aunt, but by February, after enduring a month of illness, Lizzie called by and found her aunt still so ill she was "quite unfit to sweep the floor." Lizzie demanded her aunt stop sweeping and sit down, and then she found Frank and berated him, accusing him at her most heated moment of nearly starving Phoebe to death.[141]

During the inquest, Frank said that none of his friends or family objected to Mrs Pearcey playing nurse to his wife, and that the two women appeared to "agree together very well."[142]

Perhaps that was true of Frank's friends and family, but it wasn't entirely true of Phoebe's. Though she may not have been able to articulate it then, Lizzie felt a niggling feeling: something wasn't quite right about the relationship between her uncle, aunt and the nursemaid.[143] She implored her Aunt Martha to intervene, which she eventually did, and Phoebe went to stay with family in Mill Hill. She recovered well enough, though never entirely, as Martha had testified in court.

After her recovery, Phoebe tried to put as much distance as possible between herself and her husband's lover and his family - first by requesting that they move, and then by actively refusing invitations from Mrs Pearcey and ignoring her if she happened to bump into her while out. Though Mrs Pearcey continued to visit her friends Clara and old Mrs Hogg,[144] she did not violate Frank and Phoebe's rule of invitation-only visits to their rooms. To Lizzie's knowledge, Mrs Pearcey did not visit her aunt at Prince of Wales Road after February 1890, but she seemed to find reasons to be around.

Phoebe started taking long walks with the baby, and would seldom tell Clara or Old Mrs Hogg where she was going. "She was a very reticent woman," Clara told a reporter, "and seldom spoke to anyone."[145] Frank confirmed this description of his wife, adding that Phoebe was the kind of woman who would go out but never tell you where she'd been, if she chose to mention that she'd gone out at all.[146] When questioned, she would often return monosyllabic responses.

Despite Phoebe's chilly disposition toward Frank's sister and mother, which, by March of 1890 had become "a matter of comment and regret,"[147] Phoebe and Frank's relationship seemed to have settled into a manageable - if not altogether happy - rhythm. Though impossible to know why, Frank also made less time for Mrs Pearcey that spring, which troubled her deeply. In an undated letter she wrote to Frank, she stated: "You ask me if I was cross with you for only coming for such a little while. If you knew how lonely I am surely you would not ask."[148] However often he visited her, it was never enough. Her happiness, she said in the same letter, depended on him entirely. "If it was not for your love dear, I do not know what I should really do, and I am always afraid you will take that away... I cannot live without it now. I have no right to it, but you gave it to me, and I can't give it up."[149]

As spring gave way to summer, Mrs Pearcey's loneliness compounded, and at times she was so bereft she would beg her neighbour Mrs Piddington to let her hold her baby, Charlie, which gave her some relief. Mrs Piddington commented to a reporter that in the weeks preceding the murders Mrs Pearcey was in tears walking up and down the garden. When Mrs Piddington asked why she was so sad, she was told: "no one seems to love or care for me now. I seem to have no one who cares for me now like they used to." Mrs Piddington asked whether her husband - meaning Frank Hogg - loved her. "No," Mrs Pearcey said, "he doesn't seem to lately like he did at one time; besides he is often away now, and I don't know what for."[150]

In the autumn of 1890 Mrs Pearcey enjoyed a brief reprieve when Frank invited her to go with him to the countryside on a job. Frank, who had returned to work for his brother Frederick at the family removals business, was tasked with moving a wealthy widow's belongings from Hampstead to her new house in the Bedfordshire village of Silsoe some 41 miles away. The widow had lost her husband and child, according to a report in *Lloyd's*, and had decided to retire near friends. Frank, Mrs Pearcey and an unnamed porter left Kentish Town on October 8, 16 days before the murders.

The same night, Mrs Pearcey, Frank and the porter stopped at Robert Tranfield's[151] Vine Inn at 69 Castle Street in Luton,[152] ten miles outside Silsoe. They presumably picked that location because Frank was anxious to protect the van and horses, and Tranfield had a good stable and large enclosed yard where the van would be safe. After Hogg stored the van and fed the horses, he asked Mr Tranfield if he could accommodate the three for the night. At first, Tranfield said no. He lived with his wife, Sarah, 41, and their daughters Alice, 17, Lydia, 14, Adelaide, 13, Ethel, 11, Florence, 10, and one son, Robert aged 6; there was simply no room. But Frank persisted until finally Tranfield said he could possibly accommodate *two* extra people - Frank and his missus - but not the porter. Frank wouldn't hear of splitting up, so he asked a third time. Overhearing the conversation, one of Tranfield's daughters offered to give up her bed to Mrs Pearcey, which meant they could all stay if Frank and the porter were willing to share a single bed. Frank agreed. He would put up with anything, he said, if only they would make "his good lady" comfortable.[153]

The three travellers ate dinner that night together with the Tranfield family. Mrs Pearcey was agreeable, but frequently complained that her head hurt. By ten o'clock she excused herself from the table, retiring to bed early owing to the headache. Those at the table remarked that she looked unwell. As she headed to bed Frank called to her, "Goodnight darling; you'll be all right."[154]

When it was time for the rest of the house to go to sleep, the oldest daughter, Alice, refused to sleep upstairs next to Mrs Pearcey, whispering to her mother that she had been watching their guest at the dinner table and noticed her face kept shifting in strange and unsettling ways. She was sure there was something quite wrong with the woman, and she was afraid. Her mother scolded her for being impolite and unreasonable and shooed the girl off to bed.

The following morning Hogg, his 'wife' and the porter got ready to journey up to Silsoe. Mrs Tranfield said she was astonished at the "alacrity" with which 'Mrs Hogg' climbed into the van;[155] clearly it wasn't the first time she had managed the carriage. Frank told Mrs Tranfield they'd be back that evening and asked if she would have dinner and tea ready by the time they returned. Mrs Tranfield agreed and waved them off.

As the village of Silsoe was quite small, a move of this sort was big news. The villagers were keen to see the large van, and quite surprised to find a young woman riding atop it. Hogg's lady kept her seat so expertly, several villagers told a *Lloyd's* reporter, who later came to investigate the story, they thought she must have belonged to some equestrian troupe.[156]

While Frank and the porter worked, Mrs Pearcey went into the village square and visited the shops. She stopped by the general store where she asked Mrs Flint, the shopkeeper, whether they sold milk there. As they did not, Mrs Flint pointed out where in town she could buy some. Mrs Flint later described the stranger as nicely dressed. She attracted a great deal of attention during the rest of the afternoon, as villagers spied her picking blackberries and strolling in Wrest Park.[157]

While settling the bill, the widow said she hoped Frank could get good lodgings while travelling such a distance, especially since Hogg's lady was in tow. The widow never directly inquired but assumed, as did the townspeople, that Mrs Pearcey was Frank's wife, for why else would he subject such a lovely young lady to such a distance on a bad road?

"Yes, thank you - capital," Frank answered. "We stayed at Luton, and were very comfortable."[158]

When news of the murder later broke, most villagers at first believed it was Mrs Pearcey who'd been murdered - a logical assumption, since they also believed Mrs Pearcey was Mrs Hogg. When someone realised the pretty lady who held tight to the reins of the moving van was actually the *murderess*, shock rippled through the sleepy settlement. Some of the more superstitious villagers were so struck by news that a murderess had just been in their midst, they wouldn't walk at night along the same route Mrs Pearcey had taken to pick blackberries for fear Phoebe Hogg's ghost would follow and haunt their footsteps.[159]

When Frank, the porter and Mrs Pearcey returned that night, Mrs Pearcey chatted excitedly with Mrs Tranfield about the fantastic afternoon she'd had. She told her she'd ridden a pony and taken a walk in the park. The whole group took tea together again and then enjoyed themselves with music and singing. Frank Hogg even played a little, though his ear wasn't nearly as strong as his wife's. 'Mrs Hogg' could play many songs quite well, and they worked through several popular tunes including 'Our hands have met, but not our hearts,' 'Call me back,' and, Mrs Pearcey's favourite, 'When there's love at home.'[160]

When the women were alone together, Mrs Tranfield asked how long they'd been married, receiving the reply, "five years."

Mrs Pearcey seemed better that evening than she had been the night before. She was "bright" and "cheerful" when she talked with everyone, but then a sudden seriousness punctured her cheerfulness. It was as though she was mulling something over in her mind. Mrs Tranfield described the shade that fell across Mrs Pearcey's face as dark and unsettling, just as her daughter had described it to her the previous evening.[161]

Later that night, Frank abruptly thanked the Tranfields for their generosity and said that they were not staying another night, but would head back to London - some forty miles away - immediately. Mrs Tranfield objected, saying it was far too late to drive the horses that far in the dark, but Frank said they had to get back as soon as possible. Relenting, Mrs Tranfield packed food into a basket and saw them to the door. She gave the basket to 'Mrs Hogg' specifically, and said she hoped she would keep it in remembrance of her visit to the village. Mrs Pearcey thanked her and said she would always keep it and remember the many kindnesses she had received at their home. Having readied the horses, the three climbed into the van and Frank whipped the horses into a trot, heading for St. Albans.[162]

No one knows what prompted Frank to return to Kentish Town so hurriedly, but the return to ordinary life was, for Mrs Pearcey, grim, and she slipped back into a fog of isolation and anxiety more intense than those before. Her sleep was disturbed. She suffered nosebleeds. She complained her eyesight was going and she cried as she paced the garden, according to Mrs Piddington. By all accounts, something weighed heavy on her heart, and her already fragile interior was marked with signs of a significant psychological break.

To soothe the terror of such hauntings she appealed to her mother. The Sunday before the murders, Mary paid her mother a visit. She lay down on her mother's bed and said, "It comes and goes again, but I'm never without it very long. In the dream I see a great archway and through it I go to darkness - dreadful darkness - that seems to hide something more terrible beyond."[163]

THE FUNERAL OF PHOEBE AND TIGGIE HOGG

THE funeral of Phoebe and Tiggie Hogg took place on Sunday, November 2, 1890. Frank and his family set out by cab for the undertaker's at 7.00am, hoping to avoid the crowds. Phoebe's sisters Emma and Martha Styles were waiting for him, as were her brothers Levi, James, William, Samuel and Ezekiel.[1] Lizzie and a cousin named James Wild also crowded the door. Frank must have been rather surprised when he arrived to find them all waiting, as he had not invited Phoebe's family to her funeral.[2]

S Division's Superintendent Beard was charged with directing the police presence, assisted by Y Division's Chief Inspector McFadden and Inspectors Davey and Doyle, since the cemetery lay within their territory. In all, there were 150 officers in attendance, either on foot or mounted. Inspectors Bannister, Wells and Sanctuary of S Division were also on hand, with Inspector Sanctuary in charge of the five constables in the mounted division.[3]

People watched from the windows lining the route, and congregated on the flat roofs of the shops that offered the best street view. The crowd developed in the street outside the undertaker's shop for more than an hour, by some accounts growing to more than 3,000 people.[4] As the hour drew near, men and women came "running from every direction," until the street was entirely clogged. The procession was scheduled to begin at exactly 9.00am, but the street was, at half-past, already so crowded it was virtually impassable. Police cleared the street to allow the hearse and mourning coaches by.

When Frank Hogg stepped into view the crowd booed and hissed menacingly, and police had to elbow spectators back to create a path out of the undertaker's office so he could step into the coach. As the coach lurched forward following the hearse, the crowd surged and the mounted police escorts had to drive the people back. Twelve constables guarded the coach on foot. The hooting and hissing was incessant and the crowd roared at Frank Hogg for a great distance,[5] yelling "rough summaries" of the more lewd parts of his published testimony. He was "plied on all sides with questions both painful and vulgar."[6]

No such demonstrations were made against any other member of the funeral party, and, in fact, as Phoebe's brothers got into their coach the crowd uttered words of sympathy.[7] It rained heavily and incessantly from the moment the procession began. The procession went through Camden Town, past the Britannia and Mother Red Cap pubs, onto Kentish Town Road and then to the tree-lined roadway that led to the gates of St. Pancras and Islington cemetery in Finchley.[8]

The rain was heavy and cold, but this made no difference to the crowd, who thronged the streets and side paths, following the carriages all the way to the cemetery. Gawkers came in covered wagons, pony traps, donkey carts and cabs. Some trotted alongside the carriages on foot, keeping up by running, until they were exhausted and fell out of the procession. Others were already standing at the cemetery gates, having arrived half an hour before the ceremony was scheduled to take place.

More than 1,000 people gathered at the cemetery, a considerable number that surely would have been greater still had the weather been better. Some indicated the reason for their journey with a small crepe bow fixed on their horsewhips. Women came out in numbers, and, by one reporter's estimate, expressed the greatest animosity toward Frank Hogg.

When the hearse at last arrived there was a rush to the chapel. The men in the crowd removed their caps when the wreath-covered coffin was carried across the muddied paved path, but then turned on Hogg, shouting angrily, as he descended the carriage steps to walk into the chapel.

The Reverend Herbert Charles Strickland, a nonconformist, conducted the first half of the service, to which the large congregation listened in respectful silence. But as soon as the service ended, Hogg again had to bear the walk to the coach amid a large crowd that hissed and groaned at him the whole way. The Hoggs enjoyed no peace or privacy. Spectators slogged to the graveside too, jostling and manoeuvering for a view until the muddy earth at the open pit of the grave was a slippery quagmire, making it difficult to maintain a foothold.

The sympathy for the dead was expressed as volubly as was the hostility for the living. Several moments during the graveside service were so tense that many present were sure the mob would riot. At one point in the service, Reverend Finch had to stop and appeal to the crowd to order themselves so he could finish delivering the burial rites. At the conclusion of the graveside service, the members of the family came forward to take a last look at the grave, and all did so without difficulty except for Phoebe's niece Lizzie, who had leaned heavily against one of her uncle's arms throughout the service. When she looked down into the grave, she was overcome and fainted, and had to be assisted back to one of the mourning coaches.[9]

Phoebe and her daughter were laid to rest in a plain polished elm coffin with black fittings and a brass tablet affixed to the top that read simply: "Phoebe Hogg, aged thirty-two, died October 24th 1890. Phoebe Hanslope Hogg, aged eighteen months, child of the above, died October 24th, 1890."[10]

The *Herts Advertiser* had published a rumour the day before that Phoebe and Tiggie would be buried in the quiet grounds attached to the Chorleywood church near to where her friends and family lived.[11] Whether this was true or not is impossible to verify, but the family, most of who had lived and worked the land in Chorleywood for decades, certainly would have wanted Phoebe and Tiggie close. That Frank denied her this last mercy probably added to the Styles' scorn for him, and possibly to the general public's suspicion of his involvement in the murder.

Though Frank's family described Phoebe as reticent, Phoebe's own family described her quite differently. Her brother-in-law, William Horley, who was married to her sister Emma, described Phoebe to a reporter as "kind and warm-hearted," a woman "ready to reciprocate sympathy."[12] Phoebe's mother, Emma Worrel-Styles, then an age-worn countrywoman of 69, said Phoebe was her favourite child. "A better girl and a better daughter there never was and never could be," she told a reporter after she'd learned of her murder.[13]

Reverend Finch concluded the burial service by blessing the bereaved, including Frank Hogg, which, at the mention of his name, evoked another round of hostility from the crowd, and then the families were escorted back to their mourning carriages.[14] No sooner had the last words of the Lord's Prayer escaped the chaplain's lips than the crowd rushed to get a glimpse of the coffin as clods of earth were thrown upon it.[15]

For a good while, the mourning carriage that carried Frank, Fred and Clara Hogg passed unrecognised, but when the coach entered New Hampstead Road the party was discovered again and a number of men, boys and even women ran beside it from Castle Road to Hadley Street.[16] The Hoggs escaped into the safety of brother Frederick's house as quickly as they could, but a large, angry crowd formed outside the front door and a stable of constables had to protect it to keep order.[17] The *Pall Mall Gazette* described the scene from start to finish as "disgraceful."[18] But for the police attendance, no doubt Frank Hogg would have been "roughly treated."[19]

Phoebe's father, William Styles, who was too ill to attend his daughter's funeral, never recovered from hearing the news of her murder, and died just a month later.[20]

Left: Somerled Macdonald, who discovered the body of Phoebe Hogg (© Macdonald family)

Bottom: Crossfield Road, where the body was found (© The British Library Board)

HORRIBLE MURDERS AT HAMPSTEAD

No 2 PRIORY ST KENTISH TOWN

WHERE THE MURDER WAS COMMITTED

BROKEN WINDOWS

FINDING THE BODY OF THE CHILD

141 PRINCE OF WALES RD WHERE THE MURDERED WOMAN LIVED

FINDING THE PERAMBULATOR

FINDING THE BODY.

© The British Library Board)

Left: Frank Hogg sketched in court by 'Spy'

Below: Baby Tiggie Hogg and her mother Phoebe

(All images courtesy the Mayor's Office for Policing and Crime)

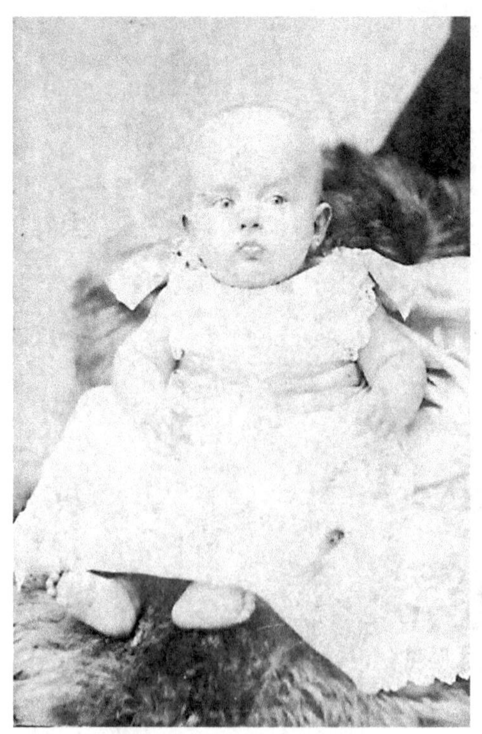

Post mortem photograph of Phoebe Hogg
(Courtesy the Mayor's Office for Policing and Crime)

Clara Hogg

Charlotte Piddington

Elizabeth Styles

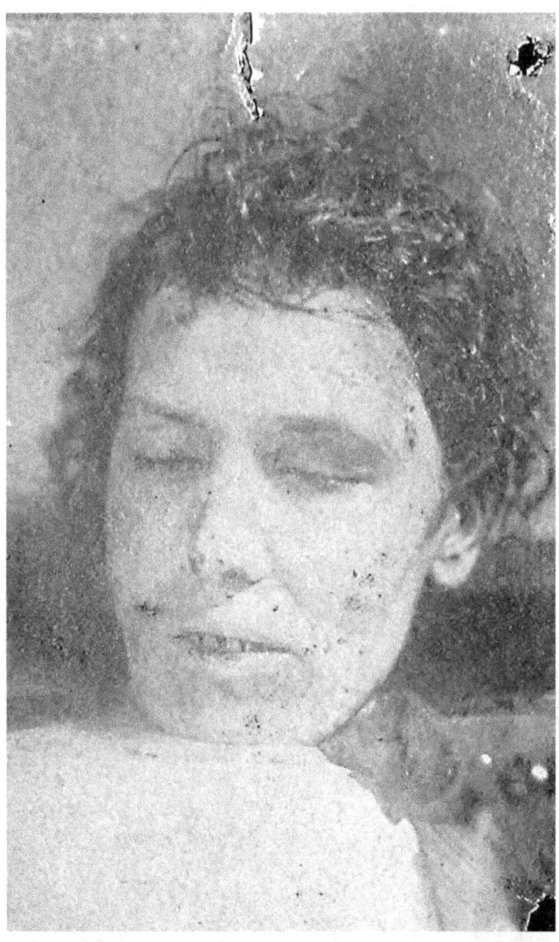

Post mortem photograph of Phoebe Hogg
(Courtesy the Mayor's Office for Policing and Crime)

Left: Inspector Thomas Bannister. Right: Mrs Pearcey's kitchen (© *The British Library Board)*

Left: Frank Hogg abused by the crowd at the funeral (© The British Library Board)
Right: Clatworthy's undertakers (© The British Library Board)

92
92 HIGH
CLATWORTHY

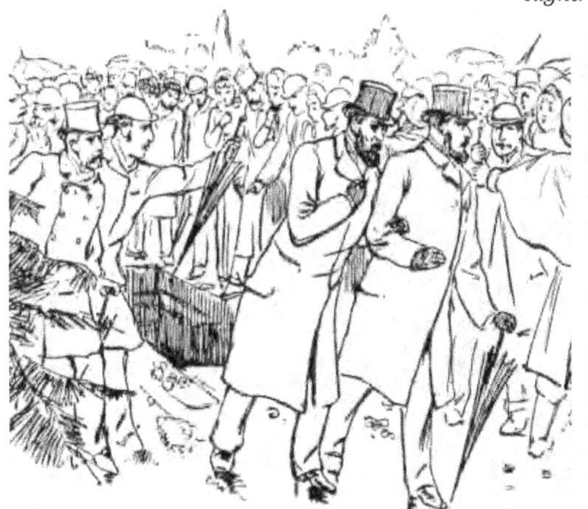

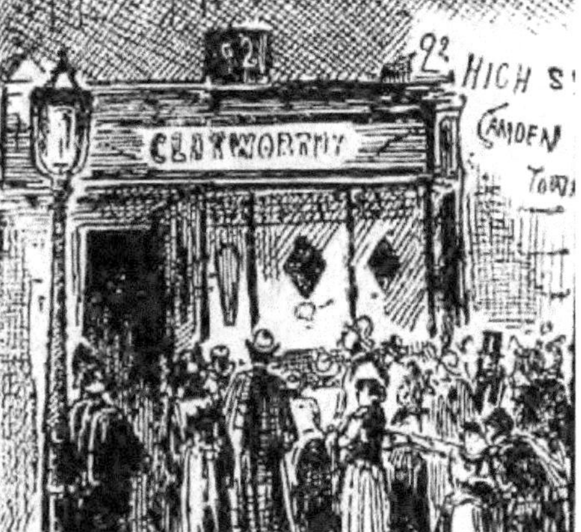

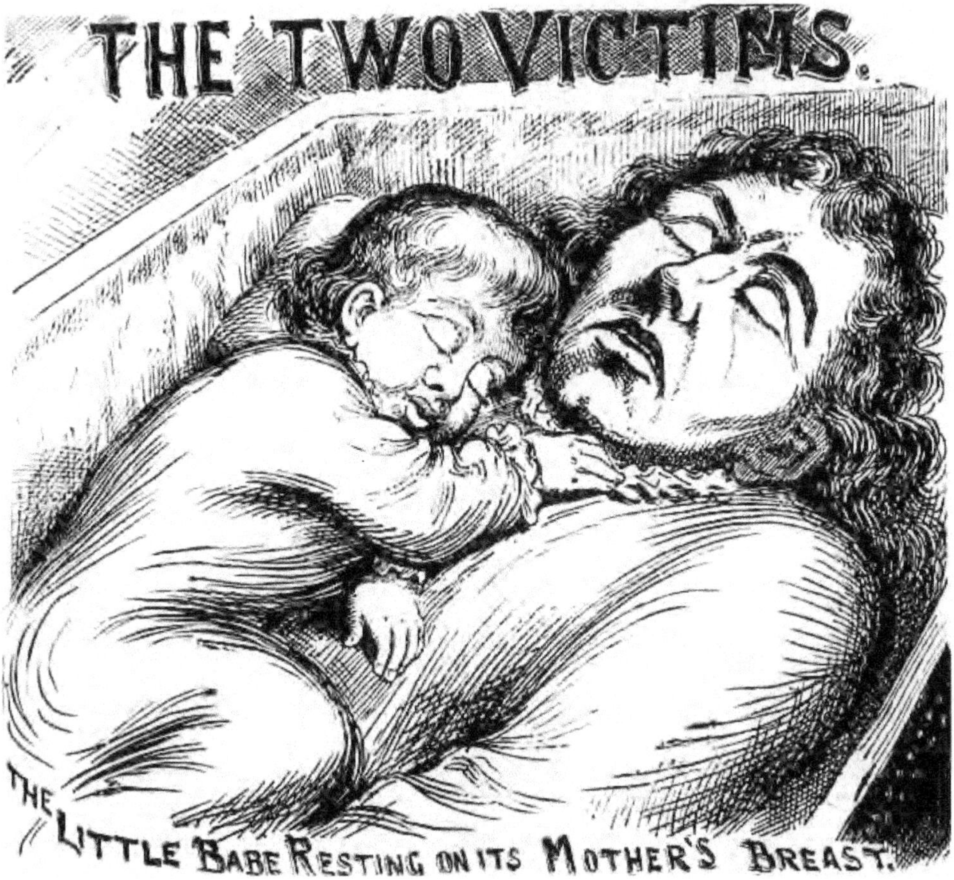
THE TWO VICTIMS.
THE LITTLE BABE RESTING ON ITS MOTHER'S BREAST.

© The British Library Board)

Mary Pearcey sketched in court by 'Spy'
(Courtesy the Mayor's Office for Policing and Crime)

Below: Author Stewart P. Evans with the rope used to hang Mary Pearcey
(Courtesy Stewart Evans)

certify that I this Day examined the Body of Mary Eleanor Pearcey on whom Judgment of Death was this Day executed in the said Prison; and that on that Examination I found that the said Mary Eleanor Pearcey was dead.

Dated this 23rd *Day of* December 1890.

(Signature) P. H. Gilbert

Certificate confirming the successful execution of Mary Pearcey

Photograph of Mary Pearcey from the collection of journalist and crime connoisseur George R. Sims

THE COMMITTAL AND TRIAL

THE Coroner's Warrant eventually moved Mary Pearcey's case on to the Central Criminal Court while further police investigation continued. On Monday, November 3, the Magistrate's hearing resumed, but there was little new evidence revealed. Mrs Pearcey arrived at the court in the prisoner's van with others under remand shortly after 11.00am. A reporter for the *Daily News* wrote that rarely had a criminal case excited greater interest than that which came before Mr Cooke at the Marylebone Police Court that day.[1]

Although no one expected the hearing to get underway before 1.00pm, by 9.00am a crowd had already assembled at the door to the court so thick that police officers had to move them on to allow the passage of street traffic. The spectators hoped to catch a glimpse of Mrs Pearcey for themselves on her arrival from Holloway Gaol,[2] for they could not rely on the press to accurately or consistently report what she said, did or even looked like, according to one frustrated reader.[3] In one incredibly inaccurate and salacious story, in fact, an overzealous reporter wrote that murder ran in the family and accused Mrs Pearcey's father, James Wheeler, of having killed farmer Edward Anstee.[4] This turned out to be a case of mistaken identities, as the man who murdered Edward Anstee was a *Thomas* Wheeler, not James. Better then, some said, for the public to come see the murderess and ferret out the truth on its own.

As it was Monday, there was a large number of mundane cases of drunkenness and assault from weekend shenanigans which had to be dealt with before the "sensational business of the day could be entered on."[5] Those who scavenged a seat inside the courtroom included miscellaneous members of the public, troops of reporters, newspaper artists, messengers, telegraph boys, witnesses, police officers and lawyers. Outside, it was so crowded and noisy that when the doors to the police court opened to let in someone with court business, a dull roar pierced the otherwise level hum of noise in the room, momentarily disrupting the proceedings. Though the courtroom inside was less noisy, it was no less packed. In fact, the courtroom was so "inconveniently crowded"[6] that Mr Clewlow, the senior court usher,[7] had to later devise a new system by which to admit pressmen so they were assured a seat.[8] Seats and tables were brought in, and every accommodation possible was made for the members of the press and others with court business, but the attempt to clear the court for the afternoon hearing of the Pearcey case was eventually abandoned, for there were simply too many people clogging the hallways to efficiently remove them.

The stir and excitement of those who attended the hearing electrified the air, and the human drama that was about to unfold promised to entertain better than any West End play. Those on the bench, in their official capacity, had the best seats by way of a special invitation, and included Sir William Melvill, solicitor to the Inland Revenue, and Viscount Royston, Viscount Dangan, Lord Greenock, Lord Cardross and Sir Charles Hartopp.[9] In the well of the court, in a prominent seat just in front of the witness box, was a Chinese Embassy attaché, whose "picturesque garb" served as a striking distraction from the otherwise mundane court attire.[10]

A writer for *Reynolds's Newspaper* wrote that such a *cause célèbre* demonstrated the very worst in human nature. He called the aristocrats in attendance "betting men," "wealthy do-nothings" and "idlers" who were there simply to stare at the "poor wretch" as she endured several hours of what was sure to be "exquisite mental torture."[11] "The whole proceedings," he wrote, "savors of the cruel and bloodthirsty glee with which the Romans of old saw a gladiator 'butchered to make a Roman holiday.'"[12] Their curiosity appalled him, and he was affronted by the magistrate's permission of it, lobbing a final insult at the judge himself, calling him a "Barnum, not a Beak."

But it wasn't just the bourgeoisie who were enthralled with the case. Only a week had passed since the terrible crime, but already a broadside ballad about the case had been written, meant to entertain the masses, but especially the lower classes who could not read or could not afford a paper in which to read about the trial. It was called 'The Terrible Murder of a Woman and Child' and was sung on the streets to the tune of 'Shelter Your Mother and Me.'[13]

When the proceedings resumed after Mr Cooke had disposed of nearly 100 night charges, remands and summonses, the side door of the court opened and a painful hush fell over the general hubbub as the "unhappy woman" stepped into the raised enclosure in the centre of the courtroom. It was half past one.

Descriptions of Mary Pearcey as she entered the courtroom varied, but the *Daily News* described her dressed entirely in black, with the exception of her hat, which was trimmed in faded blue ribbon. The newspaper described her as "slightly built" and not very tall, and not very good looking with high cheekbones, a large "prominent" mouth and a thin, long face. Her allure, said the reporter, was all in her eyes, which were "lustrous." She had a fine set of teeth too, and altogether possessed an "interesting and expressive" face, even if not handsome.[14]

As other reporters had remarked at the previous hearing and inquest, the woman who stood in the dock did not strike one as a monster capable of committing the terrible crimes for which she stood accused. In fact, Mrs Pearcey seemed gentle, and when she spoke, her voice was low, soft and musical. "It seemed absolutely incredible," one journalist wrote, "that so frail a form and so gentle a spirit as seemed to be shown in that face could by any possibility be concerned single-handed in one of the most ferocious murders of recent years."[15]

To others who observed her that day, Mrs Pearcey looked "pale" and "scared" but was also entirely self-possessed, and stood quite motionless until Freke Palmer, her solicitor, bent over and asked her if she would like to sit down. She whispered that she would. A seat was brought to her, and the proceedings began.

Mr C. F. Gill, barrister, instructed by the Treasury Solicitor, appeared for the prosecution, and Mr Freke Palmer, solicitor, defended the accused. In his opening statement, Mr Gill outlined the history of the case in what one reporter described as a "quiet, phlegmatic, business-like fashion, without the least trace of feeling either for or against the prisoner."[16] Mrs Pearcey sat and listened without so much as moving a muscle, looking at the prosecutor with a "hard stony stare of misery" as he told a most fearful story about her.[17]

The basic facts of the story were, by then, well known, but a neighbour would give new and important evidence, he said. This witness had heard the smashing of glass and the scream of a child as if in distress, and this evidence would prove the prisoner was the only person who could have committed the murder, a murder carried out in "a most brutal manner, and with the greatest amount of violence, that it is possible to believe anyone capable of."[18]

Coming to the night following the murder, said Mr Gill, it would be found that the prisoner made strenuous efforts to get rid of evidence of blood in the kitchen where the murder took place, and that the prisoner's account for the condition of the bloodied kitchen - that she had killed hundreds of mice which infested the place - was preposterous.[19]

As Mr Gill spent nearly half an hour weaving together a "dreadful array of facts," Mrs Pearcey sat "motionless as a statue," her stare fixed on the Crown lawyer,[20] except during the more lurid moments of his description, during which time a reporter saw her mouth twitch just a little.[21] She looked like someone in a trance, but she must have heard every word, for when Mr Gill concluded, she leaned over to Freke Palmer to clarify that, "Mrs Butler can tell you as to the mice" and, "it was eight o'clock, not ten, when Clara came down."[22]

Frank was the first witness to take the stand.

A reporter with the *Daily News* described him as "evidently labouring under suppressed excitement," but he delivered his version of events "faultlessly."[23]

As with Mrs Pearcey, descriptions of Frank varied by observer. A *Daily News* reporter said Frank was "intelligent-looking." He had a short, reddish-brown moustache and beard and a rather "pleasant-looking" face with a soft, "mellifluous voice." Dressed in his mourning clothes he appeared to look like a "highly respectable working man."[24]

Respectable or not, the frankness with which he delivered his testimony struck those in the courtroom as "profoundly unpleasant." It was not just the frankness with which he retold the story of his affair with Mrs Pearcey, but a strange inflection in his voice that some heard as indignation. It was as if he was asking the court, wrote one reporter, "How could you think it of me?" when pressed about his treatment of his wife, or his affair, or any other comment that cast doubt as to his character or integrity.[25]

When asked who "Tiggie" was, Frank's face puckered and his eyes filled with tears.

"It was the child," he said. "It was a pet name."[26]

His emotional reaction to the child seemed legitimate to at least one reporter in attendance, but it was the overly dramatic whimpering at the mention of his wife's name that rang discordant. Asked whether he had ever supported or financially helped the woman who he visited for sex two or three times a week - the woman who made him tea and supper, the woman who may have murdered for him - he answered, "Oh dear no," as though the very question was silly to ask.[27]

Mrs Pearcey had turned her eyes to her lover, and drank in every word he spoke in evidence against her, but never once did Frank look back at her.[28]

Freke Palmer did his best to show the court that Frank Hogg was not the respectable, pious man "foremost in the hymns and responses" of his church, as one paper described him.[29]

"Did you have reason to suspect your wife's fidelity?" Palmer asked Hogg.

"I do not know," Frank said.

Freke Palmer repeated the question.

"Yes! I had," Frank said, his composure leaving him.

"Since then had your relationship been in any way strained?"

"Not in the least." Frank turned to the Magistrate. "Am I obliged to speak in open court like this, sir? It is very painful to me."

"Yes," Mr Cooke said, "you must answer the questions."[30]

Frank burst into tears.[31]

Palmer questioned Frank about the night of the murder, the night that Mrs Crowhurst swore she saw a light moving around in Mrs Pearcey's room just after 10.00pm. Frank admitted he was there. He went to Mrs Pearcey's house around twenty past ten, but only for ten minutes or so, as he saw she was out. He took an envelope off the mantle and wrote, "20 p 10. Cannot stop longer." He then went home and went to bed.

As the shadows of that bleak November afternoon grew longer, as if to add to the gloom of the proceedings, a bell clanged mournfully in the distance.[32]

Inspector Bannister continued to hunt for hard evidence that would not simply put Mrs Pearcey at the scene of the crime, but would put the murder weapon - probably the poker found near the grate - in her hand. There was some pressure to do this, since this was a capital offence, punishable by execution, and the press and public alike would naturally be outraged if later it was discovered that an innocent woman had been hanged. Bannister and his men had already received some journalistic harassment at the expediency of the inquest: "It cannot be said that the mystery of the Hampstead Tragedy has been unravelled in a way to fully satisfy the ends of justice," opined an editor for *Lloyd's Weekly*.[33]

Hasty proceedings that favoured medical evidence and left all other fact gathering to the police set a dangerous precedent, the editor argued, and denied the public one of its greatest safeguards against crime:

> In the present instance, it is true, the alleged murderess has been arrested; though the fact by no means removes the desire for the most complete and thorough inquiry into the circumstance of one of the most atrocious crimes of modern days.[34]

What harm was there in extending the inquest by a week and learning more of the accused's past, and perhaps giving police time to find the accomplice, an eye witness, or any number of additional clues like Phoebe's ring, latchkey or purse - all of which were still missing? Such information might have significant bearing on Mrs Pearcey's mortal future.[35]

All involved in the case were surely concerned to protect and uphold an impartial process that afforded the most complete collection of evidence for the sake of bringing a murderer or murderers to justice. But the police were restrained by the limits of forensic science, and the evidence against Mrs Pearcey - though voluminous - remained largely circumstantial. "These, and other facts, which have come to the knowledge of the detectives, make it by no means certain that the guilt rests upon the accused, especially when it is considered how little real evidence there is to prove that she actually committed the murders," wrote the *Illustrated Police News*.[36]

The image of the woman in the dock, the expediency of the inquest, additional evidence-gathering expeditions at 2 Priory Street, and the growing disgust with Frank Hogg made it all but impossible for police *not* to revisit the possibility of an accomplice: "From his inquiries our representative is confident that the police have now returned to their original theory - namely, that more than one person is implicated in the crime, and it is to that end their vigorous efforts, based upon the fresh information, are now directed," continued the *IPN*.[37]

The fresh evidence of an accomplice however, was scant and suspect. An eyewitness had apparently come forward stating she saw a man wheeling a bassinette in St. John's Wood on Friday night, in the street close to where it was eventually abandoned. A reporter proposed that this man met Mrs Pearcey at Crossfield Road after Phoebe's body had been dumped, took the pram and wheeled it to Hamilton Terrace and left it there, while Mrs Pearcey disposed of the baby's body on foot. Those covering the case suggested that the letters found by the police at Mrs Pearcey's house would fill in the gaps and throw an altogether "different light upon the case,"[38] but, at the continuation of the hearing on Tuesday, November 11, no new evidence of an accomplice had surfaced.

The case was both enhanced by, and suffered from, the extensive press attention it received. Many injected themselves into the drama, raising hope they could explain the more mysterious elements of the case, such as how Tiggie was conveyed in a blood-soaked pram without getting a drop of blood on her clothes. A signalman named Gwynne who worked for the North London Railway came forward to declare he saw Mrs Pearcey carrying a "suspicious-looking bundle" in Finchley Road on the night in question, but when called to identify Mrs Pearcey in daylight, he failed to do so.[39]

Other disturbing eyewitness testimony came from Mrs Annie Gardner, who lived at 13 Crogsland Road, a few houses down from Phoebe and Frank Hogg. Mrs Gardner said she saw Mrs Pearcey pushing her "gruesome load" under the Hoggs' very windows.[40] The reporter covering the story wrote that were it true, then Mrs Pearcey would have passed not only the Hogg house, but also Frederick Hogg's house, just as Frank would have been returning from the removal job in Kensington at half past six. This turned out to be wholly wrong. Frank didn't return to Castle Road until half past seven that evening.[41]

"I thought I knew her," Mrs Gardner told the reporter, "and of course I looked right into her face to see if I did know her. I found that it was not the woman I took her to be. I turned completely round and stood perfectly still, looking after her, and said to a little girl I had with me, 'Oh, good gracious, what a load that woman has got on her perambulator. I suppose it's someone moving.'"[42]

Like Mrs Rogers, Mrs Gardner described the pram as heavily loaded and covered with a black shawl. It was rumpled and looked like many things were piled on top, and the shawl had been tucked around the items to keep anything from falling out. The woman Mrs Gardner described was heading toward Haverstock Hill. Unlike signalman Gwynne, who was unable to pick Mrs Pearcey out of a lineup of women, when Mrs Gardner was taken to the police court she clearly and quickly selected Mrs Pearcey from among the others, although it should be remembered that images of Pearcey had circulated widely by this time.

"When I identified her I saw that she had a green hat on, but I had described it as a black hat, and of course a green hat would look like a black one at night," she told the reporter.[43]

Additionally, detectives had found what the press reported as a "handmade dagger" at 2 Priory Street. The "dagger" was actually an ordinary table knife, with a white handle attached to a firm steel blade measuring about six inches long, but the back had been ground down to a sharp edge so that the knife was now essentially double-edged. The point was rubbed down so it was very sharp. The grinding wasn't professionally done though, suggesting that Mrs Pearcey may have made the dagger by hand, and with "infinite labour."[44]

The dagger was discovered in one of the initial searches of 2 Priory Street, leaning against the wall near the fireplace, behind a tea tray, but wasn't described in the press until much later. During the same search, detectives also found a button similar to those missing from Phoebe's bodice in a rubbish heap in the back yard.[45] The buttons definitively put Phoebe at the crime scene, and the dagger could easily have severed her windpipe and vertebral column, but had yet to be analysed by Dr Pepper for blood.

As police continued to uncover and catalogue an array of weapons from Mrs Pearcey's house, including a revolver and cartridges that fit it,[46] a matron at Holloway Gaol commended Mrs Pearcey for her perfect behaviour. Despite the evidence presented at the police court, the inquest, and magisterial hearings, Mrs Pearcey maintained her innocence to her solicitor, officials, and her mother, who, under the most painful of circumstances, visited her daughter in prison as often as she could.[47]

The next hearing, on November 11, was less crowded than the previous, in part due to the fact that the earlier part of the day was cold and wet, but also because by then Mr Clewlow had taken steps to accommodate the press and had arranged a seat for every accredited newspaper representative. Even though the crowds were thinner than before, there were still hundreds who congregated outside the court, attempting to get in. Mr Clewlow was offered bribes of up to several pounds per seat,[48] while others attempted to use "private influence and personal persuasion" to get into the courtroom.[49] One or two gentlemen were on the bench, one being the son of the magistrate, but the courtroom hosted no such nobility as those who attended the opening hearings.[50]

At half past one Mrs Pearcey was brought to the dock again, dressed exactly as she had been the previous week, composing herself as steadily and quietly as before, her gloved hands folded across her lap.[51]

William Henry Holmes, the boy who delivered the note inviting Phoebe to visit Mrs Pearcey, was the first witness.

"I live at 138 Prince of Wales Road. On Friday, the 24th October, somebody spoke to me about 11 o'clock in the morning. I believe the person was the prisoner in the dock. I was close to the gate of the house I live in, and was bringing something home from the market. The prisoner asked me if I was going up the road, and I said 'Yes.' She asked me if I would take a note for her. I asked her to wait while I took my things in. When I came out she was opposite my house. I went across to her, and then she gave me a penny and a note, and told me to take it to 141 Prince of Wales Road, and to ring the top bell. She told me to be sure to give it to a Mrs F. Hogg."[52]

Elizabeth Holmes, the boy's mother, then testified that her boy indeed brought home the market goods, spoke to her, and then left. "I stood on top of the area steps and saw a woman give my son a letter and a penny. He went away with the letter, and meanwhile the woman walked up and down the road." Though she said she clearly identified Mrs Pearcey from a lineup, it seems she did so only after her son had already pointed Mrs Pearcey out. Though she contradicted herself, both she and her son were quite certain Mrs Pearcey was the woman who gave Willie the penny and the note.

Annie Gardner, Dr Wells, Elizabeth Andrews, Police Constable Roser, Inspector Holland, Oliver Smith, Police Constable Dickerson, and Dr Biggs gave evidence, and then Mary's former common-law husband, John Pearcey testified.

John stood up square and broad-shouldered and delivered his testimony with his hands clasped behind his back. He was dressed in a light grey jacket with a white handkerchief peeping from his breast pocket. On one or two occasions, he answered sarcastically, seemingly apathetic toward the awful position of the woman who had "slighted his affection" in favour of Frank Hogg, whom he could see seated just behind his former lover. He told the court he had lived with Mary for three years, but then had seen her in the company of other men and so gathered up his belongings and left her, though he'd met up with her frequently since.[53]

"You are not on good terms with the prisoner?" Freke Palmer asked.

"No," John said, "decidedly not."

Mary, who was watching John Pearcey with fixed eyes, looked down.[54]

As the list of witnesses expanded, so too did some of the preliminary witnesses' stories. For example, John Pearcey had maintained that Mary told him her blinds were drawn because her young brother had died. But, during the November 11 hearing, when questioned about his last conversation with the prisoner, he added that Mrs Pearcey said she was "worried out of her life, that she wished her husband would come, but was afraid he would not as *his* brother was lying dangerously ill with typhoid fever, and it would be dangerous for him to visit her."[55] Though both stories were total fabrications (Mary did have a younger brother, but he did not die in 1890, and neither Frank nor Charles had brothers with typhoid fever), they served as examples of how Mary Pearcey embellished facts (she had a brother, and Charles was sick that week so couldn't visit) and wove them into a larger fiction that served her.

Mrs Pearcey's "confession" to the female searcher, Sarah Sawtell, was again brought up and questioned. If so important a confession were made, Freke Palmer wondered, why did she wait to report it? And why would she be instructed to withhold such important news? Sarah Sawtell's testimony was clumsy and contradictory, but unfortunately for Mrs Pearcey's defence, there was no evidence to suggest she fabricated the admission, and the gravity of the searcher's evidence "could hardly be over-estimated."[56]

The ghastly objects associated with the case were again paraded into court one by bloody one. As the pram was hoisted up to the view of the magistrate, Mrs Pearcey glanced at it, but immediately dropped her eyes.[57]

Bannister created "some little sensation" when he entered the witness box and told the court he could attest that the pram could take the weight of a fully-grown human body. "I tested the perambulator to see whether it would bear the weight of a body," he said. "I got into it myself, was covered up, and wheeled about in it. I also tested whether it was possible to wheel a similar perambulator from the street, along the passage, into the kitchen, and out again and found it could be "done with perfect ease,"[58] a sketch of the act making the *Illustrated Police News*.[59]

Bannister recounted the litany of bloodstained artifacts which had been found at the scene. He spoke of bloodied rags and knives, and various other objects: a charred bonnet, the remnants of which he pulled from a little tin box. These "mute witnesses," as one reporter for the *Daily News* called them, told the story of a murderous struggle that took place in that "dismal little back kitchen in the dismal-looking house in Priory Street."[60]

Over the course of the afternoon, as the shadows in the courtroom began to deepen, doctors gave evidence as to the "awful ferocity" with which Phoebe's head had been all but separated from her body and her daughter probably smothered, each witness linking to the next in a nearly unbreakable chain of evidence. Bannister also brought out a stack of letters addressed to Frank, marked "copies," which had been kept in an envelope recently recovered from 2 Priory Street.[61] The letters were written in Mrs Pearcey's hand, but Mr Gill didn't think it necessary to read them into evidence yet, and so they remained unstudied.

Throughout the afternoon, Mrs Pearcey sat "quite unmoved," but now and again, a reporter for the *Daily News* wrote, he thought he could see a "shadow of abject misery about the lines of [her] eyes." Surely, he wrote, this was an indication that Mrs Pearcey recognised the "dreadful peril of her position."[62] But one wonders if she did, for she stayed the legal course, despite the mounting evidence against her. What was she waiting for, hoping for? It was well within her power to change the outcome of the case, but it required her to talk about what happened that terrible day, which she remained stubbornly unwilling to do.

The case adjourned until the following Tuesday at noon.

The final day of the committal hearings was held on November 18, and ended as most believed it would, with Mrs Pearcey's trial for the wilful murder of Phoebe and Tiggie Hogg set for the next session of the Central Criminal Court. Though no one could predict the evidence that Freke Palmer would present at trial, the general consensus among the press was that the prosecution's case was solid and the fate of Mrs Pearcey was all but sealed.

At the conclusion of the hearing Freke Palmer said something to his client, and her face "blanched." Then she stood, looking "haggard and terrified," and a painful hush fell over the court.[63] Mr Cooke cautioned her in the usual manner, and asked her whether she wished to make any statement. In a low voice she replied, "No sir, I wish to reserve my defence."[64]

"And she pleads not guilty, sir," Freke Palmer added.[65]

Mrs Pearcey was at once committed. As she stepped out of the dock, a reporter noticed she nodded in a friendly way to Mr Hogg, and then disappeared from public view.[66]

As she waited in the holding room, Mrs Pearcey's much commented-on composure left her entirely. Those with her said she trembled violently and couldn't sit still for more than a minute. Her committal to trial at the Old Bailey meant that her time was running short. If she was going to change tact, now was the time. Still, she held steady.

On her mother's next visit, Mary told her what to do with the furniture and sundry items at her house and which small articles should go to which family member and what should be thrown out, should the worst happen, suggesting she still had faith in a long-end legal run. She valued the pages of music on her piano stand most, and begged her mother not to sell them, but to keep them and take care of them, as they were expensive, and she might want them again some day.

On November 25, Mary received a letter from her mother to which she replied in part, "Dear mother, do not fret for me, as I have not got anything to be afraid of."[67] But Charlotte was less naïve than her daughter, and believed there were many things to fear. These prison visits may have bolstered her daughter's spirits, but they left Charlotte wracked with grief. Sometimes, after a visit, she would stand in the hall passage of Holloway prison "lifeless," and unable to move.[68]

By the week's end, Mrs Pearcey was in "excellent spirits" again, buoyed by a long interview with Freke Palmer in which they planned her defence, such that it was. She was heard later that day singing.[69]

The press tried to anticipate the legal cards that Freke Palmer would play at trial, but Palmer declined "in any way" to indicate his line of defence, and, frankly Mrs. Pearcey hadn't left him with many cards to play. Some suggested Palmer would call into question the conduct of a person as yet suspected in the crime, or propose an alternative theory and play on the doubt that many had about Mrs Pearcey's physical ability to commit such a murder, which even her uncle William had publically questioned. In an interview with

Lloyd's, William, a tradesman in the East End, said that he used to work as an undertaker and he knew how difficult it was to lift a dead body. He couldn't understand, then, how his niece could get Phoebe Hogg's body into the pram unaided.[70] Others said Palmer would drill the fact that she had no motive for the crime. Whatever his line of reasoning, the press surmised the Old Bailey Sessions would offer disclosures of a "very startling character" that would change the complexion of the charge entirely.[71]

On November 24, 1890, exactly one month after the body of Phoebe Hogg was found butchered and dumped at Crossfield Road, the November Sessions for the jurisdiction of the Central Criminal Court were formally opened at the Sessions House in the Old Bailey.[72] The calendar contained the names of 117 prisoners for trial, with just three charged with murder and only one of those three a woman. The Recorder, who acted as a senior circuit judge, charged the grand jury. Though there were several cases about which they would hear wherein life was lost, the most serious was one with which they were already undoubtedly familiar - the case of Mary Eleanor Pearcey - charged with murdering the young married woman, Phoebe Hogg, and her daughter.

The grand jury's role was to consider the evidence such that they could determine whether a *prima facie* case was made against the prisoner and a trial justified.[73] The following day, the grand jury found a true bill against Mrs Pearcey for the murder of Phoebe and Tiggie Hogg,[74] and an application was made to fix the date of her trial.[75]

The defence brief was first offered to Mr Gerald Geoghegan but he declined, saying there wasn't sufficient time to prepare adequately for Mrs Pearcey's trial.[76] Justice George Denman attended court on the 26th to dispose of the judges' list (and assign trial dates), and did not see any reason to postpone the Pearcey trial. He made an application to fix the date for her trial for December 1. Given the quick turnaround, the brief went to Arthur Hutton instead of Geoghegan.[77]

Hutton was experienced too, and had probably defended more

murderers than any other contemporary member of the criminal bar.[78] Like Geoghegan, Hutton believed there wasn't ample time to properly review and fact-check the great mass of papers related to the case. Mrs Pearcey had been committed to trial on Tuesday, and Arthur Hutton and Freke Palmer only received copies of all the depositions that Friday.[79] But Denman didn't want to push off the business to the December sessions, which were scheduled for December 15th, because to do so may have impeded the Christmas holiday.[80] After hearing from both Hutton and the prosecuting counsel, Forrest Fulton, Denman determined that the case had received ample investigation and nine days was plenty of time to mount an adequate defence.[81]

Because of the fame of the Pearcey case, great preparations were made to prevent overcrowding at the Old Bailey, as had happened in Mr Cooke's courtroom. There were barriers erected in the corridors and no one except those on business or who had a written official order was admitted. Meanwhile, on Monday, December 1, Mrs Pearcey was transferred from Holloway Gaol to Newgate. She retained her "buoyant disposition" and told any number of visitors, including the chaplain, that she was innocent of the crime and fully anticipated an acquittal.[82]

Her mother was not as confident. Although she told a reporter she knew what "ought to be done" for her daughter - suggesting a certain calibre of barrister selected to defend her - there was no money to do it. She was upset that Mary could not be secured a "proper defence."[83] There was no one, Charlotte said, who could help them now, and she was forced to sell off all her daughter's things, even those promised to her as relics, to pay for her defence, such as it was.

"I would like to get her album which contains her photograph, and some ornaments and presents which were given to her," Charlotte told a reporter. "I would even be satisfied if I could only get that photograph of her in evening dress which appeared in *Lloyd's Newspaper*, for it was lifelike and everyone who saw it knew it at once."[84]

When the reporter asked Charlotte what, exactly, she thought

ought to be done to save her daughter, she snapped, "Why, to have the truth of the evidence against her tested. My poor daughter tells me she is innocent, and from what I know of her character I feel bound to believe her. I think she has as much right to be believed as some of the others, don't you?"[85]

Charlotte didn't elaborate why she felt Hutton and Palmer couldn't test the evidence just as well, or why they weren't fit to defend her daughter, but she was clearly distraught by her daughter's incarceration and committal to trial. It was agonising, Charlotte said, to have to see her daughter through great bars, which kept them "yards apart."[86]

Newgate Prison, where Mrs Pearcey was now held as she awaited trial at the Old Bailey was notorious, first used as a gaol in 1188, and although rebuilt in the 1780s was so dilapidated by the time of the Pearcey trial, it could only temporarily house prisoners remanded for trial in forthcoming sessions. Even in its derelict state, it was an ominous and threatening building.

"We shall never forget the mingled feelings of awe and respect with which we used to gaze on the exterior of Newgate in our schoolboy days," wrote the author Robert Thurston Hopkins. "How dreadful its rough heavy walls, and low massive doors, appeared to us - the latter looking as if they were made for the express purpose of letting people in, and never letting them out again."[87] The City of London authorities would eventually tear down parts of Newgate and Old Bailey and rebuild a larger, quite magnificent court in its place, but not without significant cost and many delays.

Mrs Pearcey was moved from Holloway Gaol to Newgate for the duration of her trial, but she was the only prisoner in its halls for the first week of December, and the facility was never fully occupied again.

Courtroom No. 1, in which Mrs Pearcey's case was scheduled to open, was perpetually dim and "very depressing" and, although it wasn't in a basement, wrote Hargrave Lee Adam in his *Old Days at the*

Old Bailey, it felt as though it was.[88] According to Adam, Courtroom No. 1 was where the most important cases were heard. He would later describe the scene on the opening day of the Pearcey trial by walking the reader into the "well" or centre of the empty courtroom, inviting them to look around, first pointing out the sound, sight, and perhaps the smell of the gas lamps that hissed overhead. So bad was the light, Adam wrote, that a reflector had to be fixed near the window, just above the jury box to the left of the centre of court, to amplify what little light got through. One might notice the bench next - an oppressive, sombre object made of dark mahogany - which ran the length of the wall at the back of the room. From his seat the judge could view, in panorama, the jury, witnesses, defendant, counsel and court, but it wasn't an expansive view. In fact, the conditions of the court, and especially the lower floor where the solicitors, lawyers, clerks and press sat were cramped, and apparently smelled when packed with people. Flowers and herbs were kept on the judge's bench, but offered minor relief on days when a notorious case like Pearcey's was heard.[89]

The dock was where the accused would stand, and directly facing was the witness box where prosecution and defence witnesses testified. Although the Old Bailey courthouse had been rebuilt several times by the time of the Pearcey trial, the basic layout of the courtrooms remained the same, designed to emphasise the contest between the judgers and the judged.[90] A sounding board hung from the ceiling over the witness box to augment witnesses' voices. The space overlooking the dock was prime real estate; it was the best seat from which to watch court tragedies unfold. Like veranda seating at an opera, a series of galleries called the "city lands" were reserved for the public; at a price, of course.[91]

Hargrave Lee Adam's quiet, private tour of the courtroom was easy and orienting for the modern reader, but the day the Pearcey murder trial opened at the 'O.B.',[92] as it was colloquially known, was anything but. The interest in the trial was "immense," and the Old Bailey was "early thronged" by pressmen and the public.[93] The court was packed with sightseers and others who had business there,

Adam wrote, and there wasn't "an inch of room to spare."[94]

Much of the public audience was composed of women.[95] "The so-called 'weaker sex' besieged the court with shameless persistency," wrote 'an indignant correspondent' to the *Pall Mall Gazette*:

> No sense of decency restrained them; no amount of personal discomfort kept them outside the doors of the grim forum. Wives came with their husbands, brothers brought the female members of their families, mothers sat side-by-side with their young daughters. Hour after hour did these ghoulish women, armed with opera-glasses, sherry-flasks and sandwich-boxes, hang with eager curiosity upon every movement and look of their miserable sister.[96]

The attendance of women to a trial wherein the antagonist and protagonist were also both female could hardly be a surprise. The Hampstead Murders was a fascinating case from beginning to end, not only because of its many mysteries and scandals, but also because its protagonist was a character unlike any that had yet been invented. Thomas Hardy, who had travelled to London on December 3, wrote to his wife that the streets around the Old Bailey were so crowded he had trouble hailing a hansom cab. Looking around the Savile Club later, he noted, "men are reading the papers everywhere," and the Pearcey trial was front-page news in many major dailies.[97]

Hardy became keenly interested in Pearcey's case and the social implications of her unusual relationship with Frank Hogg. He may have even written aspects of the case into *Jude the Obscure*, according to his biographer Martin Seymour-Smith.[98]

When the chief court usher William Field - a longtime fixture at the Old Bailey - opened the doors to Courtroom No. 1 the public flooded in. In addition to the public door were also two private entrances which led into the courtroom from antechambers. Through the first came Justice Denman, the Aldermen and the Sheriff of London, and a few ticketed visitors who filled seats upon the bench or in the adjoining private box. Through the second entrance came prosecutor Forrest Fulton, defender Arthur Hutton and the various clerks and pages who had business with the court. Mr Forrest Fulton, MP and Mr C.F. Gill appeared for the prosecution; Mr Arthur Hutton appeared for the defence, while Mr Grain and Mr Pridham-Wippell watched the case on behalf of Frank Hogg and his family. Counsel and solicitors filed into the middle chamber of the courtroom, and those interested members from the Bar filled in what few seats remained unoccupied.[99]

The tenor of excitement in the room made it difficult to believe that the finalé to this play was a matter of life and death for "one wretched being," though not all seemed excited to be there.[100] The all-male jury, who Hargrave Adam described as having been "dragged unwillingly from their daily occupations," felt the weight of their duty particularly, and looked "ill at ease and anxious."[101]

Arriving prisoners were brought into the courtroom through a series of underground passages and dark hallways, which amplified the drama of capture, confinement and public display. These hallways led, like rat tunnels, directly to the courtroom from Newgate Prison. When Mrs Pearcey was brought up from the tunnels to the dock, "every eye turned upon her."[102]

Even as the court began to settle, the last few attendees scurried in and instinctively looked to the dock to see Mrs Pearcey. Adam described her as "striking."[103] She wore a brown cloak and black dress trimmed with crepe. She wore no hat, abiding court custom, and her brown hair was attractively curled on top of her head.[104] When charged, she answered each charge in a firm, soft voice, "Not guilty, my lord." She then sat down in the chair provided for her and folded her hands in her lap.

Before the prosecution opened its case, a juror was removed and replaced. He doubted the legality of capital punishment and was substituted by someone without such qualms. Then, rather theatrically, Justice Denman said he'd received an anonymous letter with respect to the case he needed to show counsel. He was so incensed about its content that he threw it at the bar, accidentally striking the Crown Solicitor on the head with it.[105] Denman said if he could find the man who wrote it, he'd punish him severely.

No one knows what the letter sent to Denman said, but it was not the only letter received by anonymous tipsters inserting themselves into the case. One such letter told of hearing a milkman say that early on the morning of October 25, he saw Frank Hogg come out of the house where the murders took place. Another letter, addressed to Arthur Hutton, received after the trial ended, but delivered to the Old Bailey, claimed to have seen a woman turning over a pram the night of the murders. When the witness went to investigate further, he found a ring on the dead woman's finger, which he stole. In a postscript, he claimed the woman had a man with her.[106]

Forrest Fulton, the prosecutor, stood near the Clerk of Arraigns' railed desk. He was described as tall, and graceful and sported a blonde moustache.[107] He was the youngest son of Lieutenant Colonel James Forrest and Fanny Fulton. By 1890, he was an established barrister and husband to Sophia Brown, with whom he had four sons and a daughter. Fulton had been educated at Norwich School under his uncle, the Reverend Augustus Jessopp, and attended the University of London. He was admitted to the Middle Temple Bar in 1872 in his mid twenties.[108]

Fulton opened his case for the prosecution against Mary Pearcey using the accused's own words, reading three letters found at her flat. The first dated October 2, 1888 began, "My dear F. Do not think of going away for my heart will break if you do; don't go dear." As Fulton read the letter, a reporter with the *Daily News* observed Mrs Pearcey's face "quivering."[109]

Fulton believed the letters showed Mrs Pearcey's passionate attachment for Frank Hogg. He reasoned that though Mrs Pearcey *said* she could manage her lover's marriage to another woman, in practice, she could not, and her passion turned to murderous obsession. As for Frank, apart from making bad decisions to entangle himself with two women, Fulton felt "perfectly satisfied" he was unconnected to the crime.[110]

The same could not be said for his lover, against whom the chain of evidence was quite strong. By Fulton's estimation, Mrs Pearcey struck Phoebe at the back of the head with the poker several times, then cut her throat, packed her body into the pram, and then wheeled her body to Crossfield Road and dumped it before returning to Priory Street to get Tiggie, who she carried to Finchley Road and left under a nettle bush. At some point in that long night, she also left the bloody pram leaning against the wall at 31 Hamilton Terrace to confuse its connection to the crime.

The chain of evidence against Arthur Hutton's client was indeed strong, but there were three weak links in the case, as Hutton and Palmer saw it: no direct evidence against their client, no suitable motive, and Frank Hogg's reluctance to tell the whole truth and his dubious character. Hutton's strategy then would be to focus on the lack of evidence or motive and Frank Hogg's questionable character. Adam wrote in his memoir that Hutton originally wanted to argue manslaughter; he thought they might get a reduced sentence for Mrs Pearcey, but she insisted she was innocent and wouldn't hear of admitting guilt of any kind.

Arthur Edward Hill Hutton was the only son of John Hill Hutton of Houghton-le-Spring, Durham, and a well-known and respected barrister. He was born on March 17, 1859, and called to the Middle Temple bar on January 17, 1877 at just 18 years old.[111] He was described in Adam's memoir, published some thirty years after the trial, as tall, and silvery-voiced with large, gentle eyes, in one of which was affixed a monocle without which he "scarcely ever appeared in court."[112] Adam said that Hutton belonged to a new school of advocates who had evolved from the "bullying" tactics of the Dickensian character from the *Pickwick Papers*, Serjeant Buzfuz, and preferred an almost Socratic method of forensic rhetoric, relying on the elegance of a well crafted argument rather than bombast to persuade a jury. He demonstrated similar respect and deference to his client's wishes too, for he never argued the plea of manslaughter before the court, even though he believed it might save his client's life.

When Frank Hogg entered the box after each counsellor had opened, a reporter observed he and Mrs Pearcey exchanged a "long, earnest look."[113]

Arthur Hutton read aloud the letter in which Mrs Pearcey admonished Frank for thinking about suicide:

"I cannot bear to see you like you were this evening," he read. "Try not to give way. Try to be brave, dear, for things will come right in the end. Why should you try to take your life because you cannot have everything you want? Never take that which you cannot give."[114]

"Did you want to take your life at the time?" Hutton asked Hogg directly.

"I cannot recall it," Frank answered.

"Just try and recall it," Justice Denman added. "Don't let this be a mere matter of thinking. You must surely remember a thing like that?"

"I cannot recall it," Frank persisted.

"You never thought of taking your life?"

"No," Frank said.

"Then it is pure imagination on her part?" Hutton asked.

"I suppose so," Frank answered.[115]

"Under what circumstances did you make the acquaintance of the prisoner?"

"By her coming into the shop as a customer. That would be two years ago. I lived almost opposite her for nearly two years."

"Were you on extremely friendly terms?"

"Very friendly terms, nothing further. There was no intercourse at all before my marriage."

Mrs Pearcey laughed audibly.[116]

Hutton was nonplussed too. "Do you really mean to say, living opposite this woman for nearly two years and believing her to be married that there was no intimacy till December, 1888?"

"No sir, there was not. We were only friendly."

Arthur Hutton read from another of the letters, and then asked, "Do you mean to say that there has been no affection, no loving or kissing?"

"I might have kissed her," Frank admitted.

"Don't you remember? Do you think it is such a casual thing to kiss a married woman?" Hutton said.

"Well I might have."

Hutton read from the October 2 letter, wherein Mary wrote, "...if you love me as you say you do, and you went away, I should die."

Judge Denman interjected - "Had not you told her you loved her?"

"I might have told her," Frank said.[117]

Over the course of the various hearings and trials, Frank Hogg had hired representation and had been clearly coached. There was no sobbing; his forthrightness was quashed; and he proved a cold and frustratingly vague witness by the time Hutton pressed him in the witness box that day.

A now-familiar list of witnesses was called to give evidence. Clara, who recounted Mrs Pearcey's strange behaviour at the mortuary; Henry William Buxton, who worked for Frank's brother and provided Frank an alibi;[118] Willie Holmes, the boy who delivered the invitation to tea; Elizabeth Holmes, the boy's mother who saw Mrs Pearcey attempt to conceal herself after she gave Willie the note to deliver to 141; Mrs Barraud, the landlady at 141 Prince of Wales Road who saw Willie ring the bell at 141; Elizabeth Crowhurst, Mrs Pearcey's neighbour, and William Crowhurst, Elizabeth's son; Charles Britt, who saw Mrs Hogg at the door to 2 Priory Street at 3.30 on the day of the murders; Charlotte Piddington, who put the dress stand over the garden wall and heard a baby scream; Sarah Sawtell, the searcher who took Mrs Pearcey's quasi confession; Walter and Sarah Butler, residents of 2 Priory Street; Elizabeth Rodgers and Annie Gardner, who saw Mrs Pearcey pushing the pram on separate occasions on that Friday evening; Somerled Macdonald, who found Phoebe's dead body; and Arthur Gardiner, the first constable on the scene at Crossfield Road.[119]

The court adjourned for the day and the many "fashionably-attired" ladies who had been there from the opening act finally relinquished their seats.[120]

The following day's testimony opened and closed in much the same way, to a packed audience that sat rapt for hours as well-known details were again retold or slightly amended. The main attraction at a jury trial of this sort was not the evidence delivered, but the counsellor's summation of the crime, and of course, the verdict. In reviewing that evidence, Fulton contended that the prosecution had clearly proved the prisoner committed the crime for which the woman in the dock stood charged. He delivered his final summation in under an hour in a "dry, juridical, temperate and, indeed, rather a dull style,"[121] offering no grand rhetorical appeal, probably because he didn't think he needed one. The main thrust of his summation was the overwhelming evidence found at Mrs Pearcey's house, which established not only means, but also the motive for the crime. Mrs Pearcey, he contended, was clearly obsessed with Frank Hogg and she wanted the obstacle that stood between she and her lover removed. He recalled for the jury the prisoner's conversation with Sarah Sawtell, the police searcher, in which Mrs Pearcey admitted that "words" arose between she and Phoebe while having tea. There was a "strong body of evidence" he said, which pointed in one direction only, and that was straight at the woman who stood indicted in the dock.[122]

When he was finished and the courtroom brought back into silence, Arthur Hutton rose.

Every eye turned again to the young woman who sat in the dock, the light fast fading around her. Hutton made an "ingenious and clever" set of arguments that offered alternative explanations for the mounds of damning evidence against his client. What motive did she have for the crime, he asked? Mrs Pearcey would have "gained no benefit from Mrs Hogg's death."[123] He reminded the jury that, "Hogg had never promised the prisoner marriage, and she had nothing to expect in the way of marriage from him."[124] What good then would killing Phoebe and her baby do? There was also the disconnection - which the jury could clearly see now - between the savagery taken to murder Mrs Hogg and Mrs Pearcey's disposition, which, by every single account - even from those who didn't like her - was "affectionate and kindly."[125] Further, as Dr Pepper had testified, Phoebe's abscess may have made her weak, but she was clearly strong enough to push a two-year-old in a heavy pram around town. If the struggle was as grand as the prosecution proposed, wouldn't his client have suffered more than a few scratches about her hands?[126]

Hutton implored the jury to consider whether the chain of evidence Mr Fulton had laid out was *sufficiently* strong to merit a guilty verdict, for it was all circumstantial evidence, he reminded them - the most dangerous kind. If there were any breaks or strains of credulity in that chain of evidence, he said, then the jury must hesitate in their assignment of guilt, for a woman's very life was at stake.

After Hutton sat down, Justice Denman said he didn't feel competent to sum up the case at that late hour.[127] He dismissed the court until the following day with a promise to summarise what they had just heard again. The jury was put up in a nearby hotel for the night.[128]

On December 3, 1890, Courtroom No. 1 at the Old Bailey was again crowded. Freke Palmer saw his client before she was led into the courtroom, and counselled her to prepare for the worst. A reporter at court said she seemed in fair spirits, but to his anxious warning she could only return, "yes," dazedly.[129]

Just before half past ten, the jury entered the box, the dock warders took up their positions and Colonel Milman, the Governor of Holloway and Newgate Prisons, took his seat at the back of the dock, while overhead the dark public gallery was literally "crammed" with spectators, eagerly craning their necks to watch Mrs Pearcey enter.[130]

Three loud knocks on the door announced Justice Denman's approach. All in court rose and removed their hats, while Denman, the aldermen and sheriffs took their seats on the bench, bowing low to the large throng of barristers and solicitors. Then, the door at the back of the dock opened, and Mrs Pearcey stepped up, dressed as before, her hands gloved, her posture "graceful."[131]

The Judge directed her to her seat, and she dropped into the position she'd maintained all the days before, hands clasped, eyes forward. A reporter for the *Daily News* said Mrs Pearcey "never moved a muscle or gave the slightest sign of consciousness of anything going on around her."[132]

Outside, a dense fog had formed, obscuring the court and its equally grim proceedings. "On a rainy or foggy day, I don't think there is a more depressing place in the world than the old Court of the Old Bailey," the lawyer Montagu Williams, Palmer's friend and contemporary, wrote.[133] Now and then, as the gloom lifted, a little filtered light streamed down upon Mrs Pearcey, statuesque in the dock, occupying the only clear space in the court. She looked even more pathetic in the murky beam of light, the reporter observing her wrote. Yet, as desperate as her situation was, she never broke down into tears. In fact, she sat silent and motionless with a look of "blank dull misery on her pale and haggard face" throughout the judge's summation, which ended at quarter past one.[134]

Justice George Denman was a hulking man. Even in his old age, he bore the traces of a sporting youth. Indeed, he'd rowed in the Oxford and Cambridge boat race of 1841, and won the Colquhoun sculls in October 1842.[135] Denman had become "sedate and a little old-fashioned"[136] in his years on the bench, but he was still fiercely respected as much for his legal aptitude, as for his aristocratic pedigree. He was a member of Lincoln's Inn, having been admitted to the Bar on November 8, 1843 and appointed the Queen's Counsel in 1861.[137]

Denman, who had a "beautiful voice,"[138] began his summation that morning by saying that they had adjourned following an address by Hutton "as powerful and as complete and distinct" as any he had ever heard in a criminal case.[139]

It was clear to him that some time between half past three and six o'clock on October 24th, Phoebe Hogg was foully murdered. The question at hand was whether Mrs Pearcey inflicted the injuries that caused Phoebe's death. The prosecution held that the murder took place at Mrs Pearcey's house and that she alone was there at the time, and that she took steps to avoid discovery. She wheeled the body a considerable distance and left it where it was found. The defence, Denman said, suggested there were loopholes of doubt here and there and that the jury would have to take into "full and fair account" every observation of the kind that could be made. The jury should be brought to an "irresistible conclusion" that Mrs Pearcey was guilty of the murder, or else they could not find her guilty.

As for Frank Hogg, who would be the most obvious accomplice if there were one, Denman said, "no man could have given himself a viler and more loathsome character."[140] He was a witness the jury should be "slow to believe because he was so bad."[141] Though parts of his story were clearly incredible, other parts seemed reasonable, and there was no reliable evidence entered that he had anything to do with the crime.

One wonders, however, if Frank Hogg was really the dupe he pretended to be. After all, had he not encouraged Clara to visit Mrs Pearcey, it is doubtful anyone would have ever suspected her of the crime, or, if they did, it would have been hours if not days later, and she would have had time to properly dispose of and clean up all the evidence beforehand.

No matter. Denman never elaborated on the ways he felt Hogg was "so bad," but he did say he found it extraordinary that any woman should conceive such a "violent passion or lust" for a man like Hogg.[142]

This was an aspect of the Hampstead murders that perplexed many people who contemplated it: why would anyone give Frank Hogg attention, let alone murder for him? Perhaps the crime writer F. Tennyson Jesse explained it best when she wrote of the Pearcey case some years later, "Of all the strange phenomena with which the fabric of the world presents us, there is none so strange as the human heart."[143]

But Denman wasn't interested in the machinations of the heart. He had only the facts to consider. He combed through his notes line by line, mentioning the inconsistency in testimony of the boy Willie Holmes and Mrs Butler, who said they were interacting with Mrs Pearcey at exactly the same time, which clearly wasn't possible. He felt the contradiction reconcilable though by deferring to the statement Mrs Pearcey made to Sarah Sawtell. From his notes:

> Much reliance was placed on this date - which is inconsistent with the evidence of other witnesses who put the prsnr at her own house up to 12 on the 24. But the prisoner's own statement to Sawtell ([illegible]) puts the sending of a note by the boy on the 23 & I believe it did then take place.[144]

He dismissed the idea that the blood in Mrs Pearcey's kitchen could have been caused, as she had told detectives, by a nosebleed or killing mice, but he also clarified that what Mrs Pearcey had said to Sarah Sawtell - important though it was - did *not* qualify as a confession. Though it was true the case hinged largely on circumstantial evidence, most premeditated cases of murder did, given that criminals trying not to get caught cover up evidence of their crime with some success. In other words, though Inspector Bannister and his team hadn't found important clues and couldn't explain others, there was enough evidence to suggest her husband's lover, Mary Eleanor Wheeler Pearcey, did Phoebe to death at 2 Priory Street on October 24th.

Mr Hutton seems to have assumed, Denman told the jury, that unless it was affirmatively established that the prisoner had absolutely and alone, or at all events with her own hand, perpetrated the actual injuries which caused the death of the deceased, it would not be the jury's duty to find her guilty of wilful murder. "That is not the law gentlemen," he said.[145]

It was sufficient the jury should be satisfied the murder could not have taken place without the prisoner being involved in some way; to what degree was not really the question. This was quite an unfortunate legal shift for Mrs Pearcey. If the jury felt Phoebe's death could not have taken place without Mrs Pearcey standing by, or without her knowledge, or some role or assistance which enabled the murder to take place in her house then as twelve "reasonable men," they could not refrain from concluding she was guilty of wilful murder.

Denman recounted the history of the precedent so everyone

was clear. When he was a young man at the Bar, he said, one case had established beyond all doubt that a murder was planned, and though it was clearly committed by three people, because it was doubtful which of the three had inflicted the actual wound, all were acquitted. "That was so grave a scandal and was so calculated to destroy the administration of justice with due regard to the safety of the community that an Act was passed providing that accessories before the fact may be indicted and tried as principals in the felony, and if that be made out to the satisfaction of the jury a conviction would follow just as if the person accused was an actual eyewitness of the infliction of the wound."[146]

Mrs Pearcey may not have been the *only* party to the crime, but she was certainly involved, and she had attempted to destroy the proof of her involvement. Since there was no compelling support that implicated anyone else, then the law should apply only to the woman in the dock, even if it came to pass that she was assisted by someone else.

Concluding his address of nearly three hours, near 1.00pm the great bell of St. Paul's came booming dolefully through the fog,[147] and on the whole, Denman's summation was so balanced it was impossible to tell which side he believed.[148]

At 1.45 the jury retired to consider their verdict. Judge Denman kept his seat on the bench for a quarter of an hour, as though he expected the jury to return almost immediately. When they did not return, the presiding alderman and the two sheriffs then left, and the court instantly broke into a "babel of conversation."[149]

After they had been absent for about half an hour, the jury sent a note to the judge, causing "momentary excitement," but nothing came of the note, and its contents were never published. At 2.12pm came a cry of "Order" and the jury returned to court, a peculiar hush settling over the crowd.[150]

The door to the back of the dock opened and Mrs Pearcey was ushered back inside the courtroom. At the top of the steps, not quite in the dock, she stopped, as if she was uncertain of what to do. She was gently conducted to the front of the dock, a female attendant standing close to her right, and a male warder at her left, another immediately behind her, in case she fainted when the verdict was read. She stood in full view of the crowd, all of whom remained standing.[151] Though one reporter saw tears in her eyes, she maintained "complete composure" through the rest of the proceedings, the court crowded to the "very doors."[152]

The Clerk of the Court stood and called the names of each court administrator.

Mr H.K. Avory, the Deputy Clerk of Arraigns, asked if the jury had agreed upon their verdict. "We have," the foreman answered.

"Do you find the prisoner at the bar guilty of the wilful murder of Phoebe Hogg, or no?"

"Guilty."[153]

A thrill ripped through the court.[154]

"Is that the verdict of you all?" asked the Clerk.

"It is," the foreman said, nodding.

The chaplain of Newgate moved to Judge Denman's right hand, while Denman donned the small square of black silk and ceremonially placed it atop his white wig.

"Mary Eleanor Wheeler, have you anything to say why the court should not proceed to pronounce sentence of death upon you?"

She began to reply in a low but steady voice, but could hardly be heard over the excited court chatter. The usher silenced the courtroom. Justice Denman asked Mrs Pearcey to repeat herself.

"Only that I am innocent of this charge," she said weakly.[155]

"You have been found guilty after a most patient trial, and after a most powerful and able defence, and I must say that I feel it to be absolutely impossible to conceive that the death of Phoebe Hogg would have taken place without your having been an active instrument towards that death. It is a terrible case. I do not wish to add to the pangs which you must feel by saying much to you. I do say, however, that I think it is one of the many instances which have come before me, even at this very session of the terrible results of persons giving way to prurient and indecent lust. You have become a person of so little moral sense that eventually you have been an instrument, and a willing instrument, of taking away the life of a woman whose only offence was that she was married to a man upon whom you had set your unholy passion."

"Now I cannot hold out to you any hope whatever that within a very short time you will not cease to live as an inmate of this our world."[156]

Here, a reporter for *Lloyd's* noticed tears streaming down her cheeks.[157]

"You will have a certain time for preparation. God grant that you may use that time for your eternal benefit. You will have the opportunity. You will be kindly dealt with, kindly ministered to, and I trust that you will use the short time upon earth that remains for you in preparing yourself for another world. I now have nothing to do but to pass the sentence of the law upon you.

"Mary Eleanor Wheeler Pearcey, it is the sentence of this court that you shall be taken to the place from whence you came, and thence to a place of lawful execution, and there you shall be hanged by the neck until you be dead, and afterwards your body shall be buried in a common grave within the precincts of the prison wherein you were last confined before your execution; and may the Lord have mercy on your soul."[158]

The Newgate Ordinary intoned, "Amen," which the crowd fervently echoed.

The Clerk of Arraigns asked Mrs Pearcey if she had anything to say for herself in stay of execution of the judgment.

"Only that I am innocent of the crime," she said again, and without assistance, she turned around and walked down from the dock.

THE EXECUTION

"THE trial of Mary Eleanor Wheeler, alias Pearcey, for the murder of Phoebe Hogg and her child, ended yesterday at the Old Bailey in the only possible way. The unhappy woman was found guilty and sentenced to death," began *The Times*.[1] While most agreed the verdict was just, there remained a feeling that not all the facts were yet known, and parts of Denman's summation suggested to some that even he left open the possibility of a co-conspirator. A reporter for the *World* wrote that the public had a right to know what Denman meant when he said things like committing the crime "by herself or with someone else," or "so that someone else did it with her knowledge and consent."[2]

One reporter said he was disinclined to accept the prosecution's theory about how the crime was committed *because* of the way in which the crime was committed, and believed that when the truth finally came out, it would be quite different from the story told in court.[3] Another writer for *Truth* wrote that a "friend" had several interviews with Mrs Pearcey, wherein she admitted to the crime and dropped hints that someone came in and helped her clean up and dispose of the bodies thereafter.[4] But it was all speculation from then on.

As for Mrs Pearcey, she cried the entire walk back to her cell, and for some time thereafter "wept bitterly."[5] On leaving the dock after condemnation, she was taken to a specially prepared cell under the old infirmary in the basement of the male wing at Newgate. A wall separating the two rooms had been taken down and the room was then quite spacious, measuring 14 x 8 ft wide. Two female warders were with her day and night, and a rotation of six wardresses took eight-hour shifts to watch her round the clock.

The cell was heated with steam pipes and the floor covered with coca-nut matting. There was a window on the right-hand wall of the room, but it was far too high for her to see anything out of. Had she been able to see through it, she would have seen the shed in which she would be executed in a few weeks, some 30 or 40 yards off.[6] She was given a cup of tea and, within half an hour of her sentencing, had somewhat recovered her typical equanimity. At half past eight she took her supper, and talked - even joked - with her female attendants, going to bed early and sleeping "like a top" through the night.[7]

The following morning she ate bacon and an egg for her breakfast and requested an hour's walk in the prison yard. Afterwards, she seemed agitated, and anxiously paced her cell from corner to corner, at times singing to herself and at other times reciting scraps of poetry.[8]

The chaplain, Reverend H.G. Duffield, who was "unceasing in his ministrations" to her, visited, but her mind was elsewhere. The Reverend's job was to "overwhelm the man awaiting execution with religious advice and consolation, which took the form of long rigmaroles, exhortations, and prayers,"[9] but as he attempted to cajole her confession, she merely repeated what she had said for weeks - that she was not guilty. Mr Duffield was deeply sympathetic to Mrs Pearcey's situation, despite her unwillingness to confess, and felt especially bad for her mother. He had even paid Charlotte's fare home after one particularly painful visit, and had slipped her seven pence that Mary said she wanted her mother to have, telling Charlotte he was truly sorry for all she and her daughter had suffered.[10]

Sir J.C. Lawrence, the Sheriff of the County of London, Colonel Milman, Governor of Holloway and Newgate Prisons, Mr Duffield, the chaplain and several other officials went to Mrs Pearcey in her cell later in the day to tell her the date of execution had been set for two days before Christmas. She took the news "with perfect unconcern," saying only, "I thought so from his [the judge's] summing up."[11]

Some in the public didn't take the announcement of Mrs Pearcey's execution date so well, and felt it was imprudent and cruel to execute anyone, let alone a woman, so close to a holy holiday. Others argued that to change the date and forestall the inevitable was crueler still.[12]

As it had been since her arrest, her every movement in Newgate was reported in the press. "Since Thursday night her sleep has been far from undisturbed, and on Friday she became decidedly depressed. She walks feverishly across the cell, and at intervals she lies down upon her bed in hysterical sobbing," reported the *Daily News*.[13]

On Saturday, December 6, Freke Palmer interviewed his client in Newgate Prison, during which time Mrs Pearcey told him stories that may have added weight, according to the *Daily News*, to the belief that she suffered from hallucinations and a disordered mind. Palmer was already preparing his petition to the Home Secretary, and the press suspected the thrust of his argument would be that Mrs Pearcey was of "unsound mind."[14] Presciently, a reporter wrote that there would surely be some attempt to argue Mrs Pearcey's sanity on appeal, and as "the crime itself was an insane one insanely committed," then to that degree she was indeed out of her mind. "It was mad business from beginning to end."[15] But whether Palmer would be able to show that Mrs Pearcey met the *legal* standard of insanity was anyone's guess.

Palmer had indeed been busy collecting statements from

acquaintances and family, most of whom told stories that showed Mrs Pearcey was of an "excitable nature,"[16] and that her conduct and behaviour was, at times, those of "a mad person,"[17] and Palmer and Hutton must have approached this line of defence with their client at least once prior to going to trial because Mrs Pearcey had written to her mother saying her counsel wished her to admit insanity, but that she was "no more insane than the rest of them."[18] Given the treatment of epileptics and the mentally ill, or the condition of life in asylums, one could hardly blame her for not wanting to trade the rope for the straightjacket. Still, had she let counsel do their jobs, it might have saved her life.

Hutton had told H.L. Adam that he wanted to recommend the lesser charge of manslaughter and had wanted to show what happened that day was accidental. Mrs Pearcey, he would have argued, had no intention to murder at all. She had killed Phoebe in the midst of a heated argument by striking an unlucky blow.[19] But this argument never transpired in court, largely because Mrs Pearcey wouldn't let it, though no one quite knows why. Two sad consequences of her interference with counsel were that not a single witness mentioned any of Mrs Pearcey's seizures, headaches, suicide attempts, hallucinations or chronic mental health issues while on the stand, and that although 37 witnesses were called or cross-examined by counsel, none of those witnesses were actually called in Mrs Pearcey's defence. That her health issues, depression and suicidal ideation were coming out now - *after* judgment had been rendered - would make Palmer's plea for mercy based on temporary insanity a very difficult case to make.[20]

Back at Newgate, Mr Duffield gave Mrs Pearcey books to read, and read with her every day, which cheered her temporarily. She described the reverend as "exceedingly kind" and told her mother she felt consoled when he read and talked with her.[21] *Lloyd's* reported that Mrs Pearcey received the reverend gladly, and accepted his "admonitions,"[22] but they ultimately produced no effect. The reverend tried again and again to coax from her a confession, perhaps believing that to tell the truth would relieve some of the pressure of holding in such a lie, but she refused to talk about the murder to him or anyone else. She never implicated another soul, gave no plausible explanation or account of that day, and made no further admissions of guilt.

Despite bouts of depression Mrs Pearcey kept her appetite, and had plenty of food; bacon and eggs for breakfast; a chop or steak for dinner; tea and supper, and, when she chose, a "reasonable supply" of malt liquor or wine.[23] *Lloyd's* reported that Mrs Pearcey drank a bottle of ale each night before she went to bed.[24]

Throughout that first week she was the only prisoner in the gaol, as all others were kept at Holloway except during the sessions. At the end of the week, however, a fresh batch of inmates would be brought in for the December sessions, which were set to begin on the 15th. Even so, arrangements were made to maintain Mrs Pearcey's "perfect privacy."[25]

"She observes the prison rules with precision," wrote a reporter for the *Daily News*, "and lives in a comparatively methodical manner."[26]

She was no trouble to the wardresses who watched her and, in fact, officials said they never had such an obedient prisoner under their care. Her gentleness and kindness to all she encountered even caused some who observed her in her final days to doubt she could have committed the murder.[27]

On December 5, two days after her conviction, Mrs Pearcey had written to her mother asking her come visit her on Monday, December 8 and to be at the prison by 2 o'clock. An official order was enclosed in the envelope from Governor Milman authorising the visit, which was to last twenty minutes.[28] Accompanied by a niece, Charlotte arrived at Newgate Prison at five minutes past two that Monday. Administrators checked her documents and admitted Charlotte alone, while the niece was detained in the vestibule. Mrs Wheeler was escorted down a short passage to a room partitioned off in the middle by wire netting, through which it was impossible to pass anything. She was allowed to kiss her daughter, and then they each sat on the other side of the net, Charlotte by herself and Mrs Pearcey next to a wardress. Her daughter was so "down", Charlotte afterward told a reporter, that she could hardly speak.[29]

When she was finally able to talk, Charlotte begged Mary to "honestly and truthfully" tell her if she knew how the shocking crime for which she was now condemned took place.

"Mother," Mary said, "I know nothing about it."

"Do, pray, dear, tell me the truth."[30]

"Oh, mother, as I expect to meet my Maker in a few days, I cannot tell a lie. I know nothing whatever about the murder. If I knew I would, dear mother, willingly say so, for my own sake now. If I had known anything about it, I would have said so from the first."[31]

Charlotte kept at her, but the answer was always the same: "Mother, I really don't know anything about it. I have told you all I know."[32]

At one point, Charlotte tried to ask if Frank Hogg had anything to do with it, but she choked on his name.[33] Charlotte later said her daughter seemed absent-minded, as if she was trying to think of something but couldn't. She looked "ill" and "heartbroken," Charlotte said, and "spoke about our friends and family with difficulty, and entirely broke down when speaking about her youngest brother John." Charlotte left her daughter twenty minutes later "very distressed."[34]

On Tuesday, December 9, Freke Palmer wrote to the Home Office of his intention to petition for commutation of sentence, and said he would have the full petition and many affidavits of evidence that supported his arguments submitted by the Saturday following.

The sensational trial had excited the public mind, in part because it was viewed as a tragedy of "singular completeness and horror,"[35] just the kind that Madame Tussaud and Sons' Exhibition wanted for their popular Chamber of Horrors. Tussaud's opened the exhibition, which advertised the "perambulator, the furniture, and all the relics connected with the case,"[36] one week after Denman sentenced Mrs Pearcey to death.

Tussaud's had purchased all of Mrs Pearcey's belongings - utensils, the fireplace grate, even the table against which Mrs Hogg supposedly leaned when the fatal blows were struck, and the tableaux of 2 Priory Street, as well as Mrs Pearcey's wax likeness, were faithfully - and eerily - recreated.

The scene included an effigy that stood near a fire screen with her hands folded and her cold, blue marble eyes pensively staring into eternity. The tableaux included a model of the kitchen where the crime purportedly took place, as well as her piano, pictures, carpets, with the chairs arranged as they were when the police came to arrest her. Tussaud's had even purchased some of Phoebe's blood-stained garments, the actual pram in which the corpses had been transported, and the toffee bought for baby Tiggie just before she died. In one tableaux - which may have been designed later - Mrs Pearcey's wax figure stared down broodingly at a sleeping Tiggie in her crib.[37]

The money Mrs Pearcey made in selling her relics went to support her defence - by one source some £200 were paid to Freke Palmer,[38] but Frank Hogg, who sold the pram, among other items, could make no such claim, which is perhaps why the *Illustrated Police News* was outraged at finding the pram as part of the exhibit, writing:

> It would be too much to expect any great delicacy of feeling from the owner of this article, but there are a few men in existence, let us hope, who would allow such a relic of a murdered wife and child to pass into the hands of strangers for the purpose of gratifying an unhealthy curiosity.[39]

In addition to the pram, Frank sold his beard – that ancient sign of virility – which had been cut from his face by Tussaud's barber and reattached to his wax visage.[40]

The kitchen, according to *Lloyd's*, was rebuilt exactly to scale, and included all the china arranged exactly as Mrs Pearcey had left it, along with the oilcloth and all furniture arranged just as discovered by the police.[41]

Additional items on display included the prisoner's jacket worn on the day of the murder, models of the heads of the victims and the piece of toffee which Tiggie had been sucking.[42]

"Mrs Pearcey (or Wheeler) had not been sentenced to death for more than an hour for the cruel murder of Mrs Hogg at Hampstead than - Hey Presto! - her faithful presentiment in wax was set up in the midst of her late surroundings at Chamber of Horrors," wrote *Lloyd's Weekly Newspaper*.[43]

That may have been an exaggeration, but not by much. Madame Tussaud's made their living by recognising a commercial opportunity and those who were repulsed by such plundering seemed to be in the minority, for on the day the exhibit opened more than 30,000 Londoners clogged the streets trying to get into the exhibition. Three times that afternoon the street traffic had to be diverted, and twice the doors had to be closed until some people had left in order to make room for those standing outside. Though the programme of displays at Tussaud's was full, and the number in attendance as much attributed to having the day off as the Pearcey display itself (it was Boxing Day), there was a "crush" in the Chamber of Horrors to see the sad scene of Mrs Pearcey in her recreated house. And a reporter for the *Standard* went a step further, crediting her tableaux as the reasons for the record-breaking numbers of attendees.[44]

The constant stream of people kept moving past the Hampstead Tragedy scene but it was at least "three or four deep" and the press of people so intense that an extra exit had to be temporarily created to move people through safely.[45]

One of those visitors was a young boy, home from school on Christmas break. He was good friends with the Wheelers and visited Charlotte. According to an interview in *Lloyd's*, Mary had nursed the boy as an infant (in fact, it may have been the Prümmer baby Christoph) and they had grown very fond of one another as he grew up, and he continued to ask after her long after she had left the family. The boy knew nothing of her imprisonment, and asked Charlotte if Nellie was coming by for Christmas. Whenever another neighbour knocked on the door the boy jumped up eagerly to answer it, hoping to see his beloved nurse on the other side. He told Charlotte about how - just before his break - he'd eaten oranges, nuts, cakes and tea, and had been to Madame Tussaud's to see the waxworks. "We saw kings and queens, and all sorts of people in splendid dresses, and we saw Mrs Pearcey!" he exclaimed. She was the woman, the boy explained - not knowing the weight of his words - who had committed two murders in Kentish Town. She'd murdered Mrs Hogg and her baby, and wheeled the bodies away in a pram, he said. "They have got her piano and all her furniture there, too!" With the wide-eyed excitement of a boy on holiday, he finished his story by remarking that the woman, Mrs Pearcey, looked just like Nellie, his nurse.[46] His happy chatter must have felt like a blade to Charlotte's gut.

Freke Palmer submitted his petition to Home Secretary Henry Matthews as promised, but without much optimism. In practice, it was the Home Office who undertook enquiries and made recommendations regarding reprieves, although the Queen, technically, had the power to grant them. The *World* cynically suggested that perhaps the recent reprieve of Florence Maybrick had encouraged Mrs Pearcey to kill Phoebe Hogg,[47] thinking she too could get away with it, though there was no evidence at all to support such a claim.

Public antipathy to capital punishment had been slowly growing in Britain since the 1860s, when several Acts of Parliament reduced the number of civilian capital crimes to five. Though the Royal Commission on Capital Punishment (1864-66)[48] concluded there was no case for abolition, executions would no longer be public. By the late Victorian era, abolitionists were refining their arguments against capital punishment, though it would be another 74 years before those arguments would win the day. Abolitionists argued capital punishment was little more than ritualised murder disguised as justice, and no more cured the problem of serious crime than workhouses cured poverty.[49] "To enforce the full penalty for any crime is not always justice," wrote a *Reynolds's Newspaper* reporter. "On the contrary, it frequently savours of tyranny."[50]

The problem wasn't just that the idea of capital punishment struck many as morally wrong or anachronistic, but also that the law seemed to be inconsistently applied, often based on class, as seemed to be the case with Florence Maybrick. At the root of both the Pearcey and Maybrick cases, wrote an impassioned reporter for *Reynolds's Newspaper*, was lust, (though to be fair, the Maybrick murder may have been equally motivated by domestic violence).[51] Both were convicted on circumstantial evidence, the reporter noted. Both were scheduled to hang. Mrs Maybrick's sentence was commuted to penal servitude for life after her mother, a baroness, and many aristocratic friends and political acquaintances appealed to the Home Office on her behalf. The privileged classes, the reporter argued, simultaneously favoured execution as a means of dealing with criminals (especially those of the lower classes), and trusted in the advantages of their status to ensure that condemned prisoners from good backgrounds would not hang.

"If Mrs Pearcey is hanged," *Reynolds's* wrote, "it will not be because the 'majesty and dignity of the law has been outraged,' - to use a favourite Tory catchphrase - but because Mr Matthews has reached the end of his stock of consistency, and because she is a woman in a low rank of life and almost friendless."[52]

Though there was probably some truth to what the reporter claimed, Mrs Maybrick was also equally likely to have been reprieved because the physical evidence in that case was not nearly as overwhelming as it was against Mrs Pearcey. The Queen, for her part, felt that Florence Maybrick's sentence was unjustly commuted to penal servitude on a "mere legal quibble,"[53] and, presumably would have rather seen her hang.

Florence Elizabeth Maybrick (née Chandler) was a young woman from Mobile, Alabama, who had married a much older cotton broker from Liverpool named James Maybrick. Despite a socially successful partnership, their private relationship was bleak and cruel. James took a string of mistresses and was addicted to various drugs. The increasingly unhappy Florence took lovers of her own, one of whom was James' brother, Edwin. Upon hearing of his wife's indiscretions,

James beat her ruthlessly, and threatened to file for divorce and take their children.

Shortly thereafter, on May 11, 1889, James died under suspicious circumstances, and Florence was charged with his murder. She stood trial at St George's Hall in Liverpool before Justice James Fitzjames Stephen, who, after a calamitous trial full of legal blunders, questionable ethics, and negligible evidence, sentenced Florence to death before a shocked crowd. Such had been the outrage over the verdict that multiple barristers filed petitions of clemency on Florence's behalf, and Caroline Scott Harrison, wife of U.S. President Benjamin Harrison, pleaded with the Queen to spare Florence through a letter published in the *North American Review*. Four days before Florence was scheduled to die, the Home Secretary announced that she would go to prison for life, with the possibility of parole in 15 years, if she survived that long. She served her time in Woking and Aylesbury Prisons, but never saw her children again, and upon her release sequestered herself on a small farm in Connecticut, dying in 1941 at the age of 79, penniless and utterly alone.[54]

The Maybrick case is a very complicated one and brief synopses of it are almost guaranteed to omit some of the finer, important details. The point, which was almost always missed by people who compared the Maybrick and Pearcey cases, was that following Florence's conviction there remained a good deal of doubt about whether she had actually murdered her husband James. If the conviction was insecure, then she was entitled to be pardoned and freed, because the burden of proof was with the prosecution. The Home Office couldn't sort out the truth in their minds, and so reprieved her and left her sitting in prison for fifteen years - which was an equally terrible fate with lifelong consequences to follow.

This was a completely inadequate response to the problem, compounding one probable error - the conviction - with a second one - the commutation. There remained the view, echoed by the *Reynolds's* journalist, that Florence Maybrick was being judged by *moral*, rather than *legal*, standards. The key difference between Mrs

Maybrick and Mrs Pearcey was not so much about class, but guilt. There was serious doubt about Mrs Maybrick's guilt, but almost none about Mrs Pearcey's. What was most often in doubt what whether she had an accomplice, but not that she was party to the terrible crime.

Still, the comparisons persisted. Commenting on the similarity between the two cases, one correspondent wrote:

> Two women have committed the same crime for the same cause. The one, possessed of everything that might have saved her from it, has been reprieved, because of the importunities of her many friends; shall the other, possessed of nothing but her animal nature, impelling her with irresistible force to satisfy its instincts of hatred and revenge, go to her doom because she is friendless?[55]

The answer was, of course, no - she would not go to her doom because she was friendless, but because she was guilty.

One writer reminded the public of this:

> Two grounds are put forward for the sentence against Mrs Pearcey not being carried into effect. The first is that Mrs Maybrick was not hanged but was reprieved because there was a possible doubt whether the poison that she had administered to her husband had produced his death, whereas no one even affects to doubt that the evidence against Mrs Pearcey is conclusive of her guilt. The other is that Mrs Pearcey is suffering from some sort of mental condition that leads her to commit murders, and to forget that she has done so. So far as I can perceive, this singular theory is based upon the fact that Mrs Pearcey did not commit the murder, and says she did not. I need hardly point out that, if this were deemed proof of mental aberration, every murderer would only have to deny the murder not to be punished or it. The murder was an atrocious one. The murderess killed a mother and a child. She had an intrigue with the husband of the elder victim, and wished to marry him. The motive is as clear as is the guilt.[56]

The *Truth* reiterated this point:

> There are a number of very silly persons who (without having the excuse of being opposed to the infliction of capital punishment)

> make it their business to agitate against any particular murderer being hanged. If the evidence upon which the verdict was obtained is circumstantial they proceed to put forward arguments (as they are pleased to call them) to show that the evidence is not conclusive: if the proof is so damning as to render all doubt as to the act impossible they ask for a reprieve because their interesting client is not responsible for his or her actions. The nonsense that was written about Mrs Maybrick was astounding, and the attacks upon the judge and the jury who tried the case were a public scandal...[57]

Scandalous or not, Palmer persisted with his defence. The first of Freke Palmer's points in the petition sent to the Home Office was simple enough, though not very persuasive: as head of Mrs Pearcey's legal team, he hadn't nearly enough time to copy, verify or check the facts of the depositions given to police. Mary's case was committed to trial on November 18, but he and Arthur Hutton didn't receive the police depositions, which were "of great length" - 37 all told - until November 22, and the trial at the Old Bailey opened on December 1, giving Freke Palmer and his team just nine days to prepare.[58] Denman had denied Hutton's request for a temporary postponement, even though it would have cost him little to wait until the December sessions, scheduled for December 15.

The facts were technically true, but the argument was weak. He couldn't very well harp on dubious technicalities when he had had the opportunity to contest all the police evidence during a month of magisterial hearings. Had there been holes in the various witness narratives, he could have pointed them out then.

His next point was more credible. Freke Palmer argued there was not a "scintilla of evidence" that the note Mrs Pearcey sent to Phoebe was bait meant to lure her to her death.[59]

His point was well taken: no one knew what the note said, and it could have been what Mrs Pearcey told the searcher it was, an invitation to tea. She had, in fact, tried to re-establish contact with Phoebe several times in the weeks leading up to the murder, but was refused. Was this not as likely a last ditch effort to rekindle a gagged friendship as it was an invitation to her death? Further, and even more convincingly, Mrs Pearcey had made no preparations to murder Phoebe Hogg. "The place and circumstances were as ill-adapted for the perpetration of a crime as they well could be," Palmer wrote.[60]

There was no way Mary could have calculated when all other occupants of 2 Priory Street would be out of the house at the exact same time, and it was incredulous to think a cold-blooded killer would select for the commission of her crime the "crude instrumentality of a kitchen poker and a dessert knife," or the place, "a small house occupied by several lodgers."[61]

It was equally unbelievable that Mary would hamper herself by asking Phoebe to bring along the child, to whom, it was repeatedly testified, she was deeply attached.

Palmer's notes suggest that he thought the following a more likely series of events that fateful day: when Phoebe arrived at No. 2 Priory Street, there was an argument and Mary, who had a history of reacting badly to stress, slights and disappointment, was so wounded by what was said that she reacted by striking Phoebe instinctively. She may have also suffered a seizure, going into a sort of catatonic fog as it happened, which may account for why she couldn't remember anything about the commission of the crime.

Palmer's portrayal of what happened next at No. 2 Priory Street was a dangerous gamble. He reminded the Home Office that the blood spatter on the walls and ceiling were not, according to Dr Bond's inquest testimony, from arterial spray. The spatter looked more like that made by a horse's hoof splashing in mud, Dr Bond had said, suggesting Mary stomped about the kitchen in a daze. The blood spatter pattern also called into question whether Phoebe really was still alive when her throat was cut. If she wasn't alive, then maybe Mrs Pearcey cut her throat out of necessity - her body would fold and fit into the pram better - rather than cruelty. Palmer was suggesting that Mrs Pearcey committed her crimes in a state of diminished responsibility, and what appeared brutal was really just the effects of a deeply fractured mind that, in a moment of rage, entirely shattered.

And what of motive? The prosecution alleged that Mary harboured bitterness toward Phoebe and murdered her out of jealousy, hoping to reclaim her rightful place by Frank Hogg's side. But where was the evidence of this? Mary could have married Hogg had she wanted to. Her letters prove she was "passionately attached" to him, and suggested he was equally attached to her. It was Mary to whom he went seeking consolation and advice when he learned of Phoebe's pregnancy, and Mary who wrote to him just a few days before his wedding blessing the marriage, agreeing to visit, and promising to love Phoebe. A single word, Freke Palmer wrote, "would have taken him [Frank] from her rival and secured him as her own husband," but instead she "sent him back to a woman who had a better claim on him and saved this other woman from disgrace, and the child that was not yet born from bastardy."[62]

Concluding his petition, Freke Palmer also asked the Home Secretary to carefully consider the affidavits of John Pearcey, Charles Crichton and Dr George Fielding Blandford, all of whom testified to Mary's epileptic fits, or sudden and violent "paroxysms of fury," - calling to mind Lombroso's 'epileptic fury'- during and after which she had no memory of what transpired. He asked for commutation of the sentence of death for Mary who was "almost a girl" at only 24 years old, and known for her "great kindness."[63]

Freke Palmer was aware of the changing scientific, cultural and political attitudes toward capital punishment generally, and the distaste for executing women specifically,[64] but that isn't to say he was particularly hopeful that his petition, which chronicled Pearcey's chronic epilepsy, suicidal ideation and prolonged bouts of depression, would rouse the Home Secretary's sense of mercy.[65] *Lloyd's* and the *Pall Mall Gazette* covered the Pearcey case intensely, and dedicated the most column inches to Mrs Pearcey's health and mental health issues and argued alongside Palmer that "there is much to learn as to lunacy, for which hanging is no remedy."[66]

Despite such favourable coverage, Palmer was keenly aware that pleading temporary insanity at this point risked the perception of desperation, or worse, fabrication. Indeed, it seemed that Home Secretary Matthews interpreted his plea as such. "This is another example of what is becoming too common," he wrote, "i.e. of a prisoner trying a defence on the merits before the jury; and when that has failed, springing upon the S. of S. [Secretary of State] the defence of insanity, which had been carefully kept back from the jury."[67]

While Palmer was attempting to drum up compassion in Henry Matthews, he was also trying to stir public sympathy for his client; hoping public pressure may strengthen her petition. As W.T. Stead wrote, the press was the "great inspector, with a myriad eyes, who never sleeps,"[68] and Mrs Pearcey's last trial would be argued in the court of popular opinion. Freke Palmer needed someone who could convincingly sell her madness, however temporary, and stir public sympathy, and he also needed someone who knew the Lunacy Laws exhaustively. His answer was the controversial alienist, Dr Forbes Winslow.

It may have been that Forbes Winslow was not so much invited into the Pearcey case, as he inserted himself into it. Winslow had incorporated himself into the Ripper investigation two years before the Hogg murders, for example, but may have been taken less seriously by the police after Chief Inspector Swanson noticed that he had altered letters purportedly received from Jack the Ripper which foretold the murder of Martha Tabram.[69] This makes Palmer's selection of Winslow curious and somewhat questionable. Still, to be fair, the blustery, self-important and self-promoting alienist was relatively good at agitating in the press.[70] It may equally have been that, at that late hour, and given Palmer's relative inexperience in such cases, there simply was no one else. The public was insatiably curious about Pearcey's descent into madness though, and Winslow had no trouble getting his opinions into print. Perhaps the public was hoping madness could explain what the police could not.

Lyttleton Stewart Forbes Winslow was an alienist, and the son of the alienist who had contributed to the development of the lunacy laws of 1843, most famously the M'Naghten Rule,[71] which defined the threshold for criminal responsibility. The frontispiece of his autobiography, *Recollections of Forty Years*, shows a handsomely-dressed man, bald on top, with otherwise thick, curly greying hair and the full mutton-chop whiskers and moustache fashionable in his day; he quite looked the part for which he was picked to play.

A woman like Pearcey, Winslow argued, who had demonstrated strict composure during her trial and incarceration, simply didn't have it in her to bludgeon a woman to death, cut through her windpipe and vertebral column, fold and pack her virtually headless body in a pram, and then wheel that pram through London by herself.

"It was difficult to imagine," Winslow wrote in his autobiography years after the case, "that anyone who behaved herself so quietly and with so much propriety could have been guilty of such a heinous offense."[72]

If she did do it, he proposed, then she had to have committed the crime while in an "acute, violent, epileptic trance," better known as a "fugue" state.[73]

"With a distinct history of four attempts to commit suicide, with a strong hereditary predisposition to mental disorder, with strong evidence of attacks of severe epilepsy, passing on some occasions into the trance state, there is most presumptive evidence of either the act being committed whilst in this state, or to a disordered brain rendering her irresponsible for her actions," he wrote.[74]

Of course, epilepsy is a neurological disorder, not a mental disorder, but this distinction was not well established in Pearcey's day. In fact, epilepsy continued to suffer an unfortunate association with madness and murder well into the twentieth century, conceived and popularised in works of literature before it was theorised in science and medicine. Othello's murder of his beloved Desdemona, for example, is presaged during a fugue state associated with epilepsy.

Winslow first advanced his madness defence for Pearcey in a letter published in the *Evening Standard*.[75] In it, he used other cases to paint a picture of Mrs Pearcey's mental condition, though he never actually met or examined her. His goal was to forward the argument that while she may have committed the crime, she held diminished responsibility in so doing.

In 1877, the letter began, a man named Treadaway committed a murder, which became known as the "Pimlico murder." Frederick Treadaway was charged at the Coroner's Court with murdering John Collins. Treadaway was subject to epileptic seizures and suffered a strong hereditary predisposition to insanity.[76]

During the first of a two-day trial at the Old Bailey, Treadaway fell while standing in the dock and had an epileptic fit. Although Treadaway was sentenced to death at the trial, the Home Office must have been satisfied there were grounds to commute his sentence, no doubt, in part based on the testimony of Forbes Winslow, Sir Crichton-Browne, Dr Hughes Bennett and Mr Erichsen.

The Treadaway case generated discussion about the degree to which epileptics generally were responsible for crimes committed while in what Winslow and his colleagues came to call "epileptic vertigo."[77]

Similarly, and at about the same time, a man named Drant, better known as "the Chelsea murderer", was reprieved because the murder occurred while he suffered an "attack of excitement produced by epilepsy."[78]

Drant also suffered from inherited epilepsy.

Then there was the 'Otley murderer' in 1883, Winslow wrote. This man was also eventually acquitted on the ground of insanity, his mind corroded from chronic fits. The acquittal was not well received, the public believing that Taylor wasn't really mad. In the margin of the editorial where Taylor was mentioned, Charles Murdoch, a senior clerk at the Home Office, scribbled on his copy of Winslow's letter, "Taylor not a case in point – acquitted on ground of insanity. He must have been very mad – for it was not certain whether he could plead at all."[79] As it turned out, he was quite mad, as he proved some months later after his acquittal, when the "wretched man" plucked both his eyes out in Broadmoor Criminal Lunatic Asylum.[80]

Following these cases was one of a brother who murdered his sister in West England. Winslow was consulted in this case too, and the issue here was whether a crime might be committed during an epileptic trance, after which the perpetrator may suffer "total oblivion" of his surrounding circumstances.[81] According to medical testimony, Winslow wrote, the answer is that such states were quite possible. This man too was acquitted.

Winslow felt he was especially qualified to talk about epileptic trance states, since he was a physician to one of the London Hospitals for Epilepsy, at which more attendances were registered (28,000 by Winslow's count) than at any other institution in England. In his letter he wrote:

> I have taken an opportunity of investigating all cases of epilepsy, as to what patients have done in the trance state. In a vast number of cases I discovered that for some hours after a fit, though apparently conscious, they still remained in a state during which they were absolutely oblivious of what they did, though walking about.[82]

This was the thrust of his working theory about the Hampstead Murders - Mrs Pearcey had murdered Phoebe and Tiggie Hogg in an epileptic trance.

Leveraging the automatic states theory was difficult, however, because it was a theory for which science could not test. Epileptics were quite capable of committing crimes consciously and, as there were no instruments to establish with any certainty that an epileptic criminal committed a crime while *unconscious*, the "masked epilepsy," or automatic states theory, strained medical and scientific credulity. By the end of the Victorian era, it would fall out of fashion entirely in the law courts.

This did not deter Winslow. He wrote in his memoirs years later:

> I also had evidence to the effect that on other occasions after these epileptic seizures, manifestations of violence ensued, [and] an absolute loss of memory of what had happened during her paroxysm. From my experience in cases of epilepsy I can in every way endorse this. The brutality of the murder and the violence used strengthened my opinion as to the probability of the crime being committed whilst in a condition of acute, violent epileptic trance, of which I had seen many similar cases.[83]

With such "facts" before one, Winslow thought it was a "grave and serious matter" to allow Mrs Pearcey to be criminally punished, when clearly she should be sent to an asylum and studied.[84]

On December 17, Freke Palmer wrote to Secretary Matthews, pleading with him to let Dr Winslow examine Mrs Pearcey personally. He forwarded with the request the declarations of Dr Sells, Mrs Prümmer, Frank Hogg and a further deposition by Charlotte, Mary's mother. Winslow had collected all of the depositions Freke Palmer had taken on the 16th and, having reviewed them, included a deposition of his own with those sent to Secretary Matthews.

At the time of the Pearcey case, Winslow had just opened the British Hospital for Mental Disorders. It was an outpatient clinic and the first of its kind. There, Winslow practised a method of "gentle, persuasive and loving treatment" for the insane. Instead of bolts, bars and whips, patients were treated with talk, compassion, proper diet, fresh air and, if they were capable of it, sport."[85]

Winslow had also written what some considered the definitive text on the criminally insane, *The Handbook for Attendants on the Insane*, as well as dozens of other books about the definitions and causes of insanity. He later consulted with the famous criminologist Cesare Lombroso, whose theories of atavism were revolutionary (though deeply flawed and later entirely discredited), and was a friend to celebrity barristers Edwin James and Montagu Williams, for whom he often acted as an expert witness. Winslow had been called to both America and Italy to investigate major crimes, and was particularly studied in crimes involving epileptics.

Even with such credentials, the Home Office denied Winslow's request to examine Mrs Pearcey, explaining that they had decided to conduct a medical inquiry into Mrs Pearcey's mind using doctors of their own selection.

"I am directed by the Secretary of State to inform you that he has decided that a medical inquiry, authorised by the Criminal Lunatics Act, 1884, shall be held into the state of the convict's mind. He must, therefore, decline to grant the permission which you desire may be given to Dr Winslow to examine and report as to her condition," wrote Godfrey Lushington, Permanent Under-Secretary of State of the Home Office.[86]

Winslow was neither surprised, nor silenced. He composed a summative letter of opinion about Mrs Pearcey's mental condition anyway. His opinion was clear and succinct: Mrs Pearcey, an epileptic, was insane during the commission of the crime, and belonged in an asylum, not a cell, or worse still, a coffin. Winslow was irritated by his exclusion from the case, and he opened his letter to the Home Secretary dismissively:

> I do not pretend to give an opinion on the present mental state of the unfortunate woman, this must be left to those gentlemen who have been authorised to personally examine her on behalf of the Prosecution, but as no medical experts were allowed to be present on this occasion on the prisoner's behalf, I beg leave to express MY [sic] opinion on the history of the case alone, being here pleaced [sic] in the same position as those medical gentlemen employed by the government.[87]

Whether it was because of Winslow's letter, or because there was already a great deal of sympathy for Mrs Pearcey, or even growing antipathy for capital punishment generally, Freke Palmer achieved his goal of stirring public interest.

Winslow wrote in his memoirs that Palmer received nearly 2,000 letters a week after his piece appeared in the *Evening Standard* of December 12. One such correspondence read, "I will be glad to do six month hard labour in any prison in England for the respite of Mary Eleanor Pearcey, now under sentence of death. I do not know the prisoner, but this comes from a heart of pity."[88] Another letter, recalled by Winslow and, apparently, printed in *Lloyd's*, contained a note from a "Working Man" who said Mrs Pearcey should be reprieved, and enclosed five shillings for her mother.[89]

Dr P.F. Gilbert, a general doctor and the medical officer at Holloway Prison, visited Pearcey almost daily. He was assigned to Newgate because the prison was in such disrepair it needed a rotation of medical officers to service it, and since Gilbert had been Mrs Pearcey's doctor while in Holloway, it made sense that he would continue to examine and observe her at Newgate. In his report of December 16, he wrote that the prisoner had a somewhat "nervous disposition," but was not insane. He noted that Mrs Pearcey complained of a place on the top of her head that, when tapped, felt tender, but he found her skull to be in perfect working order. He concluded his report to Newgate's Governor Milman by commenting that Mrs Pearcey "eats and sleeps well." Milman sent the report to the Home Office.[90]

Charles Murdoch, acting on behalf of the Home Office, spoke to Dr Southey, the Medical Commissioner in Lunacy. Southey recommended a team of doctors with representation in lunacy, general medicine and epilepsy for the inquiry into Mrs Pearcey's mind. Southey proposed Dr Savage, late head of Bethlem, who had the largest lunacy practice in London, or, failing him, Dr Maudsley. For general medical knowledge, Southey advocated on behalf of Dr Buzzard of the Epileptic Hospital, who could speak as to epilepsy and the state of mind accompanying the disease. If Dr Buzzard was unavailable, then Sir J. Risdon Bennett, a highly distinguished physician of London for many years, should conduct the examination. In the event, Drs Savage and Bennett were selected for the task of examining Mary Pearcey, in part because Dr Buzzard turned down the commission.

On December 19, 1890, four days before her scheduled execution, the doctors visited her in the condemned cell. Freke Palmer knew Dr Savage from another case in which he had testified for the defence, and the solicitor must have been hopeful that he and Dr Bennett would agree his client was insane. His hopes were dashed, however, as Savage and Bennett's findings were even more disappointing than Gilbert's.

Before interviewing Mrs Pearcey, the doctors read all the depositions Palmer had sent to the Home Office. They also read the judge's notes, and they may have read other documents too. Contained in the reading was Dr George Fielding Blandford's deposition, in which he stated that it was an unquestioned fact that "epileptics frequently commit acts of extraordinary brutality and violence."[91]

The doctors read Charles Crichton's deposition, in which he said he found Mrs Pearcey to be "exceedingly childlike and simple."[92] In

September of 1890, they were sitting together talking when she took up a newspaper from the table and then her head shook from side to side, and she seemed to have "no idea of what she was doing." During this episode he couldn't see anything but the whites of her eyes. Charles was worried that his poor girl's mind was going.[93]

Mary complained to Crichton as often as she had to John Pearcey of the terrible pains at the top of her head. She had told them both she believed the pain was the result of an ill-formed skull. Further, both men had not just heard tell of her fits, but had experienced them first hand, especially John Pearcey. In another section of deposition, Crichton said that on October 9 of that year he went to visit her for dinner.[94] Afterwards, as she was cleaning up the table, she took a bread knife and flicked it across her hand several times like someone sharpening a knife on a whetstone. Then, Crichton said, she "flourished it" over him. He noticed her eyes "flashed." She put the knife away, but the event disturbed him and he didn't know what to make of it, especially as he found her otherwise to be kind and gentle and entirely "incapable of any act of violence towards a fellow creature."[95]

One of the difficulties for Drs Savage and Bennett, as for Judge Denman earlier, was that no one ever mentioned the word "epilepsy" during her trial.

"We find in the notes of the trial no reference to the subject of Epilepsy, not any plea on behalf of the convict, founded on assumed irresponsibility arising from mental derangement, the accompaniment or consequence of Epilepsy," the doctors wrote.[96]

Denman had written in his trial notes that neither Mrs Pearcey nor Frank Hogg had mentioned the word epilepsy, and even Mary, in her own words, had said to Edward Parsons that she "did not enjoy good health,"[97] but she never claimed she was epileptic. Further, the doctors observed no seizures during the interview with Mrs Pearcey, and she displayed no epileptic symptoms during her imprisonment in Newgate, now totaling three weeks. In looking through the paperwork, Drs Bennett and Savage concluded there was no clear indication of epilepsy in many of the incidents described, and that in many examples given, Mrs Pearcey's strange behaviour seemed to be emotionally or mentally driven. In other words, Mrs Pearcey's fits were "hysterical", they granted, but not epileptic.

Of course, the term "hysterical" was medically dubious, applied carelessly to virtually any emotional excess a Victorian woman displayed, from the inability to orgasm to murder,[98] but that was their recommendation. "Her manner was calm, free from either bravado, sullenness, or depression from conscious guilt," the doctors wrote in their memorandum to the Home Office. "She struck us as possessed of more than the ordinary amount of intelligence and readiness of mind."[99]

Even if Drs Savage and Bennett had diagnosed Mrs Pearcey as epileptic, it probably wouldn't have mattered because they didn't believe she could have murdered while having a seizure powerful enough to destroy the very memory of committing such a murder. Savage and Bennett believed, as did the judge, jury and prosecution, that Mary Eleanor Wheeler premeditated and executed the killing of Phoebe and Tiggie Hogg, alone, in her right mind, and in cold blood.

Palmer did not only rely on Winslow, but also Dr Hubert Thomas Sells, a doctor who graduated from the Royal College of Surgeons in Scotland and was a Resident Assistant at Bethlem Royal Hospital, the now infamous psychiatric hospital that is England's oldest and longest to specialise in mental illnesses. Of its many famous patients, Bethlem is where Daniel M'Naghten was housed after he shot to death Edward Drummond, mistaking him for Prime Minister Robert Peel.

Like Winslow, Sells was never allowed to visit Mary Pearecy at Newgate, and therefore never met her or observed her behaviour. Instead, he poured over the depositions which Palmer had collected from Mary's mother, relatives, lovers and acquaintances. From this close reading, Sells argued that Mary suffered from "attacks of epileptic mania", which he believed could occur before or after fits. He wrote that John Pearcey's stories of Mary trying to poison herself over trivialities was evidence of an unstable mind in itself, but that the "uncontrollable paroxysms of rage" into which she flew were familiar to Sells and others who worked with the mentally ill day in and out. He was sure she was both epileptic and maniacal. Epileptic mania, he added, often resulted in complete amnesia.

Her mother, Sells wrote, confirmed that Mary's epilepsy was real enough to cause her to fall downstairs on two occasions. Charlotte also confirmed that Mary complained of being "continually haunted by shadows of a woman." Augustine Cotterill, Mary's cousin, confirmed these hauntings. Epileptics, Sells argued, were more often susceptible to auditory and visual hallucinations and they have a most powerful effect, often causing epileptics to "commit deeds of violence or to assault people without any apparent reason."

Sells also suggested that Mary may have been slow. After all, Charles Crichton, her older lover, had described her as "child like," though other evidence and testimony counter this assessment. The instance Crichton had described of her eyes rolling into the back of her head was, Sells said, "a petit-mal" seizure in medical parlance. That she flourished the knife with no logical reasoning suggested she was acting under some "very strong insane impulses."

Doctors who worked with epileptics also believed that the slightest provocation could launch an epileptic into a rage or unprovoked assault, and that many later had no memory of the attack.

It was his opinion, Sells wrote, that Mary was indeed an epileptic and killed during epileptic mania and was therefore not responsible for her actions.[100]

Still very ill on Friday, December 19, and despite protests from her friends, Mrs Pearcey's mother made "a desperate effort" to visit her daughter, trudging through "deep and blinding snow." Her feet were soaked in a matter of minutes, as the snow was ankle deep. After she walked for some considerable time, she got a tram to take her as far as she could afford and then had to traipse the rest of the way.[102] She arrived late, but had to wait another hour before she could see her daughter while Savage and Bennett finished their examination of her.

While Charlotte waited, the gaolers who saw that she was soaked to the bone led her into a room with a large fire so she could get warm and dry. She saw Drs Savage and Bennett leave and was then allowed to see her daughter, but feared that since it was so late, her time with Mary would be cut short. She was happily surprised to find that she was allowed to stay nearly an hour after hours.

"Well mother, you are late," Mary said when the attendant finally brought Charlotte in. "But there," she softened, "you could not have seen me before, as I have just had two doctors to see me and they have been talking very kindly to me for more than an hour. They were very nice gentlemen indeed."[102]

She asked whether her mother had seen Mr Palmer, her solicitor. Charlotte said she had not, and that she wasn't sure whether he could do anything else for her now.

"Well, mother, I am innocent, and even if it comes to the worst, and I am sent into eternity, I shall not be afraid to meet my Maker."[103]

In her opinion, Charlotte told a reporter for *Lloyd's* later, her daughter seemed to have no distinct recollection of what took place on the evening of the murder. When she tried to give some account of it, what she said was inconsistent with the evidence given at trial, and so Charlotte let it go that visit, and asked no more questions about it.

"Mother, my time, I believe, is getting very near, and I have a few remembrances to send to all my relations and friends," Mary said.[104]

She expressed disappointment that one particular relative had not been to see her, and then they talked a little about family matters before Mary asked her mother to send her love to a large number of relatives and friends. She hoped they would think kindly of her in her misfortune. At five o'clock, the wardress said their time was up. Mary affectionately wished her mother goodbye from behind the iron grating, through which they could not even shake hands.[105]

"Mother, don't fret. Remember, I am in the Lord's hands now. I am quite prepared, and not afraid to meet Him."[106]

Charlotte then kissed her daughter through the small piece of netting in the wirework and left somewhat consoled by the fact that her daughter seemed "resigned," but cheerful.[107]

"I did not think it well to raise in her mind any false hopes," she told a reporter afterward, "for it would only be a greater blow to her should the last doom come. I wish her mind now not to be disturbed any more."[108]

The whole crime was a mystery to Charlotte, she said, because it was so opposed to her daughter's "former gentle character."[109] She was particularly vexed by her daughter's reticence to talk about the case, though, which she felt was also opposite her typical candour and truthfulness. "Either her character is entirely changed," Charlotte said, "or else the whole thing is more a dream to her than a reality."[110]

While Charlotte reported that her daughter had gathered courage and was resigned but at peace, *Lloyd's* reported that outside of her mother's company Mrs Pearcey was "low and despondent." The wardresses had been instructed not to speak with her unless she initiated conversation first, and so at times she would sit for hours without talking or moving. She went to bed at 10.00pm each night and slept soundly until seven in the morning, her sleep entirely unbroken. At eight she was served breakfast, and had eggs, bacon, a bloater, or some other relish. At one, she had a hot dinner, and during the cold weather she had a small bottle of ale every day, reported *Lloyd's*.[111] She was allowed to take exercise for half an hour after each meal, but as a rule didn't go out after breakfast, preferring to walk during the middle of the day. She had tea at six o'clock, and a bread and butter or cheese supper with another bottle of ale before going to bed.[112]

On Charlotte's next visit, Mary asked to see her uncle again, and then asked to see Frank Hogg.

"I want to see Hogg very particularly," she said, "I wish someone would go and get him to come and see me."[113]

"What do you want to see Hogg for?" Charlotte snapped. "If I can help it, you will not see him."

"Mother, my time is getting very short now, and I want to see him particularly, very particularly. I know I am going down into the pit. I have these visions constantly, and I can see the pit so plain."

"If there is anything you have to say you ought to say it now, and let it be sent to the proper authorities for consideration before it is too late. What do you want to see Hogg about?"

"I want him to produce something."

Mary explained she wanted him to produce a photograph of a man who used to keep company with Mrs Hogg before Hogg married her, when she was a servant for a woman named Miss Wilson in Hampstead.

Charlotte didn't know what to do with these new details, if they were even true. Mary described the man as fair, and not as tall as Mrs Hogg. She didn't know his surname, but understood his first name to be James. She said he used to visit Phoebe at 2 Priory Street unbeknownst to Frank. In fact, Mary had given Phoebe her own latchkey to take him in whenever she liked, if she herself was out.

Was James the killer, or was it another composite story that Mary Pearcey laced together - part fact, part fantasy? Mary felt strongly that Phoebe's ring ought to have been found. If it could be traced, she said, then perhaps it would show who was really connected to the murder.[114]

"You ought to have told me everything you could before," Charlotte scolded, "and if there had been anything I could have done for you I would have done it."

"Mother," came the reply, "don't fret. I have been led into a snare; but never mind. I am in God's hands and all will come right in the end."[115]

On Wednesday, Charlotte visited her daughter once more, and asked her directly to give an account of her day and night on Friday, October 24, the day Phoebe was murdered. Whereas Mary had been reticent before, this time, she agreed to talk.

She said she was in the house until noon, and then went to Great College Street to buy a mousetrap. She went back to 2 Priory Street and cooked her dinner, then went out at 3 o'clock to Foster's, a wine merchant. At around 3.50, she went to Mrs Fleming's, and then to Moore's, the linen draper's, and then left about 4.10. She said she went home and lit the fire for tea. Mrs Hogg arrived shortly thereafter, and wanted to know if she would lend her a shilling and mind the baby while she went to fetch her black bag. She had said she couldn't, because she was about to go out again. She said they both left 2 Priory Street at the same time - Mary to get some fish, and Phoebe to... who knows where?

The story didn't make sense on several levels, and was inconsistent with evidence given by eyewitnesses in almost every way, but Mary continued.

When she returned from the fishmonger, she and Mrs Crowhurst walked into the house at the same time, one after the other. Mary saw Mrs Hogg - presumably alive - behind the door with the pram. Apparently, she turned around and went back out, perhaps thinking Phoebe was visiting with her mystery man, James.

Mary said that at quarter past six she took the tram from Camden Road station to Euston Road, then a bus to Oxford Street. She walked toward Marble Arch and back up Regent Street to Great Portland Street, where she stopped to watch a Punch and Judy show. She went into an Italian restaurant and afterwards took the bus from Great Portland Street back home to Priory Street, getting there at 8.40pm.

When she arrived she saw the postman, who delivered a registered letter. She went into the kitchen and lit the lamp to read the letter, which was from Charles Crichton. She slipped it into the pocket of her grey dress, leaving the envelope on the kitchen table. She left the lamp lighted. A few minutes before 10 o'clock she went out again, this time to Castle Road to see if the vans were in because she was, presumably, expecting or hoping that Frank would visit her after work. She came back - having just missed Frank - and then went to the Eagle public house for a whiskey, staying about twenty minutes, and then went home. She went into the kitchen again and the lamp was still burning. She went to bed and slept soundly in her own bed for the rest of the night.[116]

Charlotte never pressed her daughter to explain how it was possible to have missed the overwhelming blood evidence in the kitchen, or the neighbours' testimony that they heard people moving about Mrs Pearcey's rooms all night, as if cleaning up. She did not insist she explain the shattered kitchen windows, the burned letters, the bloodstained pram, the buttons from Phoebe Hogg's bodice found in her kitchen grate, the shrine of obsession under her bed, or the fact that at least one man, Charles Britt, saw Phoebe enter Mary's house, but no one saw her leave.[117] She was apparently so nonplussed by the story, she didn't say anything else to her daughter that visit.

Though she promised to visit again, Charlotte was so ill she could not get out. In her stead she sent another relative, and a very old friend of hers, to visit her daughter, imploring her to tell Mary how sorry she was that she could not come.[118] It was nearly eight o'clock on Saturday, December 20th when the relative returned from visiting Mary at Newgate. The relative said they had had a long interview, and that she had never seen such "terrible changes" in Mary.[119]

When she came to the wire grating to speak to the relative she was weak and bent "nearly doubled."[120] Her face was "wan and pale and she had fallen away so that she scarcely seemed able to speak - she shook and trembled in such a terrible manner."[121]

The relative thought Mary had wanted to say something to her, but the wardress stood closer than she had before. Mary explained the tightened surveillance: there had been several inquiries from authorities as to how the facsimiles of her letters, and photographs and bits of conversation had found their way into *Lloyd's* and, presumably, other newspapers. In consequence, the authorities had given strict orders that nothing further of a similar nature should occur.

Mary told the relative that she felt resigned to her fate, whatever it might be, but she had her forebodings that her end was near.[122] She explained she'd received notice from prison officials that if she wanted friends or family to see her, they would all have to be at the gaol at 10 o'clock on Monday morning, and if there was no respite, she would need to be prepared to say farewell to all.[123]

"Tell mother to be sure to be here by ten at the latest, so as to be with me as long as possible, as I am told the business of the preparations will then begin."[124]

Mary told her relative she'd requested that this last visit with her mother be in private. This was her "last request," in fact. She wanted it to be as she was when she was a child, "without these iron bars, and when no one is by." She then told the relative to give her love to her mother and to tell her "how I love her, but that I speak the truth when I tell her I am innocent."[125]

"If you are innocent," pressed the relative, "then why don't you say who did the murder?"

"No." Mary said.

–"No! And she will not if she has ever promised her word not to do so," Charlotte exclaimed when told of this later.

The relative had asked Mary whether Hogg was the murderer.

"No," she replied, "Hogg was not in it."

They wished each other goodbye, and as the relative left the Deputy Governor of the prison said he expected there might be a telegram from the Home Secretary about the appeal for a reprieve. If there was, he said, he promised to telegraph it to her family the moment it came.[126]

Charlotte listened to the relative, but was in "great bodily pain and mental affliction," according to a reporter who was also there.[127] She cried through the entire interview with the reporter thereafter.

"People think it is a hard thing to lose a child on a deathbed," Charlotte said, "but if my daughter were lying dying on this bed that trial would be nothing to the trial of her dying where she is."[128]

Charlotte seemed comforted knowing that Mary would see her father and "two little sisters who died young,"[129] and that they would be reunited soon, for she felt it wasn't long until she would "follow her."

But that comfort paled against the regret that chewed at her inside for turning her daughter away on the Sunday before the murders. Had she let Mary stay, even for a day or two, she told the reporter, she felt she could have prevented the murders altogether. Mary had begged her to stay, saying she was ill and unhappy, and feared she would be lured away somewhere where there was a chasm from whence she could never return.

Charlotte recalled the day to the reporter.

"Well dear," Charlotte had replied dismissively, "if you think it is not safe to go anywhere don't go."[130]

At this, Mary burst into sobs and lay down on the bed.

"Oh mother," she cried, "my poor head. It seems as though it is opening at the top, and when I think of it all I am afraid if I go I shall go down into the chasm. Yes, mother; I feel if I follow on I shall go into the chasm."[131]

She told Charlotte she didn't want to go back to "that house" for fear that something "dreadful" would happen.[132] Mary had apparently been talking of getting a house down in the country. It is possible that she was preparing to escape after she murdered Phoebe and Tiggie, which might explain why there were so few items of clothing in her flat, and why she had several pawn tickets and so much money in her purse. But it's more probable that her "house in the country" tale was yet another outlaying fragment of detail woven into an incomplete and incongruous alibi; on balance, pure invention.

Charlotte was uncomfortable at the talk of hauntings and chasms, and advised her daughter to take medicine. She said Mary's foreboding was simply the leftovers from a lucid dream, but her daughter was insistent it was no dream and that she saw "visions in that house night and day."[133] Charlotte conceded that her daughter looked "strange," that day, as if she was watching something or someone move around her.[134]

Charlotte gave her daughter a gentle shake of encouragement. "Come, rouse up out of this," she said. After a while Mary seemed more like herself, nattering on about her "niece", meaning Tiggie, who was such a "dear little darling." She described how she stuck her little arms out every time she saw Mary, and gave her sweet kisses.[135]

"You could not help but love her if you saw her," she said.

But, nearly as soon as she'd come to, she went back to that dark place again.

"But it is these visions that I constantly see that upset me so," she said. "I never can lie down on my pillow but they appear to me directly. No matter where I am, there is the big, tall woman with the large eyes always before me. When I go to bed at night there first come two or three balls of light which get clearer and clearer till they get as bright as the moon, and then the figure of the tall woman comes, with her two hands up on each side of her head, and lower down, but a great deal dimmer, is the figure of a little baby. Then there is another figure beckoning me on. I don't want to follow, and sometimes turn my eyes away; but they look me in the face, and seem to draw me on to some place where I shall be shut up with bars before me, and where there is a deep pit into which I can see I shall be dropped down if I follow on."

Charlotte had rebuked her daughter to stop talking such nonsense or else people would think her mad,[136] and that was the end of the conversation.

Charlotte told the reporter for *Lloyd's* that she hoped her cautionary tale would induce mothers across the country to never refuse their children shelter, even if that shelter was meagre. She explained her daughter's foretelling as the "vision" she had of what was to become of her. In hindsight, Charlotte now realized, Mary had described the "great stone walls" of Newgate, the iron bars of the condemned cell and the great pit into which she would be cast. Charlotte was as tormented at her daughter's end as she was at her beginning. She felt she had failed to protect Mary and was anguished by the belief that had she done more, she might have saved her daughter from the terrible fate that now awaited her.

"Oh how that poor girl cried to me that afternoon. She said, 'Mother, I know I did wrong when I left my home and went with strangers. But when I had done it I felt I could not come back. You have never been out of my thoughts all these years, wayward as I was, but I have suffered for it. But you forgive me, don't you, mother?'"

"Yes, my child; and I wish you could stay, but you see how it is."

Mary agreed to go, but said she felt she would be "let into something." She then kissed Charlotte goodbye and left. She never illuminated further what she meant or thought about the visions, but Charlotte said that when she first saw her daughter in Holloway Gaol Mary had said, "Well, mother, you see now it was no dream."[137]

While awaiting the decision from the Home Office, Mrs Pearcey wrote a letter to one of her female attendants from the Marylebone Police Court: "Thanks to you very much for your kindness to me and all belonging to me. It was so kind of you." She also wished to thank the assistant gaoler, Barrett, who had given her part of his dinner.[138]

On Saturday, December 20, around 10 o'clock at night, Freke Palmer received an envelope from the Home Office. The following morning, the Home Secretary's decision was front-page news. *Lloyd's Weekly Newspaper* ran the headline: Mrs Pearcey's Fate.[139]

The official letter read:

> Whitehall, 20th December, 1890.
>
> Sir - With reference to the representations and memorials which you have submitted in behalf of Mary Eleanor Pearcey, or Wheeler, now under sentence of death in Newgate Prison for murder, I am directed by the Secretary of State to say that, after medical inquiry and the most careful consideration of all the circumstances in the case, he regrets that he has been unable to discover any sufficient grounds to justify him in advising her Majesty to interfere with the due course of law.
>
> I am, sir,
> Your obedient servant, Godfrey Lushington.

Freke Palmer was, understandably, "bitterly disappointed."[140] A copy of the response was sent to Governor Milman, who enquired as to whether Mrs Pearcey was awake, but as she was not he thought it would be cruel to wake her just to deliver the bad news.[141]

It was the Reverend Duffield, the following morning, who told Mary Pearcey that all appeals for human mercy were at an end. At the news, she turned in her seat and passed her hand across her brow.[142]

Freke Palmer received another letter that day that read:

> Dear Sir
>
> Owing to certain information that I have gleaned I write to you owing to Mrs Pearcey's sad fate. I heard that a certain milkman that serves the Kentish Town district with milk and he says that he can swear that he saw Mr Hogg come out of the house where the murder was committed at 5 or ¼ past the morning after the murder. He told this to a person which he serves at Wellesley Road and which number I do not exactly know. If you would try and look for that certain milkman it would no doubt lead to the conviction of an accomplice in the crime. So trusting you will make urgent inquiries about the above,
>
> I remain Yours & C –a Lover of Justice.[143]

Palmer wasted no time, and dashed off a note to the Home Office, enclosing the anonymous letter in his post.

Shortly after 10 o'clock on a bitterly cold Monday morning, Freke Palmer conducted a parting interview with his client. Since the day was so cold, their conversation took place in the chief warder's room, which was warm and well lit.[144] Palmer later told a reporter that Mrs Pearcey entered the room with a "certain amount of cheerfulness," remarking on the bad weather. She first wanted to talk about the few trinkets that remained after the Tussaud sale, and who would get them. They weren't worth any real money, but they were valuable sentimentally. She wished a ring to go to her mother, and a Bible to her sister, but her next request was peculiar: she wanted Palmer to place an advertisement in the Madrid papers, addressed to certain initials with the line, "Have not betrayed."

Palmer was naturally surprised. He asked whether this request was to do with the case.

"No." Mrs Pearcey said.

"Do you admit the justice of the sentence?"

"No," she replied. "I do not. I know nothing about the crime."

"But," Palmer urged, "even if you did it in a trance you must have some idea or shadowy recollection of the matter?"

"I know nothing about it," she repeated.

Surely he was frustrated, but what could he do against such restraint?

"Under those circumstances let me ask whether you are satisfied with what we have done for your defence and the efforts we have since made on your behalf."

"I am perfectly satisfied," she said. "I don't think any more could have been done."

He pleaded once more. "If you have any facts to reveal, and will let me know them, even at this late hour, I will lay them before the Home Secretary in the hope of obtaining mercy."

"I have nothing more to say," Mrs Pearcey answered. "Don't forget about those things," she said. "Good-bye."

And then she went again across the yard to her cell.

Freke Palmer didn't tell Mrs Pearcey about the anonymous letter, probably because he did not wish to give her false hope at that late hour. There was also no mention of the 2,000 letters he'd received each week offering sympathy, money or support, with some of the money directed toward Charlotte specifically. These facts would not save her, but they might have given her a little peace.[145]

As one of her last acts of charity, Mrs Pearcey wrote her solicitor a letter in which she thanked him for all he had done for her. She said she found it hard to say what she intended to say, but that she couldn't thank him enough for his service. "I would much better die now than be in prison all my life," she wrote.[146]

Charlotte rose at seven o'clock on Monday morning, and, after getting a cup of tea, she and her youngest daughter started off for Newgate Prison shortly after eight. Charlotte was determined to have as much time as she could with her daughter, and to be at the prison on time.[147] The weather again slowed their journey, the fog so dense they had to grope their way along. After they travelled some distance by train, they changed to an omnibus, but took the wrong one, so had to head for Bishopsgate, which caused them to be nearly an hour and a half late to the prison.[148] Mary took no breakfast, just a little water, feeling her position acutely. She grew impatient waiting for her mother. When her mother and sister at last arrived, they were told they could only have 40 minutes of the allotted two hours together.[149]

Mrs Wheeler and her youngest daughter were escorted into the chaplain's room. When Mrs Pearcey saw them she greeted them "very affectionately," embracing and kissing them, and taking them each by the hand. She sat between them, nuzzling against her mother's breast, like she must have as a child. Her last wish had been granted.[150]

They spent some time in what Charlotte called "silent grief" and then Mary said, "Well, mother, my time is very near now when I shall see you no more. But I feel resigned now. I am trusting in a merciful Saviour, and I feel that God will forgive me all my sins, and that I shall go to heaven, and that I shall meet my father and my two little sisters there before you. Yes, I shall see them first."[151]

"Well Nellie," Charlotte responded, using her daughter's childhood nickname, "if you are guilty I hope you will confess."

Emphatically, Mary said, "Mother, I am not guilty; I am innocent. You do not think I am guilty, do you?"

"No child; I do not think you are guilty if you say you are not at such a solemn time as this."

"Mother, they wanted me to plead insanity; but I would not have that plea at all. I know I am not insane. I am no more insane than any of them, and I was not going to be sent into the presence of my Maker with a lie in my mouth. Besides, if my life had been spared on that plea I should only have been sent among a lot of convicts and criminal lunatics, and I might have grown as wicked as the worst of them, and have had a long life of misery. No, I am innocent of the real murder, but rather than be shut up with a lot of convicts I would sooner die than live."[152]

For a little while, they talked about business arrangements. Mary had sent her mother a little money each week to help her pay for rent. She was now concerned about how Charlotte would get on now without her support. She sent her love to all her relations and friends, and expressed hope that they would not think her guilty of the "terrible crime imputed to her."[153]

She asked her mother to be kind to her sister and brothers, and Charlotte assured her she would. She then took her sister's hands, and hugged her, and said, "And now, dear, you will be a good girl, won't you, and not fall into any temptation? And above all, dear, you will be kind to mother, will you not?"[154]

Young Charlotte said she would.

They all kissed each other.

Mary could only manage "good-bye, Mother,"[155] and then Charlotte and her youngest daughter left the gaol getting back home again, Charlotte scarcely knew how.[156]

Mary Pearcey had repeatedly requested permission for Frank Hogg to visit her. She sent a letter to the Hogg family, in which she expressed a hope that they did not consider her guilty of so foul a crime. She asked Clara to write to her, and asked to be remembered. The post also contained the order and the invitation for Frank to visit her. Frederick intercepted the communication.[157]

The visit from Frank was arranged to take place between two and four on Monday afternoon, and she was "quite built upon seeing him once more," wrote a reporter for *Lloyd's*.[158] As two o'clock drew near, and then passed, and then three drew near and passed, Mrs Pearcey grew somewhat "nervous and impatient."[159] When four o'clock came and went and Frank was still not there, she was seized by a terrible fit of dejection. She laid on her bed with her hands over her face sobbing, unable to speak.[160] When the storm passed she rose, her face calm, and read at the table in her cell, determined to "harden her heart," supposed one reporter, and maintained "the strictest silence."[161] She mentioned her agony only once to her solicitor in a letter which she penned him that day. In it, she wrote that Frank's visit was the last kindness he could have done for her, but that she forgave him, even for denying her this, though, "he might have made death easier to bare [sic]." Concluding she said that she was "justly punished for ever thinking anything about him."[162]

After realising that Frank was not coming to see her, she wrote a second letter to Clara stating that her brother was perfectly innocent of any complicity in the crime. Mrs Pearcey had mistakenly thought that the handwriting on the returned order was Frank's,[163] but it wasn't. It was Frederick who had returned the permission to visit on his brother's behalf, as Frank was out of London by then. Frederick then wrote to Frank and told him what had happened.

Acting upon the advice of her relatives, Clara Hogg replied to Mrs Pearcey's letter by return post. It seems she, too, perhaps seeking closure for the family, tried once more to cajole from Mrs Pearcey the truth about what happened to Phoebe and the baby. Clara said she could not believe that she could be guilty of the crime, but that she surely knew something about it, and if she did, she should tell them. She added, for a little extra pathos, that old Mrs Hogg was ill.[164]

On December 22, 1890, Mrs Pearcey replied to Clara's letter.

> Dear C.—
>
> I have just received your kind letter, and I am so very sorry, dear, to hear the mater is not so well. O if I could only have seen Frank for a few minutes; but, my dear friend, I am justly punished for my sins. As I know your brother Frank did not have anything to do with that dreadful crime - I mean the death of his wife or her child, I want all the world to know, when I am gone out of it, what I have to say. As I hope for pardon as a sinner before my God I say he (Frank Hogg) did not have anything to do with it, nor did he know anything about it. What I write here is the truth, as I hope to be forgiven by our SAVIOUR. I should not have written you this if you had not answered my letter so kindly, and I do think you love me a little. I did so want to see Frank and tell him all I know. That is why I sent for him, and when the order came back without him I thought all of you did not care what became of me; so, dear C., I thought I would go out of this world and not clear Frank's name. But, my dear friend, when your letter came to me, I knew then I loved you all too much to go out of the world to meet my God and not say before I went that Frank was innocent in word or deed. Let the world say what they will - I mean the people in it, Frank was a good husband to his wife, and would have been a better one if she had only been a good wife, and stayed at home and looked

> after him as a wife should have done, instead of being out when he came home, and having nothing ready for him. Dear C., you lived in the same house, and know I am speaking the truth. Where is there a man that would stand such a life? But you know Frank did, and not complain about her. Dear C., my head is so bad this evening, but I am trying to finish this letter to you, my dear friend. I hope one and all will have pity on him when they read this, for they will some day know the truth of every word I am writing. God knows I am speaking truly - it is the last good act I can do for all the kindness you and the mater has shown me. Now, dear friend, I must say good-bye to you and the mater in this world, hoping and praying to meet you again in a better land than this one. Say good-bye to F. and the mater for me.
>
> With love and best wishes from a great sinner.
>
> Monday evening, 9.55 p.m. M.E.[165]

James Berry, the man sent to execute Mrs Pearcey, had arrived late on Monday afternoon, December 22. His southbound train had been delayed for several hours due to heavy snowfall. He was an average looking man with small eyes, set into an otherwise unremarkable face covered with a beard and full moustache. His hair, which had thinned early, was cut short and neat above his ears.[166]

Over an eight-year career as England's official executioner, Berry would hang 197 people, five of them women. He shared with Mrs Pearcey a place in Madame Tussaud's wax gallery, where he and other famous hangmen such as William Marwood perpetually stared at those they had executed. Mary Pearcey was the last woman he would execute before resigning in 1892 due to alcoholism and inappropriate "tell-alls" held at local pubs after an execution.[167]

When Berry arrived at the prison that day, he dropped his bags in the room in which he would sleep and went to the execution shed, where he inspected new "innovations" made to the scaffold at Newgate. Formerly, hangmen would calculate the length of rope needed by the height and weight of the convict, any excess of which was allowed to hang loose down the prisoner's back. The Government had recently adopted a new bracket, however, which was attached to the beam and stored any extra rope in a system of slots, pins and locks, so only the exact amount of rope needed was exposed. This was the first time the new system would be employed at Newgate.[168]

James Berry wrote in his diaries that Mrs Pearcey was "the most beautiful woman" he hanged. Her "big blue eyes with a languishing look in them, masses of wavy hair and lips like Cupid's bow were the attractions that made many a man fall in love with her in the days of her youth,"[169] he supposed. He went on to write that she had a long and shapely neck, and "though there was never anything of the artist or the poet in James Berry, I tell you I was spellbound when I saw her in the condemned cell."[170]

At some point, Berry consulted his table of drops, and confirmed that at 9 stones, Mrs Pearcey would need a rope of six feet.[171] The noose used at the time by British hangmen had no knot, they having long ago abandoned the "cowboy coil" still used by American executioners, in favour of a rope with a metal eye built into it, through which the running end of a hempen rope was threaded. A rubber washer adjusted against the rope and was placed under the prisoner's neck to hold it steady at the mark.

The long drop method of execution was designed to break a prisoner's neck quickly and painlessly. As the prisoner's body accelerated, the metal eye fetched up against the chin, forcing the head backward and snapping the neck just at a certain vertebrae, which would rupture the spinal cord causing instantaneous unconsciousness and immediate death.

The long drop method of execution was vastly more humane as compared to the short drop, which had been in general use until the latter part of the 19th century. The short drop sometimes killed quickly, either by breaking the neck or cutting off blood supplies to the brain, but it didn't kill consistently. Sometimes the short drop killed by asphyxiation, which could take as much as 15 agonising minutes, and sometimes by decapitation, which was quick, but unnecessarily gruesome.[172]

At half past nine on Monday night, warders escorted Mrs Pearcey to the condemned cell, a "stone dungeon, 8x6 feet wide, with a bench at the upper end. It contained a rug, Bible, prayer book, and an iron candlestick affixed to the wall. The moon could shine through on a clear night from the small, high window in the back of the cell, but the moonlight was filtered between a double row of heavy, crossed iron bars."[173] Hargrave Adam, who was close to Pearcey's barrister, Arthur Hutton, said that after her imprisonment Mrs Pearcey liked to feed the birds at Newgate from her cell window. This may have been true in general population cells, but it could not have been true once she was moved to the condemned cell, for the window was much too high to reach, even if a bird should light upon it.[174]

For hundreds of years the viewing public took great pleasure in public executions, which were attended by crowds in the tens of thousands, with politicians and the nobility paying great sums for those spots closest to the noose. Executions were theatre, and the moments leading up to the climactic act were exhaustively described in broadsheets and penny dreadfuls, as well as the more respectable newspapers. Most often, reportage featured "confessions" by murderers accompanied by detailed accounts of their execution, if not always reported first hand. When public executions were banned in 1868, the press's role incorporated a new function: it would continue to entertain the masses with its lurid descriptions of crime and criminal proceedings, but it would also now serve as a proxy witness, offering public guarantee of fair practice, and attenuating the very concern Justice George Denman voiced in his vote on the Criminal Act two decades previously.

Mary Pearcey's execution, however, was slightly different still. The High Sheriff of London, Sir James Whitehead, who had the responsibility of ensuring capital sentences were properly executed, denied the press access to her execution completely. Since the passage of the Private Executions Act it was customary to allow two reporters to represent the press at hangings, which served as an important check against political and police corruption. But there were so many applications from newspapers all over the country to attend Pearcey's execution that Whitehead was worried what he regarded as a "solemn" affair would devolve into a media circus. And so, he denied all press access.[175]

On Whitehead's orders, Mrs Pearcey had been moved to the male ward on her last night at Newgate. This too was uncustomary, but this would afford her the small mercy of a walk of less than twenty yards to the execution shed through a private door in the cell wall the following morning, rather than suffering a passage through "birdcage" walk, the long hallway of narrow arches that led to the scaffold.

Soon after 10 o'clock, Reverend Duffield entered the condemned cell. He had an earnest conversation with Mrs Pearcey, and urged, "Do not be launched into eternity with anything on your mind which you can now explain."

She replied calmly, but faintly, "I have nothing to explain. I am not guilty."[176]

Reverend Duffield relented after half an hour, and left Mrs Pearcey's cell a few minutes after eleven o'clock.

Mrs Pearcey went to bed at half past eleven, forgoing her last meal. She couldn't sleep, waking up every half an hour or so. At about half past three in the morning she gave up sleep completely, stood, dressed and asked for a cup of tea. From time to time she talked with her wardresses, but otherwise read.

Around six o'clock Duffield visited her again, and she received him calmly, always evading conversation on the subject of the murder. The chaplain had hoped the weight of such a trying moment would have provoked her confession. Solemnly, he pointed out her position once more and urged her to make some reparation to the Hogg family by gifting them the truth. But all he could get from her was that it was absurd to think Frank was connected to the crime. She was, just as one of her uncle's had predicted she would be, determined to "keep her mouth closed until the end."[177]

A little after seven o'clock, Duffield left so that Mrs Pearcey could take her breakfast, but she still could not eat and just sipped a little tea from a steaming mug until he returned to pray with her. They recited the Lord's Prayer together, and close to eight o'clock he urged her once more to confess.[178]

"The foot of the executioner is almost at your door," he said. "Now

I ask you for the last time is there anything you have to say to me?"

"No."

"Do you admit the justice of your sentence?"

"Yes, but the greater part of the evidence was false."

"Then you mean to say by that that you are guilty?"

She shook her head 'no' and sat down, not another word passing through her lips before she hanged.[179]

Despite a "bitter frost, a sulphury fog, and slippery streets,"[180] knots of people gathered at the Old Bailey before seven o'clock in the morning. Many of those gathered were women, some of whom made ribald jokes while they waited, and seemed to feel no pity at all for their sister who was about to be no more. It was largely a quiet crowd though, composed of "penny dreadful"-type boys, out-o-work men, costers,[181] mechanics, factory girls and working women. There were a few "silk hats and kid gloves" visible, but by and large the "ladies" who had thronged the court during Mrs Pearcey's theatrical trial were noticeably absent.[182]

Not all were there to cheer her death. A street urchin who had planted himself at the front of the crowd said, "Poor Mrs Pearcey."[183] Another woman said she couldn't help but come, having looked down at her own small daughter just that morning and feeling an overwhelming sympathy for Mrs Wheeler.

"I just wished my girl 'ud die rather than come to such a end," she said.

A reporter for the *Pall Mall Gazette* asked the woman if she knew much about Mrs Pearcey's mother.

"Only that she's very poor, and that this poor creature left her 'ome at seventeen all through a man."[184]

By the time Mr Gilbert, the prison doctor, arrived, there were at least three hundred people gathered at the Old Bailey entrance, and at twenty minutes to eight a buzz of voices among the crowd indicated the arrival of Under Sheriff Metcalfe, who walked quickly into the porter's room and then into the reception room where

Governor Milman stood waiting. Sir James Whitehead, the Sheriff, arrived soon after, and the crowd had by then grown so large that a force of constables was ordered to maintain a clear thoroughfare and keep the mob calm.[185]

A few minutes before the top of the hour, Under Sheriff Metcalfe, Colonel Milman and executioner Berry followed the High Sheriff of London, Sir James Whitehead, into Mary Pearcey's cell. The single mourning bell of St. Sepulchre's church "rang out sharply on the morning air."[186]

When they entered, she quietly rose, and the female warders gathered around her.

"This is Berry," whispered one.

"I know," she answered, as she took his proffered hand.[187]

Sir James Whitehead asked whether she had anything to say. She said no, and then took a little tea. She turned to her warders who had been her constant companions since her imprisonment and bade them "Good-bye." The warders, who had grown to like her were deeply affected. The night before, Mrs Pearcey purportedly told her attendants she would give Berry no trouble, as she wished to "die like a man."[188] Still, when Berry moved to pinion her, two wardresses flanked her to walk her to the gallows. She refused their aid, preferring to walk alone and unsupported into the corridor, she said, as she had into the courtroom.

"You have no need to assist me," she said. "I can walk by myself."

One warderess said she didn't mind and was ready and willing to walk alongside her. She embraced each of her attendants, and they returned her affection.[189]

Scarcely a word was said as she was pinioned,[190] which only took a few seconds. At that time, it was customary to pinion the prisoner with his or her hands in front - to facilitate prayer in the final moments - by means of a waist-belt to which wrist straps were attached. Some years later this method was abandoned, and the prisoner was pinioned behind with a single leather strap, which was quicker and less conducive to resistance. Berry used a modified belt originally made for Mrs Frances Stewart, the only other woman to be executed within the walls of Newgate.

As they walked across the yard, a certain other assemblage of gentlemen watched the procession pass in silence. They walked across the corridor into the exercise yard beyond and Berry drew the white cap over Mrs Pearcey's eyes, so she could not see the gallows.[191] Guided by Berry, warders led Mrs Pearcey directly under the rope. "I was pleased to see that her step never faltered," Berry later wrote.[192]

The shed was lit by gas. Those there to officiate the execution were already inside. In addition to Milman, Reverend Duffield and Dr Gilbert, also in attendance were Mr Frederick Kynaston Metcalfe, the Deputy Under Sheriff for the County of London and Colonel Henry Smith, Commissioner of the City of London Police. The chaplain stood just in front of Mrs Pearcey and recited passages from the burial service.

When Mrs Pearcey was secure upon the trapdoor, the female warders who had accompanied her left and two male warders took their places while Berry fixed the rope around her neck. Not a word passed after leaving the cell. The only sound in the room was the minister's voice reciting the liturgy.

As soon as the strap was affixed around her dress, just below the knees, Berry touched the warders, who stepped back, and then, he pressed the lever down, the doors snapped opened - bang! - and Mary Eleanor Wheeler disappeared into the dark cavern below, her hands still clasped.[193] It was over quickly.

Berry confessed in his memoirs that he "did not like to kill" this beautiful woman "but the law had said she must die, and how could he stand in the way?"[194] He felt, as many others did in the absence of either a more suitable explanation or confession, that there just must have been something "wrong somewhere in her composition,"[195] but this was a small consolation.

Outside, since half past seven,[196] the crowd had grown and along the streets boys and men, women and girls rushed in, arriving "breathless,"[197] hoping to glimpse the flagstaff as the black flag raised. A policeman walked by calling, "Pass along; move away," and "don't stand hare[sic]," but despite the injunction, the crowd grew until it filled all the space from which anyone could see much of anything. It was a quiet crowd that waited, wrote the reporter, despite the "cold, frosty morning with nothing to look at but the grim walls of the prison, and the fluttering of the gentle pigeons that make their home in its shadow."[198]

The crowd looked on with "strained watchfulness," as the ropes on the flagpole began to quiver.[199] The black flag rose slowly to the top of the pole, provoking a subdued "hum" among the people outside.[200] Some reporters said a "loud, exulting cheer" rose up from the immense crowd, which then stretched away from the entrance to the Old Bailey to the Holborn end of the prison. The cheering was a "strange chorus of satisfaction," the reporter wrote, that Mrs Pearcey had paid the ultimate price for her crime.[201] Others reported that only a few, faint cheers rose up from the small boys[202] and the gathering then loosened and began to disperse,[203] as the black flag flapped in the winter wind.

A reporter amid the crowd was outraged by those first few shrieks of delight. He reflected solemnly that just a few minutes before Mary Eleanor Wheeler was a living, sentient being, and now she was not.[204] Another reporter among the crowd said people made more sympathetic, rather than condemnatory comments. Even beyond the immediate area of the gaol one could still hear, in passing groups of men that lingered, chatting over the terrible murder, "Poor thing! Poor thing! And only twenty-four; only twenty-four!"[205]

Mrs Pearcey hung for an hour, and then her dead body was taken down. Mr Gilbert, the medical officer of the prison, issued a formal certificate, certifying she was dead, and her body was placed in a shell to await the coroner's inquest.[206] At noon, Mr Langham, coroner for the City, held an inquest in Courtroom No. 3 at the Old Bailey.[207] Those present included Governor Milman, the Reverend Duffield and Dr Gilbert. The press wanted access to the inquest but were again refused, this time by the coroner. The jury went into the gaol to see Mrs Pearcey's body, which was lying in a shell on the floor of the scaffold beneath the beam. Those at the inquest who saw the body in the shell noticed discolouration in her face, but also an expression, according to one *Lloyd's* reporter, "foreign to Mrs Pearcey's countenance during all the anxious days of the trial,"[208] but he didn't elaborate as to what he thought that expression meant. Her long, luxuriantly curling hair was spread down her back and over her shoulders, and her hands were soft and at her side. She wore no boots, which were at the foot of the coffin, ready to be buried with her, and her feet appeared small and well shaped. She was dressed in the striped gown she wore at the trial.[209]

Close observers looking into the bottom of Mrs Pearcey's plain coffin that day could see great lumps of lime, while in the corner were two or three bags of the same material which were going to be emptied into the coffin before burial. The lid had a large number of holes bored into it, and when it was fastened down several buckets of water would be poured in after it was hauled to the burial site on the prison grounds.

As the jurymen entered the passageway leading from the gaol to the court to view the body they would have passed the already open grave, which measured about 7 feet deep. Mrs Pearcey's grave was the same as had been used for one Wiggins, who was executed in 1867 for the murder of Agnes Oaks, his paramour, at Limehouse. When the earth of Wiggins' grave was disturbed, there was hardly a trace of him, the lime having so effectively disintegrated his remains.

Dr Gilbert confirmed the cause of death, a dislocated neck. To be sure, one of the jurymen moved Mrs Pearcey's head this way and that.[210] The coroner explained that the jury must be satisfied that the sentence was duly executed upon one condemned to death, and they were, the execution having been technically perfect, according to Dr Gilbert, who said, he'd never seen a better execution, in fact.[211] Signing the Coroner's Inquisition Certificate which was then sent to the Home Office, the jury adjourned for the Christmas holiday.

Five bushels of lime were spread beneath Mrs Pearcey's coffin and the same quantity placed above it. The earth was filled in, the flagstone re-laid, and the spot marked with a 'P.' Had Governor Milman not spared Mrs Pearcey the march through Birdcage Walk, she would have walked over the very stones beneath which she now lay.[212]

After the execution, a reporter caught up with Reverend Duffield. He asked if Duffield believed Mrs Pearcey confessed when she said the "sentence was just but the evidence false." Duffield told the reporter he couldn't believe anything Mrs Pearcey said, for she had been fencing in her words all along. The reporter noted that Duffield looked "extremely ill," and suspected his illness was due to the anxiety he felt not having significantly improved Mrs Pearcey's spiritual condition before death. "It is impossible," the reporter wrote, "to estimate the care and anxiety which such an office imposes upon a conscientious man."[213]

After the execution James Berry went to the Old Bell Tavern near St. Bride's Church, sat at a small table dressed in a tall hat and an enormous cloak, writing, reading over, and then scratching through lines of the manuscript that would become his autobiography. He held a long pipe in one hand and alternately picked up the pen and a pint of beer in the other. He was writing a book about hanging. "I am sick at heart," he recorded, "I am always like that after an execution."[214]

Berry eventually rejected the notion of capital punishment as justice altogether, trading the rope for the pulpit. He became a preacher because it was only through religion, he said, that he was ever able to get "a moment's peace in life."[215]

On the day of the execution, Freke Palmer was also interviewed, and discussed the request Mrs Pearcey had made to insert the cryptic advertisement in the Madrid papers.

"What did Mrs Pearcey really say, Mr Palmer?"

Palmer told the reporter that she'd asked him to put in the London newspapers - and any other paper read in Madrid - an advertisement addressed to particular initials.

"Did that refer to the crime?" the reporter asked.

"Not at all. I asked her that, and she said, 'No.'"

"Did you ask her what it referred to?"

"Yes; I said to her, 'Does it refer to the marriage you have told me took place between you and a certain gentleman?' She replied, 'Yes.'"

"What are the facts?"

"She had told me she was a married woman, but would not divulge the particulars."

"How much do you know about it?"

"Only this. She told me she was married in some chambers at Piccadilly to a gentleman in the presence of his valet, by a clergyman in robes."

"Did she give you the name of her husband?"

"No; she said she could not, as she had taken an oath never to divulge it."

"How long did she live with him?"

"Not long. He left her shortly after the marriage, but contributed to her support for a few months. Since then she has not heard of him."

"I suppose you have often pressed her for further particulars?"

"Yes, but she would never give them. She would only repeat 'I have taken an oath never to divulge.' I have tried to trace the marriage, as it might have been very important in reducing the supposed motive for the crime."

Palmer had told his client that he thought the marriage may not have been legal and may have been "only a form gone through."[216]

Mrs Pearcey believed the marriage was perfectly legal and seemed "depressed" by the idea that she might have been deceived, yet again.[217] She thought this 'husband' might be in Madrid.

The reporter asked Palmer for his personal opinion of Mrs Pearcey.

"It always seemed to me," Freke Palmer started, "that her lot had been a very hard one, that she had been badly treated by many people. In fact, the whole world appeared to be against her and none for her. She was a woman of some character and of great intelligence."

She was not a "common low character" as people made her out to be, Palmer said. "Although her character will not bear investigation."[218]

Mary Pearcey's mother had also been interviewed about her daughter's strange final request, but offered very little insight, saying only that her daughter was adamant she had married a "gentleman" whom she called Charles. Charlotte presumed this was the man who fathered the child Mary claimed to have had while abroad. The baby died, she had told her. As to the credence of the story, Charlotte confirmed that Mary did have, at one time, splendid clothes and talked about tours she had been on with her husband and had especially enjoyed travelling up the Pyrenees.[219]

Freke Palmer faithfully carried out Mary Eleanor Wheeler's dying request. The following morning, on Christmas Eve, 1890, in the Madrid and London newspapers could be found the following advertisement:

M.E.C.P. - Last wish of M.E.W.;
Have not betrayed.

In *The Sunday Times*, four days later, a small excerpt appeared that is the only evidence found which may shed light on what the initials M.E.C.P. stood for. It reads in full:

> A correspondent, dating from Perpignan, writes as follows:- "We both thank you for trying to save Mrs 'Pearcey'- Mdme. Previst (Miss M.E. Wheeler)." Our correspondent, who merely signs with a Maltese Cross, no doubt refers to our article of the 14th, and we can only conjecture that "Previst" was the real married name of the woman who was hanged as Mrs Pearcey.[220]

Perpignan is a southern French city near the Mediterranean coast and the border of Spain, framed by the peaks of the Pyrenees.

POSTSCRIPT

Hemingway said the writer's job is to tell the truth, to write one true sentence, the truest sentence that you know. But writing the truth about a liar is rather difficult.

We live in an age where accessing, organising and closely reading the reports, census data and juridical notes from famous trials has never been easier. And yet, while the historical record of the case is fairly complete, the historical record of Mary Pearcey's life is frustratingly fragmented. Not even the best of modern technology can yet solve some of the case's greatest mysteries, and one of my hopes is that those with old papers or genealogical connections to the characters in this tale will come forward and share those documents, which may help explain some of the more baffling questions that remain unanswered.

Of the mysteries yet to be solved...

Who was M.E.C.P.? What didn't Mrs Pearcey betray? Was she ever truly married, and if so to whom? Did the advert in *The Sunday Times* mean she travelled the continent with Charles Crichton, or some other man? What might that imply about other almost-truths? Where did Frank Hogg disappear to, and what became of his life after the death of his wife and child? Was there an accomplice, and if so, to what degree did Mrs Pearcey murder, or simply assist in murder? Was she jealous, mentally ill, epileptic, or all three? How did she induce a woman who feared her to visit for tea, and what could Phoebe have possibly said that enraged Mrs Pearcey to the point of killing?

Rumours that Pearcey was Jack the Ripper sprouted soon after her execution, and have never entirely died away. A London correspondent of the *Western Daily Mercury* suggested people that wanted to explore these theories should contact Inspector Bannister, for he, too, had his own suspicions about a connection between Pearcey and the Ripper. Perhaps it was a slow news day. The *Pall Mall Gazette*, writing a year after the murders, suggested the brass rings recovered from the crime scene and the ring never recovered from Phoebe's body was the connection between Mrs Pearcey and the Ripper.[1] But such evidence is thin.

Had Pearcey been the Ripper, she would have been the first and perhaps only of her kind, and what a story that would be. Maybe it was just that the theory of Jack-be-Jill was too novel and intriguing for writers to let go. In 1939, the *Nottingham Evening Post* ran an article with the headline "Jack the Ripper: New Theory of Notorious Crimes. Should it have been 'Jill'?"[2] This article covered William Stewart's recently-released book *Jack the Ripper: A New Theory*, which was that the Ripper was indeed a woman. Stewart expanded and sharpened Conan Doyle's original thesis, postulating that if the Whitechapel murderer was a midwife, she could have killed and walked through London as though invisible. At the end of his book, Stewart made a reference to Mary Pearcey, reminding readers that she had savagely cut Phoebe's throat in a Ripper-like way and had also dumped the corpses in dark places. It was a scintillating insinuation, but entirely untrue, and important only in so much as it helped paint a more realistic picture of women who kill. Women, as it turns out, have the same criminal potential as men.

It should go without saying - yet I will say it here definitively - that Mary Pearcey was not Jill the Ripper. In brief: the way in which she murdered was different; the type of person she murdered was different; motives for murdering were different, and where she murdered was different. The only commonality between the Hampstead and Whitechapel cases was that there was some overlap in the cadre of reporters and police assigned to work them.

Intense interest in the Pearcey case diminished over time, but her crime never entirely went out of style. The length of a murderess's stay in the Chamber of Horrors is but one indication of her continuing prominence and our fascination with women who kill, particularly.

Only four exhibits survived the Chamber of Horrors beyond 1970, Mrs Pearcey's tableaux being among them. The Hampstead Murders became part of Victorian pop-culture briefly, when a woman said to another to watch out or "I'll Mrs Pearcey you."[3] And In 1931, a short piece in the *L.A. Times* called "She Couldn't Do It" by Walt Mason looked at the Pearcey case, and noted that it was fashionable in the early 1900s to shudder when Pearcey's name was mentioned. Pearcey's notoriety is one reason it is surprising to find she has no entry among the red volumes of *Notable British Trials*.

On June 28, 1914, another version of the Pearcey story ran in the *Washington Post*, and another that same year in *The Weekly Record*. The Pearcey case suffers something of a Lazarus effect, resurrecting every so often on television (*Ladykillers*)[4] and reality television (*Bloody Marys, Investigation Discovery*), the stage, the canvas and in print.[5] In the original Crime Museum at New Scotland Yard, commonly known as the Black Museum, photographs of the victim and the murderess were supposedly once on display.[6] Recently, the execution rope James Berry used to dispatch Mrs Pearcey was part of a display of gruesome nooses at the Crime Museum Uncovered exhibition.

Clearly, Mrs Pearcey has haunted us for years, but why? Why does the Pearcey case still fascinate 120 years on? Is it because primary mysteries of the case have yet to be solved, or because Mrs Pearcey has become something of a folk heroine? The fascination with Pearcey seems to centre around her strength of character and the matchlessness of her crime. She is an example of the type of woman that scholar Elisabeth Bronfen, while discussing destructive femininity, said would 'break conventions or commit a crime punished with death, such as adultery, infanticide or murder, as an expression of liberating subjectivity, or assuming authorship and responsibility for her destiny.'[7] One explanation for Mrs Pearcey's actions, then, was an irrational attempt to escape from a situation in which she felt she could no longer continue, and no longer control. Bronfen might review Pearcey's case and conclude the murders were an attempt to reverse a situation - Frank's withdrawal of love - that was psychologically intolerable to her. This was a motive altogether different from the most commonly ascribed her: jealousy, or, as the writer F. Tennyson Jesse more beautifully called it, the 'impulse of love.'[8]

We should be careful here though to not make a martyr of her even as she fascinates, as one contemporary writer cautioned.[9] Writing in 1900, a reporter for the Spanish newspaper *El Motin* compared Mrs Pearcey to another famous murderess of the era, Teresa Parras, who also stared down the scaffold bravely, he wrote.[10] But paying the Devil his due isn't bravery. Let us not forget that Mrs Pearcey gruesomely murdered, enabled or helped cover up the murder of a woman and her child. And what can we say about whom she helped, if she did?

I have tried to keep conjecture to a minimum in this book, but for a moment let's recount the proofs that might help us calculate the probability of Hogg's involvement.

Mrs Pearcey told Frank he had more power over her than anyone else on earth, and that there was nothing he could ask of her that she wouldn't do, implying, perhaps, he might have asked her to do something rather extraordinary. Frank took Mrs Pearcey problems for her to solve - how best to deal with Phoebe's unexpected pregnancy, for example - and was quite happy to let her relieve him of other responsibilities, such as caring for Phoebe when she became ill. Is it not reasonable to think that he asked of the most capable person he knew to take care of the most persistent problem he had?

It seemed that Mrs Pearcey believed that something about the case, or someone connected, would come to light and save her. It's probably why she refused to let Palmer and Hutton plead the lesser charge of manslaughter. When she realised no one was coming to her defence, she told her mother she had been led into a snare. Of course, if it was Frank who had ensnared her, he would have been only one of any number of men who had done so. Even Freke Palmer noticed that for all her intelligence, Mrs Pearcey had a blind spot when it came to beguiling men.

When she realized Frank wasn't coming to save her, the only

choice left that seemed to fit her psychology was to martyr herself, to "die like a man" having not betrayed confidences. Perhaps I am the only one who read her repeated insistences of Frank's innocence as a little too vigorous?

As for Hogg, he was a suspicious character from beginning to end. It is one thing to disagree with your wife for sending letters to her family, but quite another to not invite them to her funeral. That he went to Mrs Pearcey's house the night of the murders and walked about but didn't find anything unusual strikes me as strange. His direction to Clara to see Mrs Pearcey the next day was also shady. Had he not involved her so early, she probably would have never been implicated or, if so, long after she had time to get rid of the evidence. The sudden trip two weeks before the murders to Silsoe seems to me stranger still. If we're entertaining speculation for a moment, a trip to the country alone was the perfect opportunity to plot a murder.

Frank's cold indifference to Mrs Pearcey once in court; his repeated lies; his coached responses at the Old Bailey; his dramatic wailing when asked about his wife; the manner in which the body was butchered and conveyed; and his immediate disappearance from Camden cause me to pause and ask myself whether Frank Hogg wasn't a sly fox all along.

But here we must stop imagining alternative possibilities and get back to the facts, and, in my estimation the facts suggest that Pearcey withheld the name of her secret accomplice because there was none; denied Freke Palmer the satisfaction of pleading insanity because she was quite sane; and absolved Frank Hogg of guilt because he was innocent. And the truth is, agreeing on her guilt or sanity doesn't make her crime any less exceptional. The murder of Phoebe and Tiggie Hogg was unusual in that, if jealousy was her motive, it is almost always the jealous husband who kills his wife's lover.[11] Her gender also made her exceptional. By the 1890s, women on trial at the Old Bailey (for any number of crimes, let alone murder) represented less than 10 per cent of all defendants.[12] Finally, the manner in which she murdered and transported her victims was very unusual,[13] - epic even, according to F. Tennyson Jesse[14] - marking this Gothic tale one for the ages, and its protagonist among the "front rank of murderesses."[15]

The persistent belief that Mrs Pearcey had an accomplice may have had more to do with the social construction of femininity in the Victorian era than the evidence available. It may also have had to do with the ways that communities respond and process violent crimes. As in modern cases of extreme and terrifying violence, it is often difficult for neighbours, family and friends to believe someone with whom they were close committed an offence because of what it says about them. In other words, murder is disruptive to the psyche of a community because it fractures the narrative classes of people tell themselves *about* themselves. It is unnerving to learn how little we really know of those from whom we borrow dress stands.

What I am willing to concede is that Mrs Pearcey may have deserved a fate other than death. Of course, it is easy to re-read history and her antagonists more sympathetically than a contemporary could have. The Pearcey story contained all the elements of the tragic, marked as it was by pity and fear. Undoubtedly, Mary Pearcey would have benefitted from medication to control her seizures and any one of several mental illnesses from which she likely suffered. Modern forensics would have exonerated her, or definitively settled her involvement in the butchering of Phoebe Hogg's body. And had she killed half a century later, she wouldn't have been put to death at all.

And this, I think, is really why Mrs Pearcey's case continues to titillate and dazzle us. Her case demands that we acknowledge love can serve as the wellspring of both generosity and inhumanity. Who among us has not loved something or someone so completely, that it stripped us bare of reason? And what are we to do - how do we rehabilitate or fairly punish those who use the heart as a weapon? As we turn our gaze to Mary Pearcey again and again, perhaps we fear looking too closely at her, and those like her in our own time, for fear we might catch a glimpse of ourselves in the reflection.

NOTES AND REFERENCES

The Crime

1 *Lloyd's Weekly Newspaper*, October 26, 1890.

2 *Portsmouth Evening News*, October 25, 1890.

3 *Lloyd's Weekly Newspaper*, October 26, 1890.

4 *Pall Mall Gazette*, October 25, 1890.

5 Ibid.

6 Old Bailey Proceedings Online, November 1890, trial of Mary Eleanor Pearcey (t18901124-43).

7 *Lloyd's Weekly Newspaper*, November 2, 1890.

8 *Lloyd's Weekly Newspaper*, October 26, 1890.

9 *Portsmouth Evening News*, October 25, 1890.

10 *Lloyd's Weekly Newspaper*, October 26, 1890.

11 Ibid.

12 The Old Bailey transcripts have both Gardiner and Inspector Wright sending for an ambulance.

13 Old Bailey Proceedings Online, November 1890, trial of Mary Eleanor Pearcey (t18901124-43).

14 Some newspapers reporting on the murder in editions of October 25, 1890 mentioned that the word 'Phoebe' was marked on her handkerchief. (The *Portsmouth Evening News*, time stamping their report with '3.10pm', spelled it Fibe, and the *Gloucester Citizen* spelled it Febe.) But it's worth noting that the *Sheffield Evening Telegraph* reported that the Press Association announced the identity of the victim at 4.00pm. The victim's name was not available to the press at 3.10pm on Saturday, but by 2.00pm the body had already been identified at the mortuary. The fact that Phoebe's first name was correctly reported in certain newspapers before her identity had been officially announced indicates that the named handkerchief existed. It's possible that

the fact that the handkerchief had a name on it was withheld by the police, but it is not described by the police in their evidence at the Old Bailey, and one would have thought that it ought to have been, if it had existed.

15 *Lloyd's Weekly Newspaper*, November 2, 1890.

16 *Lloyd's Weekly Newspaper*, October 26, 1890.

17 Ibid.

18 *Sheffield Evening Telegraph*, October 25, 1890.

19 Ibid.

20 *Aberdeen Evening Express*, October 25, 1890.

21 *Lloyd's Weekly Newspaper*, October 26, 1890.

22 *Sheffield Evening Telegraph*, October 25, 1890.

23 *Portsmouth Evening News*, October 25, 1890.

24 *Pall Mall Gazette*, October 25, 1890.

25 *Portsmouth Evening News*, October 25, 1890.

26 *Lloyd's Weekly Newspaper*, November 2, 1890.

27 Old Bailey Proceedings Online, November 1890, trial of Mary Eleanor Pearcey (t18901124-43).

28 *Portsmouth Evening News*, October 5, 1890.

29 *Lloyd's Weekly Newspaper*, October 26, 1890.

30 The undertaker calculated her height at 5ft 7in but said he couldn't quite tell owing to her head, meaning he couldn't get an exact calculation because by the time he collected the body rigor mortis had set in and her head drooped to the side owing to the cut in her neck, which had severed the vertebral column.

31 *Portsmouth Evening News*, October 25, 1890.

32 *Nottingham Evening Post*, October 25, 1890.

33 *Pall Mall Gazette*, October 25, 1890.

34 *The Echo*, September 17, 1888.

35 *Lloyd's Weekly Newspaper*, October 26, 1890.

36 Either Bannister is misremembering, or the reporter is misquoting, but either way, the timeline is off by several hours. The body was found at 7.30pm and Roser clearly states in his trial testimony that he found the pram at 10.30pm that night, just after he'd gone on duty.

37 *Lloyd's Weekly Newspaper*, October 26, 1890.

38 *Aberdeen Evening Express*, October 25, 1890.

39 *Lloyd's Weekly Newspaper*, October 26, 1890.

40 *Portsmouth Evening News*, October 25, 1890.

41 Melville Macnaghten, *Days of My Years* (1914).

42 *Herts Advertiser*, November 1, 1890.

43 *Sheffield Evening Telegraph*, October 25, 1890.

44 Ibid.

45 *Lloyd's Weekly Newspaper*, October 26, 1890.

46 *Aberdeen Evening Express*, October 25, 1890.

47 The *Portsmouth Evening News* reports his name was Inspector Collis, but surely they are referring to Thomas Hollis of T Division, who testified about his plan made of the crime scene.

48 *Portsmouth Evening News*, October 5, 1890.

49 *Derby Daily Telegraph*, October 27, 1890.

50 *Lloyd's Weekly Newspaper*, November 2, 1890.

51 *Lloyd's Weekly Newspaper*, October 26, 1890.

52 Hanslope was a family name of Frank's mother's side.

53 Her middle name was the maiden name of Frank's mother.

54 *Daily News*, November 4, 1890.

55 *Lloyd's Weekly Newspaper*, November 2, 1890.

56 Mulcaster said a woman with a baby girl in a pram stopped at her shop and bought a pennyworth of butterscotch. Mrs Hogg was also thought to have stopped at a fruiter's shop at Chalk Farm Road and bought some grapes. (*Portsmouth Evening News*, October 30, 1890).

57 *Freeman's Journal*, October 28, 1890.

58 Old Bailey Proceedings Online, November 1890, trial of Mary Eleanor Pearcey (t18901124-43).

59 *Lloyd's Weekly Newspaper*, November 2, 1890.

60 *Belfast News-Letter*, October 27, 1890.

61 *Morning Post*, October 28, 1890.

62 *Lloyd's Weekly Newspaper*, October 26, 1890.

63 *Evening Standard*, October 27, 1890.

64 Now Ivor Street.

65 *Pall Mall Gazette*, October 29, 1890.

66 Now called West Kentish Town.

67 *The Times*, October 29, 1890.

68 Ibid.

69 Old Bailey Proceedings Online, November 1890, trial of Mary

Eleanor Pearcey (t18901124-43).

70 *The Times*, October 29, 1890.

71 *Lloyd's Weekly Newspaper*, October 26, 1890.

72 Clara's testimony is uncertain about whether Mrs Pearcey offered to buy the papers, or whether she was asked. She commented several times, however, that she was deeply distraught over hearing of the news, and could not recall exactly how each event unfolded one month later during her trial.

73 Judge's notes: HO 144/237/A52045.

74 Old Bailey Proceedings Online, November 1890, trial of Mary Eleanor Pearcey (t18901124-43).

75 *Lloyd's Weekly Newspaper*, November 2, 1890.

76 Inspector Bannister had worked on many cases in his time within S Division and had received a commendation early in his career for acting bravely when he rushed into a burning house to save two children and their mother from the fire. Sir James Ingham mentioned about Bannister's heroism in the most "complimentary terms", acknowledging that Bannister saved the children at great risk to himself. The children's mother, regrettably, had died in Bannister's arms. Most of Bannister's other cases were rather routine, some even comically absurd, such as a case in September 1890 when three men were accused of using a monkey to facilitate a rigged gambling scheme at Barnet Fair. More seriously, he had also led the investigation into what the media called the Kilburn Tragedy, a crime wherein a 34-year-old clerk named Leonard Bowes Handforth attempted to murder his wife and her mother. Handforth then unsuccessfully tried to commit suicide.

77 *Oxford Dictionary of National Biography*.

78 Old Bailey Proceedings Online, November 1890, trial of Mary Eleanor Pearcey (t18901124-43).

79 Bannister later sought permission from Frank Hogg to take a cast of his wife and daughter's head, which may exist in New Scotland Yard's Crime Museum.

80 Old Bailey Proceedings Online, November 1890, trial of Mary Eleanor Pearcey (t18901124-43).

81 Ibid.

82 Some papers even report one of the women - presumably Pearcey - even fainted. cf *Sheffield Evening Telegraph*, October 25, 1890.

83 Old Bailey Proceedings Online, November 1890, trial of Mary Eleanor Pearcey (t18901124-43).

84 *Derby Daily Telegraph*, October 27, 1890.

85 Melville Macnaghten, *Days of My Years* (1914).

86 For example, Macnaghten thought the baby had been found in its pram on Hampstead Heath, but the pram was found in St. John's Wood, nearly two miles away.

87 Melville Macnaghten, *Days of My Years* (1914).

88 *Lloyd's Weekly Newspaper*, November 16, 1890.

89 This should be read with suspicion. Macnaghten's memoir, *Days of My Years*, is mired with inaccuracies and outright fabrications. According to *Lloyd's Weekly Newspaper* of November 2, 1890, Lizzie was in fact questioned on the Saturday morning, but by Inspector Miller, not Macnaghten. When told that her aunt may have been murdered, Lizzie volunteered, "Well, if it is her, I know who did it." When Inspector Miller asked her who, she replied, "Mrs Pearcey." Whether told to Macnaghten directly or not, the information would have got back to Macnaghten and in consequence, his suspicions about Mrs Pearcey were probably heightened. Macnaghten probably shared this information with Bannister. Further, at the inquest, Bannister testifies, "The two females, Mrs Pearcey, Mr Hogg, and the niece, Lizzie Styles, were taken to the police-station for examination" (*Lloyd's Weekly Newspaper*, November 2, 1890), so Lizzie might have cornered Macnaghten before they went back to tell Frank Hogg his wife was murdered, but it could have as well happened in a different sequence; the record is unclear. But, in consequence of this and the discovery of the affair between Frank and Mrs Pearcey, Bannister probably nursed a deep suspicion about Mrs Pearcey and so, indirectly, Lizzie's testimony was one of the things that prompted Bannister to search Mrs Pearcey's house later that day when Lizzie, Clara, Frank, and Mrs Pearcey went back to the station for questioning.

90 Melville Macnaghten, *Days of My Years* (1914).

91 Ibid.

92 Ibid.

93 *Lloyd's Weekly Newspaper*, November 2, 1890.

94 In May 1887 workers pulled a bundle containing the torso of a female from the Thames at Rainham. Throughout May and June, numerous parts from the same body showed up in various parts of London, until a complete body, minus head and upper chest, was reconstructed.

95 Paul Begg, Martin Fido and Keith Skinner, *The Jack the Ripper A to Z* (1991).

96 In his report sent to Assistant Commissioner Robert Anderson, Bond wrote that the Whitechapel murderer must have been a man of "physical strength" and "great coolness." He was probably "inoffensive looking, probably middle-aged, and neatly and respectably dressed." Lauren Barrow, Ron Rufo and Saul Arambula, *Police and Profiling in the United States: Applying Theory to Criminal Investigations* (2014); Tim Newburn, Alan Wright and Tom Williamson, *Handbook of Criminal Investigation* (2007). For a more complete description of Bond's career with Scotland Yard, see Adam Wood's article 'The Matter with Dr Bond' in *Ripperologist* No. 150, June 2016.

97 *The Lancet*: Obituary of Dr Thomas Bond (1901) Vol. I, p. 1721.

98 Katherine Ramsland, *Beating the Devil's Game: A History of Forensic Science and Criminal Investigation* (2007).

99 J. Dixon Mann in the Introduction to his *Forensic Medicine & Toxicology* (1893).

100 Charles Tempest Clarkson and J. Hall Richardson, *Police!* (1889).

101 Tom Cullen, *When London Walked in Terror* (1965), p. 225. Note: Cullen's source was not Sir Conan Doyle himself, but his son, Adrian Conan Doyle. Note that any hypotheses that Mrs Pearcey could have been such a woman were developed much later, around the 1930s.

102 Dr Bond eventually committed suicide after a severe bout of insomnia and depression. As no definitive biography exists on Bond, it is impossible to know whether his depression was caused or exacerbated by the kind of work he did, though he wouldn't be the first to admit the gravity of his work took its toll. See also Stewart P. Evans, *Executioner: The Chronicles of James Berry, Victorian Hangman* (2004) and *The Scalpel of Scotland Yard* by Douglas Browne and EV Tullet, chronicling the suicide by gassing of British pathologist Bernard Spilsbury in 1947.

103 *Lloyd's Weekly Newspaper*, October 26, 1890.

104 Old Bailey Proceedings Online, November 1890, trial of Mary Eleanor Pearcey (t18901124-43).

105 Ibid.

106 Ibid.

107 *Sheffield Evening Telegraph*, October 27, 1890.

108 Ibid. There were conflicting reports about whether Mrs Pearcey whistled or played the piano. By the time Macnaghten wrote his memoirs in 1914, this scene was embellished into Mrs Pearcey "strumming away at popular tunes." Later, he said that when

Mrs Pearcey was asked for an explanation of the blood she chanted, "Killing mice, killing mice, killing mice," and went on playing the piano. Bannister testified at the Old Bailey that she wasn't whistling tunes, but whistling to herself.

109 Old Bailey Proceedings Online, November 1890, trial of Mary Eleanor Pearcey (t18901124-43).

110 Ibid.

111 Ibid.

112 Ibid.

113 *Daily News*, October 27, 1890.

114 *Western Mail*, October 27, 1890.

115 Old Bailey Proceedings Online, November 1890, trial of Mary Eleanor Pearcey (t18901124-43).

116 *Western Mail*, October 27, 1890.

117 Dr. Pepper would later analyze the clothes Mrs Pearcey was wearing when taken into police custody. Though he certainly found spots, smears and drops of blood on her grey skirt and flounce, it was hardly "saturated" in blood. Further, by the time Mrs Pearcey was taken into custody, whatever blood from the scene her skirt absorbed had certainly dried.

118 Old Bailey Proceedings Online, November 1890, trial of Mary Eleanor Pearcey (t18901124-43).

119 cf *Western Mail*, October 27, 1890.

120 *Morning Post*, October 28, 1890.

121 *Lloyd's Weekly Newspaper*, October 26, 1890.

122 Ibid.

123 Ibid.

124 Ibid.

125 Ibid.

126 Ibid; 1861 Census.

127 *Yorkshire Post and Leeds Intelligencer*, October 27, 1890.

128 *Illustrated Police News*, December 20, 1890.

129 *Lloyd's Weekly Newspaper*, October 26, 1890.

130 *Daily News*, November 12, 1890.

131 Ibid.

132 Old Bailey Proceedings Online, November 1890, trial of Mary Eleanor Pearcey (t18901124-43).

133 *Daily News*, November 12, 1890.

134 *Daily News*, October 27, 1890.

135 *Daily News*, November 12, 1890.

136 The assistant's name does not appear to have been reported.

137 Reports of the Meetings & Discussions Held in London August 10-17, 1891, p. 23.

138 Conservation Area Statement. Hampstead. Conservation & Urban Design Team London Borough of Camden Environment Department. London, p. 20. The mortuary was later converted to become the New End Theatre, which operated from 1974 to 2011.

139 G. Sims Woodhead MD: *Practical Pathology* (3rd Edition, 1892), p. 4; Pages from a Tiemann Company catalogue circa 1878 showing post-mortem instruments. See www.medicalantiques.com/civilwar/Articles/Post_Mortem_instruments.htm.

140 *Lloyd's Weekly Newspaper*, October 26, 1890.

141 *British Medical Journal*: Obituary of Augustus Joseph Pepper, F.R.C.S. December 28, 1935.

142 Jane Robbins, *The Magnificent Spilsbury and the Case of the Brides in the Bath* (2010).

143 As the autopsy records no longer exist, this information was actually taken from the court testimony of Clatworthy, the undertaker.

144 E. Ashworth Underwood, 'Rudolf Virchow', *Encyclopedia Britannica*. www.britannica.com/biography/Rudolf-Virchow.

145 J. Dixon Mann, *Forensic Medicine and Toxicology* (London: Charles Griffin, 1893).

146 Old Bailey Proceedings Online, November 1890, trial of Mary Eleanor Pearcey (t18901124-43).

147 *Daily News*, October 27, 1890.

148 Old Bailey Proceedings Online, November 1890, trial of Mary Eleanor Pearcey (t18901124-43).

149 Ibid.

150 Ibid.

151 Ibid.

152 Ibid.

153 Ibid.

154 Whether this is true or not is difficult to tell. Lizzie Styles, Phoebe's niece who lived nearby, was visited by the police on the Saturday. She may have been told not to say anything to any other family member until they had confirmed Phoebe's identity, so it is

possible that on the Sunday afternoon, when the brother popped by for a visit, he truly didn't know about his sister's murder. That said, it seems that the whole family had been barred from such visits months before and so one wonders why he would just "pop in".

155 *Lloyd's Weekly Newspaper*, 2 November, 1890.

The Inquest

1 Clare Graham: *Ordering Law: The Architectural and Social History of the English Law Courts* (2003), p. 157.

2 *Sheffield Evening Telegraph*, October 27, 1890.

3 Ibid.

4 *The News & Observer*, October 29, 1890.

5 Robyn Anderson, *Criminal Violence in London, 1856–1875* (PhD thesis). University of Toronto, 1990.

6 *Sheffield Evening Telegraph*, October 27, 1890.

7 *Evening News and Post*, October 27, 1890.

8 *Women's Penny Paper*, December 13, 1890, p. 120.

9 *Singapore Free Press and Mercantile Advertiser*, February 24, 1932, p. 16.

10 Eleven years after he represented Mrs Pearcey, Freke Palmer represented Maud Amelia Eddington, a 22-year-old singer who shot her lover, John Bellis, and was caught before she could shoot herself. Through deft and tireless legal work, Palmer supported Eddington's barrister, Lord Coleridge, in preparing a case that eventually saved her from the death penalty. She was sentenced to 15 months' hard labor for attempting suicide, a defence that resonated since she claimed that Bellis had been killed in a struggle that took place as she drew out a gun with which to shoot herself.

11 The only record of payment to Freke Palmer was the proceeds from the sale of Mrs Pearcey's relics to Madame Tussaud's. The receipt suggested a sum of £200 was collected, according to the *Leeds Mercury* of December 30, 1890, but in the Home Office files there is a record, signed by Mary, that says she only received £25 from Madame Tussaud & Sons Ltd for all her "furniture and effects now at my rooms at No. 2 Priory Street Kentish Town".

12 Neil R.A. Bell, Trevor N. Bond, Kate Clarke and M.W. Oldridge, *The A-Z of Victorian Crime* (2016).

13 *Evening Telegraph*, October 27, 1890.

14 *Singapore Free Press and Mercantile Advertiser*, February 24, 1932, p. 16.
15 *Manchester Guardian*, December 28, 1890.
16 *North-Eastern Daily Gazette*, October 27, 1890.
17 *Bristol Mercury & Daily Post*, November 1, 1890.
18 *Sheffield Evening Telegraph*, October 27, 1890.
19 *Lloyd's Weekly Newspaper*, November 23, 1890.
20 *Sheffield Evening Telegraph*, October 27, 1890.
21 *Lloyd's Weekly Newspaper* November 23, 1890.
22 *Daily News*, October 28, 1890.
23 *Lloyd's Weekly Newspaper*, November 2, 1890.
24 Ibid.
25 *Sheffield Evening Telegraph*, October 27, 1890.
26 *Daily News*, October 28, 1890.
27 *Lloyd's Weekly Newspaper*, November 2, 1890.
28 *Pall Mall Gazette*, October 29, 1890.
29 *Pall Mall Gazette*, October 30, 1890.
30 *Evening Standard*, October 28, 1890.
31 *The Times*, October 29, 1890.
32 *Lloyd's Weekly Newspaper*, November 2, 1890.
33 Ibid.
34 Ibid.
35 Ibid.
36 *Devon & Exeter Gazette*, October 31, 1890.
37 *Lloyd's Weekly Newspaper*, November 2, 1890.
38 *Devon & Exeter Gazette*, October 31, 1890.
39 *The Times*, October 29, 1890.
40 Ibid.
41 *Lloyd's Weekly Newspaper*, November 2, 1890.
42 *The Times*, October 29, 1890.
43 Ibid.
44 *Lloyd's Weekly Newspaper*, November 2, 1890.
45 *The Times*, October 29, 1890.
46 *Lloyd's Weekly Newspaper*, November 2, 1890.
47 Ibid.
48 *Daily News*, November 12, 1890.

49 *Pall Mall Gazette*, December 1, 1890.

50 *The Times*, October 29, 1890.

51 *Lloyd's Weekly Newspaper*, November 2, 1890.

52 *Devon & Exeter Gazette*, October 31, 1890.

53 There is minor discrepancy here in the reports. *The Times* reports that the conversation happened at the gate; the *Cornwall Gazette* reports it happened at her front door. Either way, it seems to have happened outside the house.

54 *Lloyd's Weekly Newspaper*, November 2, 1890.

55 *Daily News*, November 12, 1890.

56 There is some discrepancy here about the brother's age: 14 or 40, as reported in the *Devon & Exeter Gazette*, but the end result is the same: Mary Wheeler had neither a brother of 14 nor 40 who died in October of 1890.

57 Interestingly, the *Cornwall Gazette* of October 30, 1890 reports that the 'gentleman caller' - Charles Crichton - could not identify either ring, and one would think if he'd given her the gold ring, he could identify it.

58 *The Times*, October 29, 1890.

59 *Devon & Exeter Gazette*, October 28, 1890.

60 *North-Eastern Daily Gazette*, October 27, 1890.

61 *Lloyd's Weekly Newspaper*, November 2, 1890.

62 In some articles Martha is described as a dressmaker; others don't specify, just stating that she was in service.

63 *Illustrated Police News*. November 22, 1890. This image of Martha Styles was probably sketched while at the Old Bailey, but it's one of the few images we have of her, and it's probable that she dressed similarly for all the trials and inquest. The *Evening News* (October 30, 1890) shows her wearing the same hat.

64 *Lloyd's Weekly Newspaper*, November 2, 1890.

65 Martha testified she wasn't sure if she remembered the note saying 'your' or 'our' little darling. (*Lloyd's Weekly Newspaper*, November 2, 1890.)

66 *Lloyd's Weekly Newspaper*, November 2, 1890.

67 *The Times*, October 29, 1890.

68 *Cornwall Gazette*, October 30, 1890.

69 *Lloyd's Weekly Newspaper*, November 2, 1890.

70 Ibid.

71 *Lloyd's Weekly Newspaper*, November 16, 1890.

72 *Lloyd's Weekly Newspaper*, November 2, 1890.
73 Ibid.
74 *Cornwall Gazette*, October 30, 1890.
75 *Lloyd's Weekly Newspaper*, November 2, 1890.
76 *Cornwall Gazette*, October 30, 1890.
77 *The Times*, October 29, 1890.
78 Ibid.
79 Ibid.
80 *Daily News*, October 27, 1890.
81 *Devon & Exeter Gazette*, October 31, 1890.
82 *Portsmouth Evening News*, October 30, 1890.
83 *Lloyd's Weekly Newspaper*, November 2, 1890.
84 *The Times*, October 29, 1890.
85 *Bristol Mercury & Daily Post*, November 1, 1890.
86 *The Times*, October 29, 1890.
87 *Cornwall Gazette*, October 30, 1890.
88 Ibid.
89 Ibid.
90 *Lloyd's Weekly Newspaper*, November 2, 1890.
91 *The Times*, October 29, 1890.
92 Ibid.
93 Ibid.
94 *Lloyd's Weekly Newspaper*, November 2, 1890.
95 *The Times*, October 29, 1890.
96 *Leeds Mercury*, November 4, 1890.
97 *Lloyd's Weekly Newspaper*, November 16, 1890.
98 Ibid.
99 *Pall Mall Gazette*, October 29, 1890.
100 *Cornwall Gazette*, October 30, 1890.
101 *Bristol Mercury & Daily Post*, November 1, 1890.
102 *Lloyd's Weekly Newspaper*, November 16, 1890.
103 Ibid.
104 Ibid.
105 Ibid.
106 Ibid.
107 Ibid.

108 Ibid.
109 *The Times*, October 29, 1890.
110 *Lloyd's Weekly Newspaper*, November 2, 1890.
111 Ibid.
112 Ibid.
113 *The Times*, October 29, 1890.
114 Ibid.
115 Ibid.
116 Margaret Roberts and Michael Wink (eds.), *Alkaloids: Biochemistry, Ecology, and Medicinal Applications* (1998), p. 20.
117 *The Scotsman*, October 19, 1890.
118 *The Times*, October 29, 1890.
119 *Lloyd's Weekly Newspaper*, November 2, 1890.
120 Ibid.
121 *Cornwall Gazette*, October 30, 1890.
122 *Lloyd's Weekly Newspaper*, November 2, 1890.
123 Ibid.
124 *Pall Mall Gazette*, October 30, 1890.
125 *St. Pancras Guardian*, November 9, 1890.
126 Ibid.
127 *Evening Standard*, October 30, 1890.
128 *Pall Mall Gazette*, October 30, 1890.
129 *Evening Standard*, October 31, 1890.
130 Ibid.
131 Ibid.
132 *Pall Mall Gazette*, October 31, 1890.
133 *Evening Standard*, October 31, 1890.
134 Ibid.
135 *Pall Mall Gazette*, October 31, 1890.
136 *Lloyd's Weekly Newspaper*, November 2, 1890.
137 *Hull Daily Mail*, October 27, 1890.
138 *Daily News*, October 10, 1890.
139 *Daily News*, October 27, 1890.
140 *Lloyd's Weekly Newspaper*, November 2, 1890.
141 *Daily News*, October 27, 1890.
142 *Pall Mall Gazette*, November 1, 1890. Evidence would later show

that this early reporting of the number of buttons was not quite right, but that finding the buttons was an important clue all the same.

143 As it turned out, the missing button, which was found among the ashes of the dustbin, not in the grate, was identical to one on the left sleeve of Phoebe's jacket. The button on the right sleeve was still missing from the jacket and police made the link between the buttons as both belonging to Phoebe and as evidence that someone had tried to erase that fact.

144 *Evening Standard*, November 1, 1890.

145 *Bristol Mercury & Daily Post*, November 1, 1890.

146 *Lloyd's Weekly Newspaper*, November 2, 1890.

147 Old Bailey Proceedings Online, November 1890, trial of Mary Eleanor Pearcey (t18901124-43).

148 *Evening Standard*, November 1, 1890.

149 Ibid.

150 *Lloyd's Weekly Newspaper*, November 16, 1890.

151 Ibid.

152 *Lloyd's Weekly Newspaper*, November 2, 1890.

153 Ibid.

154 Ibid.

155 Ibid.

156 Ibid.

157 Ibid.

158 Ibid.

159 Ibid.

160 Ibid.

161 Ibid.

162 Ibid.

163 Ibid.

164 Ibid.

165 *Reynolds's Newspaper*, November 2, 1890.

166 Ibid.

167 Ibid.

168 *Lloyd's Weekly Newspaper*, November 2, 1890.

169 *Herts Advertiser*, November 1, 1890.

170 *Evening Standard*, November 1, 1890.

171 *Illustrated Police News*, November 8, 1890.

172 *Evening Standard*, November 3, 1890.

173 *Lloyd's Weekly Newspaper*, November 2, 1890.

174 *Evening Standard*, November 1, 1890.

175 *Pall Mall Gazette*, October 31, 1890.

176 *Lloyd's Weekly Newspaper*, December 21, 1890.

177 Ibid.

178 *Evening Telegraph*, October 27, 1890.

The Murderess, The Lover and The Wife

1 Birth Certificate.

2 Baptism record.

3 *Canterbury Journal, Kentish Times & Farmers' Gazette*, March 24, 1866.

4 *Lloyd's Weekly Newspaper*, November 16, 1890.

5 *Lloyd's Weekly Newspaper*, November 30, 1890.

6 *Lloyd's Weekly Newspaper*, December 14, 1890.

7 *Lloyd's Weekly Newspaper*, October 30, 1890.

8 *Lloyd's Weekly Newspaper*, December 14, 1890.

9 *Lloyd's Weekly Newspaper*, November 30, 1890.

10 *Lloyd's Weekly Newspaper*, December 14, 1890.

11 Havelock Ellis, *Studies in the Psychology of Sex* (1927), Vol. 5, p. 218.

12 *Lloyd's Weekly Newspaper*, December 14, 1890.

13 James and Elizabeth would part some time before 1860, when Elizabeth married one John Jenkins.

14 Record of marriage.

15 *Lloyd's Weekly Newspaper*, December 30, 1890.

16 *Lloyd's Weekly Newspaper*, December 14, 1890.

17 *Lloyd's Weekly Newspaper*, November 16, 1890.

18 Ibid.

19 *Lloyd's Weekly Newspaper*, December 14, 1890.

20 Ibid.

21 The alternative spelling of this street was 'Gloucester'. The street is now called Settles Street.

22 Sally Mitchell, *Daily Life in Victorian England* (2nd Edition, 2008), p. 92.

23 Lavinia Mitton, *The Victorian Hospital* (2008), p. 37. Quoting

Dickens from *The Uncommercial Traveller*.

24 Ibid.

25 Jonathan Reinarz and Leonard Schwarz (eds), *Medicine and the Workhouse* (2013).

26 Lavinia Mitton, *The Victorian Hospital* (2008), p. 38.

27 Death Index.

28 HO 144/237/A52045.

29 The *Lloyd's* reporter said the "direct evidence" of this suicide attempt was "not so strong" as the others; the others being witnessed by John Charles, her mother and a neighbour. *Lloyd's Weekly Newspaper*, December 14, 1890.

30 Eva LaPlante, *Seized: Temporal Lobe Epilepsy as Medical, Historical, and Artistic Phenomenon* (2000).

31 Ibid.

32 Ibid.

33 Eva LaPlante, *Seized: Temporal Lobe Epilepsy as Medical, Historical, and Artistic Phenomenon* (2000).

34 Roy Porter, *Madness: A Brief History* (2002), p. 12.

35 Keith Joseph, 'Introduction' in *Samuel Smiles, Self Help* (1859, 1986 edn).

36 S.G. Howe, *On the Causes of Idiocy* (Edinburgh: Maclachlan & Stewart, 1858), p. 2.

37 Francesco Monaco and Marco Mula, 'Cesare Lombroso and Epilepsy 100 Years Later: An Unabridged Report of his Original Transactions', *Epilepsia* 52, no. 4 (2011), 679-688.

38 Nellie Bly (aka Elizabeth Jane Cochrane Seaman), *Ten Days in a Mad-House* (1887).

39 Baptism records.

40 1871 census.

41 Information from birth and baptism records. The third boy, John, is something of a mystery. He does not appear in the official census data until 1881, where he is listed as 6-years-old and born in Limehouse, but in the Booth archival record, taken in 1889, John is listed as 10-years-old, so one of the two documents is wrong. Further, census data beyond 1881 doesn't list James John Henry Wheeler at all, though he does show up in the Booth records as a 17-year-old who was commissioned to the Navy. There is also a record of an enlistment in the right name, but the date of birth is wrong. Ancestry.com.

42 Baptism record of James John Henry Wheeler.

43 Baptism record of Charles Thomas William Wheeler.

44 *Lloyd's Weekly Newspaper*, November 30, 1890.

45 Ibid.

46 *Illustrated Police News*, November 22, 1890.

47 *Lloyd's Weekly Newspaper*, November 30, 1890.

48 *Illustrated Police News*, November 22, 1890.

49 Electoral Registers, 1832-1965.

50 *Lloyd's Weekly Newspaper*, November 30, 1890.

51 Testimony of Alice Prümmer, December 16, 1890. HO 144/237/A52045.

52 *Daily News*, November 13, 1890.

53 Robert Taylor, *White Coat Tales: Medicine's Heroes, Heritage, and Misadventures* (2007), p. 158.

54 Testimony of Alice Prümmer, December 16, 1890. HO 144/237/A52045.

55 Simon Shorvon, *Handbook of Epilepsy Treatment* (2nd Edition, 2010), p. 231.

56 The exact month of her dismissal is difficult to discern, but in the 1891 census the child, Christoph, is 9-years-old, which means that he was born in 1882. The Prümmers are recorded living on Whitehorse Street in 1881, which means that July, 1882 for Mary's dismissal is a reasonable guess. This event is recorded in Notes from No. 26 of the Booth Journals from Stepney Union from May, 1889 and the 1891 census.

57 *Lloyd's Weekly Newspaper*, December 14, 1890.

58 *Lloyd's Weekly Newspaper*, November 30, 1890.

59 Signed affidavit of Mrs Buckley, December 16, 1890. HO 144/237/A52045.

60 *Lloyd's Weekly Newspaper*, December, 14, 1890.

61 *Lloyd's Weekly Newspaper*, November 30, 1890.

62 Ibid.

63 Notes from No. 26 of the Booth Journals from Stepney Union from May, 1889.

64 *Lloyd's Weekly Newspaper*, December 28, 1890.

65 *Lloyd's Weekly Newspaper*, November 30, 1890.

66 Notes from No. 26 of the Booth Journals from Stepney Union from May 1889.

67 *Lloyd's Weekly Newspaper*, December 14, 1890.

68 Affidavit of John Lawrence Bosley, December 11, 1890. HO 144/237/A52045.

69 *Lloyd's Weekly Newspaper*, December 7, 1890.

70 *Lloyd's Weekly Newspaper*, December 14, 1890.

71 Ibid.

72 *Evening Standard*, November 13, 1890.

73 *Illustrated Police News*, November 22, 1890.

74 *Lloyd's Weekly Newspaper*, November 30, 1890.

75 There is one document from the Queensland State Archive's Registers of Immigrant Ships' Arrivals with a passenger listed as Mary Wheeler, age 18, who departed in Glasgow and arrived in Cooktown on January 21, 1883. The ship was in terrible condition, but it was not lost at sea, and it is most likely this is not related to the case. Queensland State Archives; Registers of Immigrant Ships' Arrivals; Series: Series ID 13086; Roll: M1700.

76 *Lloyd's Weekly Newspaper*, November 30, 1890.

77 Ibid.

78 In most accounts, this happens at the Wheeler house. In the *Daily News* of November 13, 1890, this story is told to her mother at the hospital.

79 *Lloyd's Weekly Newspaper*, November 30, 1890.

80 Ibid.

81 *Daily News*, November 13, 1890.

82 *Daily News*, November 12, 1890.

83 Affidavit of John Charles Pearcey. Signed December 10, 1890. HO 144/237/A52045.

84 Ibid.

85 Ibid.

86 Ibid.

87 Ibid.

88 Ibid.

89 Ibid.

90 *Daily News*, November 12, 1890.

91 Ibid.

92 Birth Index.

93 J.H.H. Gaute and Robin Odell, *Lady Killers* (1980). This description seems to be best supported by statements made from Phoebe's niece, Lizzie Styles, and her sister, Martha, during and after the

trial, who, clearly, had an axe to grind with the Hogg family.

94 *Lloyd's Weekly Newspaper*, November 2, 1890.

95 J.H.H. Gaute and Robin Odell, *Lady Killers* (1980). From the letter dated October 2, 1888.

96 *Evening Standard*, December 2, 1890.

97 *Lloyd's Weekly Newspaper*, November 2, 1890.

98 From a letter dated October 25 as quoted in *Evening Standard*, December 2, 1890.

99 *Lloyd's Weekly Newspaper*, November 2, 1890.

100 Ibid.

101 From a letter dated October 25 as quoted in the *Evening Standard*, December 2, 1890.

102 *Pall Mall Gazette*, December 1, 1890.

103 From a letter dated October 25 as quoted in the *Evening Standard*, December 2, 1890.

104 Death of James Hogg registered in 1st Quarter 1880.

105 1881 Census.

106 *Morning Post*, October 28, 1890.

107 1881 Census.

108 *Morning Post*, October 28, 1890.

109 J.H.H. Gaute and Robin Odell, *Lady Killers* (1980).

110 1881 Census.

111 *The Times*, December 4, 1890.

112 *Daily News*, December 2, 1890.

113 Steven Denford, *Streets of Kentish Town* (Camden History Society, 2005), p. 70.

114 Steven Denford, *Streets of Kentish Town* (Camden History Society, 2005), p. 9.

115 John Richardson, *Camden Town and Primrose Hill Past* (2002).

116 Mary had initially occupied an upstairs room, but subsequently moved downstairs. When this took place however, is unknown.

117 *Lloyd's Weekly Newspaper*, November 16, 1890.

118 Ibid.

119 *Daily News*, December 2, 1890.

120 *Lloyd's Weekly Newspaper*, November 2, 1890.

121 *Daily News*, December 2, 1890.

122 For example, the *Freeman's Journal*, October 28, 1890 (and several

other papers that relied on wires) erroneously printed that Charles Crichton was Mary Pearcey's legal husband. For a day, they called her Mrs Crichton. They also reported that she'd known Charles for three, four and five years, depending on the account.

123 *Morning Post*, October, 28, 1890.

124 Ibid.

125 *Devon & Exeter Gazette*, October 28, 1890.

126 *Daily News*, December 2, 1890.

127 *Evening Standard*, December 2, 1890.

128 J.H.H. Gaute and Robin Odell, *Lady Killers* (1980), pp. 99-100. There are slightly different versions, but Gaute and Odell's seems to be the most complete. For another see *Daily News*, December 2, 1890.

129 J.H.H. Gaute and Robin Odell, *Lady Killers* (1980).

130 Phoebe's name is misspelled as Phebe on the marriage certificate.

131 This is according to his sworn testimony taken on December 16, 1890. Also part of the Home Office record.

132 In some instances in the historical record this is spelled Phebe.

133 Board of Guardian Records, 1834-1906 and Church of England Parish Registers, 1754-1906. London Metropolitan Archives, London.

134 Old Bailey Proceedings Online, November 1890, trial of Mary Eleanor Pearcey (t18901124-43).

135 *Morning Post*, October 28,1890.

136 J.H.H. Gaute and Robin Odell, *Lady Killers* (1980).

137 Old Bailey Proceedings Online, November 1890, trial of Mary Eleanor Pearcey (t18901124-43).

138 *Lloyd's Weekly Newspaper*, November 2, 1890.

139 Old Bailey Proceedings Online, November 1890, trial of Mary Eleanor Pearcey (t18901124-43).

140 *Evening Standard*, December 2, 1890. It was never consistently confirmed whether it was two or three weeks.

141 *Lloyd's Weekly Newspaper*, November 2, 1890.

142 Ibid.

143 Ibid.

144 *Evening Standard*, December 2, 1890.

145 *Freeman's Journal*, October 28, 1890.

146 *Lloyd's Weekly Newspaper*, November 2, 1890.

147 *Freeman's Journal*, October 28, 1890.

148 John Laurence, *Extraordinary Crimes* (1931), p. 217.

149 Ibid. Also read aloud in court: See Old Bailey Proceedings Online, November 1890, trial of Mary Eleanor Pearcey (t18901124-43).

150 *Lloyd's Weekly Newspaper*, November 16, 1890.

151 *Lloyd's* erroneously spelled his name 'Transfield.' But his real name was Robert Tranfield and the 1891 census has him listed as 48 years old and a "licensed victualler" or pub owner. Census Returns of England and Wales, 1891. Kew, Surrey, England: The National Archives of the UK (TNA): Public Record Office (PRO), 1891.

152 1891 Census.

153 *Lloyd's Weekly Newspaper*, November 23, 1890.

154 Ibid.

155 Ibid.

156 Ibid.

157 Ibid. The Earl Cowper (Francis Thomas de Grey Cowper) had a country seat at Wrest Park in Silsoe (now a Grade I listed country house). It is surrounded by the 92 acres of Wrest Park gardens and parkland, also Grade I listed, which edges the village of Silsoe. Therefore, Mary Pearcy was strolling and riding in Wrest Park, which at the time and locally may have been known as Earl Cowper park.

158 *Lloyd's Weekly Newspaper*, November 23, 1890.

159 Ibid.

160 Ibid.

161 Ibid.

162 Ibid.

163 Guy B. Logan, *Rope, Knife and Chair: Studies of English, French and American Crimes* (1928), p. 171. NB: this book was written nearly thirty years after the Hampstead murders, and while it is in line with the sentiment of other predictions Mary made to her mother, it may not be the exact phrasing used by Mary Pearcey.

The Funeral of Phoebe and Tiggie Hogg

1 Phoebe had another older brother, Joseph, who was not recorded as being in attendance.

2 *Evening Standard*, November 3, 1890.

3 Ibid.

4 Ibid.
5 Ibid.
6 *Illustrated Police News*, November 8, 1890.
7 *Evening Standard*, November 3, 1890.
8 Ibid. Islington cemetery was the first municipally-owned cemetery in London. It bordered the ancient Coldfall Wood, a stunning, though overgrown, landscape of sycamore and ash, hawthorn and willow trees appropriately coloured autumn grey, gold and brown.
9 *Illustrated Police News*, November 8, 1890.
10 Ibid.
11 *Herts Advertiser*, November 1, 1890.
12 *Pall Mall Gazette*, November 1, 1890.
13 *Lloyd's Weekly Newspaper*, November 2, 1890.
14 *Evening Standard*, November 3, 1890.
15 *Illustrated Police News*, November 8, 1890.
16 It's unclear where this road was, but it was probably a variant of Kentish Town Road.
17 *Evening Standard*, November 3, 1890.
18 *Pall Mall Gazette*, November 3, 1890.
19 *Evening Standard*, November 3, 1890.
20 *Nottingham Evening Post*, December 3, 1890.

The Committal and Trial

1 *Daily News*, November 4, 1890.
2 Ibid.
3 *Pall Mall Gazette*, November 6, 1890
4 *Herts Advertiser*, December 13, 1890.
5 *Daily News*, November 4, 1890.
6 Ibid.
7 *Daily News*, November 12, 1890.
8 *Daily News*, November 4, 1890.
9 Ibid.
10 Ibid.
11 *Reynolds's Newspaper*, November 9, 1890.
12 Ibid, quoting from Lord Byron's poem *Childe Harold's Pilgrimage*.
13 *The Echo*, November 1, 1890.
14 *Daily News*, November 4, 1890.

15 Ibid.

16 Ibid.

17 Ibid.

18 Ibid.

19 Ibid.

20 Ibid.

21 *Illustrated Police News*, November 8, 1890.

22 *Daily News*, November 4, 1890.

23 Ibid.

24 Ibid.

25 Ibid.

26 Ibid.

27 Ibid.

28 Ibid.

29 *Lloyd's Weekly Newspaper*, November 2, 1890.

30 *Leeds Mercury*, November 4, 1890.

31 *The Graphic*, November 8, 1890.

32 *Daily News*, November 4, 1890.

33 *Lloyd's Weekly Newspaper*, November 2, 1890.

34 Ibid.

35 Ibid.

36 *Illustrated Police News*, November 8, 1890.

37 Ibid.

38 Ibid.

39 *Daily News*, November 10, 1890.

40 Ibid.

41 *Lloyd's Weekly Newspaper*, November 23, 1890.

42 *Daily News*, November 10, 1890.

43 Ibid.

44 Ibid.

45 Ibid.

46 Old Bailey Proceedings Online, November 1890, trial of Mary Eleanor Pearcey (t18901124-43).

47 *Daily News*, November 10, 1890.

48 *Daily News*, November 12, 1890.

49 *Daily News*, November 19, 1890.

50 *Daily News*, November 12, 1890.
51 Ibid.
52 Ibid.
53 Ibid.
54 Ibid.
55 Ibid.
56 Ibid.
57 Ibid.
58 Ibid.
59 *Illustrated Police News*, November 22, 1890.
60 *Daily News*, November 12, 1890.
61 Ibid.
62 Ibid.
63 *Daily News*, November 19, 1890.
64 *Blackburn Standard & Weekly Express*, November 21, 1890.
65 *Reynolds's Newspaper*, November 23, 1890.
66 *Daily News*, November 19, 1890.
67 *Lloyd's Weekly Newspaper*, November 30, 1890.
68 Ibid.
69 *Lloyd's Weekly Newspaper*, November 23, 1890.
70 *Lloyd's Weekly Newspaper*, November 30, 1890.
71 *Cornwall Gazette*, November 20, 1890.
72 *The Times*, November 24, 1890.
73 Ibid.
74 *Pall Mall Gazette*, November 25, 1890.
75 *The Star*, November 25, 1890.
76 *Daily News* November, 26, 1890.
77 Ibid.
78 H.L. Adam, *Old Days at the Old Bailey* (1935), p. 6.
79 *Pall Mall Gazette*, November 26, 1890.
80 Ibid.
81 *Birmingham Daily Post*, November 27, 1890.
82 *Lloyd's Weekly Newspaper*, November 30, 1890.
83 Ibid.
84 Ibid.
85 Ibid.

86 Ibid.

87 R. Thurston Hopkins, *Life and Death at the Old Bailey* (1935), p. 23.

88 H.L. Adam, *Old Days at the Old Bailey* (1935), p. 5.

89 Ibid.

90 Clive Emsley, Tim Hitchcock and Robert Shoemaker, "Historical Background - History of The Old Bailey Courthouse", Old Bailey Proceedings Online.

91 R. Thurston Hopkins, *Life and Death at the Old Bailey* (1935), p. 25.

92 H.L. Adam, *Old Days at the Old Bailey* (1935), p. 6.

93 *Pall Mall Gazette*, December 1, 1890.

94 H.L. Adam, *Old Days at the Old Bailey* (1935), p. 5.

95 *Pall Mall Gazette*, December 1, 1890.

96 *Pall Mall Gazette*, December 4, 1890. This seems to be a reprint of a report in the *Evening Standard*, which had similarly described the scene during the Adelaide Bartlett trial and thus should be read as commentary rather than eyewitness description. For more see Judith Flanders, *The Invention of Murder* (2011), p. 411.

97 Thomas Hardy was 16 the first time he watched a woman hang. Her name was Elizabeth Martha Brown, and she'd murdered her husband, John. Thousands of spectators gathered to watch William Calcraft hang her on August 9, 1856, Hardy among them. He later recalled Elizabeth's "fine figure" silhouetted against the grey mist of a rainy morning. Still impressed by the event years later, he recalled, "the tight black silk gown set off her shape as she wheeled half round and back." Lady Hester Pinney, *Thomas Hardy and the Birdsmoorgate Murder 1856* (1966), p. 2.

98 Martin Seymour-Smith, *Hardy* (1994). Seymour-Smith is describing the attempts of others to determine who Hardy was alluding to when he said in the first edition of Jude the Obscure that the narrative had been partly 'suggested by the death of a woman' in 1890. Michael Millgate's suggestion that it was Mary Pearcey is noted by Seymour-Smith, who also observes that it is not the only suggestion available, and that it is 'a shot in the dark'. He doesn't dismiss it and finds some strengths in it, but he acknowledges that the true source of inspiration might be any 'one of ten thousand news items' which came to Hardy's attention that year.

99 R. Thurston Hopkins, *Life and Death at the Old Bailey* (1935), p. 32.

100 R. Thurston Hopkins, *Life and Death at the Old Bailey* (1935), p. 30.

101 H.L. Adam, *Old Days at the Old Bailey* (1935), p. 6.

102 *Daily News*, December 2, 1890.

103 H.L. Adam, *Old Days at the Old Bailey* (1935), p. 7

104 *Pall Mall Gazette*, December 1, 1890.

105 Ibid.

106 The note, which was not publicised but kept in the Home Office files related to the trial read: "Dear Sir, I can not keep silent any longer about he murder case and I want to tell and clear myself. I am frightened that I shall be hanged if I write my address to you, but I on Friday evening Oct 24th in Crossfield road noticed a woman turning over a perambulator and hurrying away and I went to see the place and I am ashamed to tell but I was starving at the time and took the ring off the woman who was dead. John Maple PS: There was a man with her." The Maple letter was later sent to Robert Anderson to follow up. Inspector Bannister replied to the request for a further inspection of the letter after the trial at the Old Bailey ended. He said that he and his team of detectives had made "every possible effort" to find the missing ring. They'd searched the flats at 2 Priory Street inside and out, searched multiple neighbourhoods, made special inquiries with various pawnbrokers and, frankly, he failed to see "what further enquiry" could be made about the ring or the letter, or indeed Mr Maple. Inspector Bannister thought the letter was a hoax. If Mr Maple suddenly had a change of heart about stealing the ring such that it compelled him to write and post a letter, why wouldn't he have included the pawnbroker's address where he pawned the ring?, Bannister reasoned. As the letter was anonymous, it was "totally unworthy of notice," as far as Bannister was concerned. Besides, the note from Mr Maple, added Superintendent Beard in a postscript in his report, was only "one of many letters written by eccentric and unprincipled persons" who wanted to be part of famous murder case.

107 H.L. Adam, *Old Days at the Old Bailey* (1935), p. 7.

108 By any standards, Fulton was a man of ambition. In 1886, he had been elected to the Commons with a majority of 727 votes, but he made "no particular mark" in Parliament, and was unseated in the next election of 1892, though only by 33 votes. In 1896, he would preside over the trial and wrongful conviction of accused swindler Adolph Beck, but his mishandling of that case resulted in severe chastisement from the Committee of Inquiry established to look into the case, and eventually reforms to protect against

similar miscarriages of justice. Despite this setback, Fulton was knighted and ended his career prestigiously as the Recorder of London. See 'Obituary: Sir Forrest Fulton Thirty Years On', in *The Times*, June 27, 1935; 'Fulton, Sir (James) Forrest', in *Who Was Who*, Oxford: OUP (2007).

109 *Daily News*, December 2, 1890.

110 *Pall Mall Gazette*, December 2, 1890.

111 *Solicitors' Journal and Reporter*, November 25, 1882, Vol. 27, p. 57.

112 H.L. Adam, *Old Days at the Old Bailey* (1935), p. 6.

113 *Bristol Mercury*, December 2, 1890.

114 *Daily News*, December 2, 1890.

115 Ibid.

116 *Bristol Mercury*, December 2, 1890.

117 *Daily News*, December 2, 1890.

118 According to Henry William Buxton, who worked for Frank Hogg's older brother, he and Frank started on jobs at 10 in the morning on Clarence Road in Kentish Town. There, they loaded the removing vans and went to Cromwell Mansions in South Kensington. On the way to Cromwell Mansions, however, the shaft broke and delayed them by about an hour and a quarter. Buxton went back to Kentish Town with the cart to fix it, and they eventually arrived at Cromwell Mansions at around the same time Phoebe Hogg arrived at 2 Priory Street, or 4.00pm. They stopped for tea at a coffee house on Silver Street and arrived back in Kentish Town at Frank's brother's shop at a quarter past seven, and immediately started on another job on Leighton Road. The sum of Buxton's testimony was that he was with Frank from nine o'clock in the morning to a quarter past seven the night of the murders.

119 *Daily News*, December 2, 1890.

120 *Hull Daily Mail*, December 2, 1890.

121 *Daily News*, December 3, 1890.

122 *Lloyd's Weekly Newspaper*, December 7, 1890.

123 *The Times*, December 3, 1890.

124 Ibid.

125 Ibid.

126 Ibid.

127 *Pall Mall Gazette*, December 3, 1890.

128 *The Times*, December 3, 1890.

129 *Daily News*, December 4, 1890.

130 Ibid.

131 Ibid.

132 Ibid.

133 Montagu Williams, *A Magazine of Record and Review*, Vol. XI. Sept-December, 1892, p. 359.

134 *Daily News*, December 4, 1890.

135 In total, Denman rowed in 101 races - losing only 13 - and when he spoke of his own accomplishments, he boasted of his boating triumphs before those he enjoyed in court.

136 H.L. Adam, *Old Days at the Old Bailey* (1935).

137 He was the twelfth child, and seventh son, of Baron Thomas Denman and his wife Theodosia Anne, born on December 23, 1819. The young Denman graduated from Trinity College, Cambridge in October 1838. In February 1852, at 33, Denman married Charlotte Hope of Liverpool and they had six children. Their eldest son, G. L. Denman, would be appointed a Metropolitan Police magistrate in the same year as the Pearcey trial. During his early years practising law Denman acted as a law reporter, learning to take meticulous notes by shorthand, which served him well during the Pearcey trial, as his notes were just shy of verbatim quotes. That meant he didn't have to rely on memory to recall what this or that person said; he merely had to find the reference for it and then could read it, as if a stenographer had written it down for him. In 1859, Denman was elected Member of Parliament for Tiverton, and he held the seat until 1872. While in Parliament, he became interested in the reform of the law of evidence in criminal trials. The Evidence Further Amendment Act of 1869, later known as Denman's Act, was of his entire making and allowed witnesses of no religious belief to "affirm" instead of taking the oath in court, which meant parties otherwise prohibited from giving evidence in a criminal trial, based on an inability or unwillingness to swear on the Bible, could now testify. William Carr, 'Denman, George (1819–1896)', *Oxford Dictionary of National Biography*, 2004-2008.

138 William Carr, 'Denman, George (1819–1896)', *Oxford Dictionary of National Biography*, 2004-2008.

139 *Hull Daily Mail*, December 3, 1890.

140 Ibid.

141 Ibid.

142 *Hull Daily Mail*, December 3, 1890.

143 F. Tennyson Jesse, *Murder and Its Motives* (1958), p. 152.
144 HO 144/237/A52045
145 *Daily News*, December 4, 1890.
146 Ibid.
147 Ibid.
148 Ibid.
149 *Lloyd's Weekly Newspaper*, December 7, 1890.
150 Ibid.
151 Ibid.
152 Ibid.
153 *Daily News*, December 4, 1890.
154 Ibid.
155 Ibid.
156 Ibid.
157 *Lloyd's Weekly Newspaper*, December 7, 1890.
158 *The Times*, December 4, 1890.

The Execution

1 *The Times*, December 4, 1890.
2 *St James's Gazette*, December 9, 1890.
3 *Auckland Times*, December 5, 1890.
4 *Truth*, January 8, 1891.
5 *Lloyd's Weekly Newspaper*, December 7, 1890.
6 Ibid.
7 Ibid.
8 Ibid.
9 Charles Duff, *A Handbook on Hanging* (1928), p. 97.
10 *Lloyd's Weekly Newspaper*, December 14, 1890.
11 *Daily News*, December 5, 1890.
12 *Illustrated Police News*, December 13, 1890.
13 *Daily News*, December 8, 1890.
14 Ibid.
15 *Auckland Times*, December 5, 1890.
16 *Daily News*, December 8, 1890.
17 Ibid.
18 *Lloyd's Weekly Newspaper*, December 28, 1890.

19 H.L. Adam, *Old Days at the Old Bailey* (1935), p. 6.

20 *Lloyd's Weekly Newspaper*, December 14, 1890.

21 *Lloyd's Weekly Newspaper*, December 21, 1890.

22 Ibid.

23 *Daily News*, December 8, 1890.

24 *Lloyd's Weekly Newspaper*, December 21, 1890.

25 *Daily News*, December 8, 1890.

26 *Daily News*, December 9, 1890.

27 *Reynolds's Newspaper*, December 21, 1890.

28 *Daily News*, December 9, 1890.

29 Ibid.

30 Ibid.

31 Ibid.

32 Ibid.

33 Ibid.

34 Ibid.

35 *The Times*, December 4, 1890.

36 *Lloyd's Weekly Newspaper*, December 7, 1890.

37 R.H. Lewis, *Victorian Murders* (1988), p. 112. The following information about Madame Tussaud's purchase of the goods comes from documents cited in Chapman's *Mme Tussaud's Chamber of Horrors*, pp. 99-100, but Chapman is unreliable. She cites *Lloyd's* of November 24, 1890 as the paper from which she pulled most of the details that follow, but that isn't right. Some judgments then need to be made about who might have sold what and when, based on who probably owned the goods, the available source data, and advertisements. The *Leeds Mercury* of December 30, 1890 noted that on display, along with Mrs Pearcey's tableaux, were the receipts for the purchase, signed by Mrs Pearcey and her landlord. Joseph Tussaud's comment can be found in the *Pall Mall Gazette* on October 28, 1892 under the headline 'The Value of the Murderers' Relics.' Pamela Pilbeam's *Mme Tussaud and the History of Waxworks* (2003), p. 179, is also a good source. Frank Hogg's moustache, and the price of the pram, can be found in the *Western Mail*, 'Hogg Sold His Beard', December 24, 1890. No other source suggests that Hogg sold his wife and child's clothes, and Madame Tussaud's did not display a receipt from Hogg, but the clothes are itemised in the advertisement, and it appears likely that he was entitled to sell them.

38 *Leeds Mercury*, December 30, 1890.

39 *Illustrated Police News*, December 13, 1890.

40 *Western Mail*, December 24, 1890; *Lloyd's Weekly Newspaper*, December 21, 1890.

41 *Lloyd's Weekly Newspaper*, December 21, 1890.

42 *Lloyd's Weekly Newspaper*, December 7, 1890.

43 As quoted in Chapman's *Mme Tussaud's Chamber of Horrors*, pp. 99-100. To be read with suspicion.

44 *Evening Standard*, December 27, 1890.

45 Ibid.

46 *Lloyd's Weekly Newspaper*, December 28, 1890.

47 *The World*, December 10, 1890, p. 16.

48 Great Britain. Royal Commission on Capital Punishment (1864-66). Royal Commission on Capital Punishment together with the minutes of evidence and appendix. (Parliamentary Papers, Session 1866, vol. 21).

49 *Reynolds's Newspaper*, December 14, 1890.

50 Ibid.

51 For a more complete look into the Maybrick murder, read Kate Colquhoun's *Did She Kill Him? A Victorian Tale of Deception, Adultery and Arsenic* (2014).

52 *Reynolds's Newspaper*, December 14, 1890.

53 Kate Colquhoun, *Did She Kill Him? A Victorian Tale of Deception, Adultery and Arsenic* (2014), p. 313.

54 Kate Colquhoun, *Did She Kill Him? A Victorian Tale of Deception, Adultery and Arsenic* (2014).

55 Letter sent to a rival newspaper, commented on by *Lloyd's Weekly Newspaper*, December 14, 1890.

56 *Truth*, December 11, 1890.

57 *Truth*, January 1, 1891.

58 Petition to Henry Matthews from Freke Palmer. Received by the Home Office on December 15, 1890. HO 144/237/A52045.

59 Ibid.

60 Ibid.

61 Ibid.

62 Petition to Henry Matthews from Freke Palmer. Received by the Home Office on December 15, 1890. HO 144/237/A52045.

63 Ibid.

64 Judith Knelman, *Twisting in the Wind: The Murderess and the English Press* (University of Toronto Press, 1998), p. 16.

65 There is a long and well-documented historical connection between epilepsy and madness. For a quick introduction into this connection, see Roy Porter's excellent and short book *Madness: A Brief History* (2002).

66 *Pall Mall Gazette*, December 23, 1890.

67 Metropolitan Archives Binder 2, p. 12; note from Home Secretary Matthews written at the bottom of Dr Gilbert's assessment of Mary Eleanor Wheeler.

68 W.T. Stead, 'Government by Journalism' (as quoted in Martin L. Friedland, *The Trials of Israel Lipski* (1984), p. 127.).

69 Molly Whittington-Egan, *Doctor Forbes Winslow: Defender of the Insane* (2000), p. 192.

70 Robin Odell, *Jack the Ripper in Fact and Fiction* (2008 edn), p. 18.

71 In 1843, Daniel M'Naghten shot and killed Edward Drummond, private secretary to Prime Minister Robert Peel, believing it was Peel himself whom he'd shot. Forbes Winslow Sr had taken great interest in the case; prior to the shooting, he had written and published several articles on the legality of executing the insane, one of which had been read by Chief Justice Nicholas Tindal, the judge in the M'Naghten case. Realising Winslow was in the audience, Tindal asked the physician to come to the witness box and give his professional opinion. M'Naghten was acquitted largely on Winslow Sr's testimony, and the psychiatrist became an instant authority on criminal lunacy.

72 L. Forbes Winslow, *Recollections of Forty Years* (1910), p. 166.

73 Ibid. Victorian psychiatry theorised that epileptics could enter a "fugue" state, murder and then exit the state with no memory of the act. Modern psychiatry calls this state dissociative fugue or psychogenic fugue and it is listed in the DSM-5. Though exceedingly rare, it is characterised as a short-term, reversible amnesia that can last hours to days. There are several case studies of dissociative fugue states, most interestingly experienced by the Grande Dame of murder writing, Agatha Christie. See: Cecil Adams, 'Why Did Mystery Writer Agatha Christie Mysteriously Disappear?', *The Chicago Reader*, April 2, 1982.

74 L. Forbes Winslow, *Recollections of Forty Years* (1910), p. 163.

75 *Evening Standard*, December 12, 1890.

76 In his letter, Winslow misspells the man's name as 'Tredaway'. The murder was actually committed in December 1876, although

the trial took place in 1877.

77 Ibid.

78 Ibid.

79 HO 144/237/A52045.

80 *Evening Standard*, December 12, 1890.

81 Ibid.

82 Ibid.

83 L. Forbes Winslow, *Recollections of Forty Years* (1910), p. 165.

84 *Evening Standard*, December 12, 1890.

85 L. Forbes Winslow, *Recollections of Forty Years* (1910), p. 370.

86 *Daily News*, December 18, 1890.

87 Misspelled in the original.

88 L. Forbes Winslow, *Recollections of Forty Years* (1910), p. 166.

89 Ibid.

90 Correspondence from Dr Gilbert dated December 16, 1890. HO 144/237/A52045.

91 Affidavit of George Fielding Blandford, December 13, 1890. HO 144/237/A52045.

92 Affidavit of Charles Crichton, December 10, 1890. HO 144/237/A52045.

93 Ibid.

94 Ibid. The date here is suspect because Mary was purportedly returning from the trip she took with Frank to Silsoe. It could be that either he got the dates wrong, the press reported the dates of the trip incorrectly, or they actually returned home in time for his visit, though it was uncommon for Charles to visit on a Thursday.

95 Ibid.

96 Correspondence from Drs Savage and Bennett dated December 16, 1890. HO 144/237/A52045.

97 Old Bailey Proceedings Online, November 1890, trial of Mary Eleanor Pearcey (t18901124-43).

98 The original Greek word 'hystera' simply meant uterus. Women who couldn't or didn't orgasm and suffered emotionally because of it were said to suffer "uterine melancholy".

99 Correspondence from Drs Savage and Bennett dated December 16, 1890. HO 144/237/A52045.

100 Affidavit of Dr Hubert Thomas Sells, December 16, 1890. HO 144/237/A52045.

101 *Lloyd's Weekly Newspaper*, December 21, 1890.
102 Ibid.
103 Ibid.
104 Ibid.
105 Ibid.
106 Ibid.
107 Ibid.
108 Ibid.
109 Ibid.
110 Ibid.
111 Ibid.
112 Ibid.
113 Ibid.
114 Ibid.
115 *Lloyd's Weekly Newspaper*, December 25, 1890.
116 *Lloyd's Weekly Newspaper*, December 21, 1890.
117 Old Bailey Proceedings Online, November 1890, trial of Mary Eleanor Pearcey (t18901124-43).
118 *Lloyd's Weekly Newspaper*, December 21, 1890.
119 Ibid.
120 Ibid.
121 Ibid.
122 Ibid.
123 Ibid.
124 Ibid.
125 Ibid.
126 Ibid.
127 Ibid.
128 Ibid.
129 We know of one sister who died young: Amelia. But Charlotte, Mary's other known sister, was still alive. It is practically impossible to tell whether this is a journalistic misreading or whether there was another child who died young.
130 *Lloyd's Weekly Newspaper*, December 14, 1890.
131 Ibid.
132 Ibid.
133 Ibid.

134 Ibid.

135 Ibid.

136 Ibid.

137 Ibid.

138 *Illustrated Police News*, December 20, 1890.

139 *Lloyd's Weekly Newspaper*, December 21, 1890.

140 Ibid.

141 *Pall Mall Gazette*, December 22, 1890.

142 Ibid.

143 HO 144/237/A52045

144 *Lloyd's Weekly Newspaper*, December 28, 1890.

145 Stewart P. Evans, *Executioner: The Chronicles of James Berry, Victorian Hangman* (2004), p. 267.

146 H.L. Adam, *Police Work from Within: With some reflections upon women, the law, and lawyers.* Ontario Legislative Library, p. 187. Online version.

147 *Lloyd's Weekly Newspaper*, December 28, 1890.

148 Ibid. There are differences in the accounts; in the *Evening Standard* they arrived only half an hour late. *The Times* says they arrived at 11.20 and were only given 20 minutes (December 23, 1890), but I think Charlotte had been shown kindness before by the gaolers and suspect that 40 minutes was a more reasonable amount of time for a final goodbye.

149 *Evening Standard*, December 23, 1890.

150 *Lloyd's Weekly Newspaper*, December 28, 1890.

151 Ibid.

152 Ibid.

153 Ibid.

154 Ibid.

155 *Pall Mall Gazette*, December 23, 1890.

156 *Lloyd's Weekly Newspaper*, December 28, 1890.

157 Ibid.

158 Ibid.

159 Ibid.

160 Ibid.

161 Ibid.

162 H.L. Adam, *Police Work from Within: With some reflections upon*

women, the law, and lawyers. Ontario Legislative Library, p. 187. Online version.

163 Ibid.

164 *Lloyd's Weekly Newspaper*, December 28, 1890.

165 Ibid.

166 Stewart P. Evans, *Executioner: The Chronicles of James Berry, Victorian Hangman* (2004).

167 Ibid.

168 *Lloyd's Weekly Newspaper*, December 21, 1890.

169 Stewart P. Evans, *Executioner: The Chronicles of James Berry, Victorian Hangman* (2004), p. 267.

170 Ibid.

171 Stewart P. Evans, *Executioner: The Chronicles of James Berry, Victorian Hangman* (2004), p. 335.

172 Geoffrey Abbott, *The Book of Execution: An Encyclopedia of Methods of Judicial Execution* (1995).

173 R. Thurston Hopkins, *Life and Death at the Old Bailey* (1935), p. 21.

174 H.L. Adam, *Police Work from Within: With some reflections upon women, the law, and lawyers*. Ontario Legislative Library, p. 187. Online version.

175 *Lloyd's Weekly Newspaper*, December 21, 1890.

176 *Lloyd's Weekly Newspaper*, December 28, 1890.

177 *Lloyd's Weekly Newspaper*, November 30, 1890.

178 *Lloyd's Weekly Newspaper*, December 28, 1890.

179 Ibid.

180 *Pall Mall Gazette*, December 23, 1890.

181 Ibid.

182 Ibid.

183 Ibid.

184 Ibid.

185 Ibid.

186 Ibid.

187 Stewart P. Evans, *Executioner: The Chronicles of James Berry, Victorian Hangman* (2004), p. 267.

188 *Daily News*, December 24, 1890.

189 Ibid.

190 *Lloyd's Weekly Newspaper*, December 28, 1890.

191 Ibid.

192 Stewart P. Evans, *Executioner: The Chronicles of James Berry, Victorian Hangman* (2004), p. 268.

193 *Daily News*, December 24, 1890. The press were not allowed to see the body despite repeatedly asking Colonel Milman, who said he had no authority to overturn the High Sherriff's order to ban media. Therefore, what we know of how she looked in death is second and third hand.

194 Stewart P. Evans, *Executioner: The Chronicles of James Berry, Victorian Hangman* (2004), p. 267.

195 Ibid.

196 *Pall Mall Gazette*, December 23, 1890.

197 Liverpool Mercury, December 24, 1890.

198 *Pall Mall Gazette*, December 23, 1890.

199 Liverpool Mercury, December 24, 1890.

200 *Pall Mall Gazette*, December 23, 1890.

201 Liverpool Mercury, December 24, 1890.

202 *Pall Mall Gazette*, December 23, 1890.

203 There are conflicting stories about the general mood and tenor of the crowd on the day of her execution, with some reporting a general hum, and others, such as the *Dundee Courier & Argus* of December 24, 1890, reporting more melodramatically, but perhaps incorrectly, "a fierce delight" rippled through the people.

204 *Lloyd's Weekly Newspaper*, December 28, 1890.

205 *Pall Mall Gazette*, December 23, 1890.

206 Ibid.

207 *Daily News*, December 24, 1890.

208 *Lloyd's Weekly Newspaper*, December 28, 1890.

209 Ibid.

210 Ibid.

211 J.H.H. Gaute and Robin Odell, *Lady Killers* (1983), p. 107.

212 *Lloyd's Weekly Newspaper*, December 28, 1890.

213 Ibid.

214 Stewart P. Evans, *Executioner: The Chronicles of James Berry, Victorian Hangman* (2004), p. 317.

215 Stewart P. Evans, *Executioner: The Chronicles of James Berry, Victorian Hangman* (2004), p. 315.

216 *Lloyd's Weekly Newspaper*, December 28, 1890.

217 Ibid.

218 Ibid.

219 Ibid.

220 *The Sunday Times*, December 28, 1890.

Postscript

1 *Pall Mall Gazette*, February 14, 1891.

2 *Nottingham Evening Post*, March 9, 1939.

3 *Reynolds's Newspaper*, December 16, 1890.

4 *Ladykillers* was a Granada Television drama series (1980-81) featuring famous murder cases involving women. 'Killing Mice' (aired on August 10, 1980) was an adaptation of the Mary Pearcey case. It starred Joanna David as Mary Pearcey and Ronald Lacey as Inspector Bannister.

5 www.mirror.co.uk/news/uk-news/exclusive-jill-the-ripper-625801.

6 Stewart P. Evans, *Executioner: The Chronicles of James Berry, Victorian Hangman* (2004), p. 269.

7 Elisabeth Bronfen, *Over Her Dead Body: Femininity, Death and the Aesthetic* (1992), p. 219.

8 F. Tennyson Jesse, *Murder and Its Motives* (Pan Books, 1958).

9 *St James's Gazette*, November 4, 1890.

10 *El Motin*, July 21, 1900.

11 J.H.H. Gaute and Robin Odell, *Murder 'Whatdunit'* (St. Martin's Press, 1982).

12 Judith Flanders, *The Invention of Murder* (2011), p. 409.

13 Judith Knelman, *Twisting in the Wind: The Murderess and the English Press* (University of Toronto Press, 1998), p. 8.

14 F. Tennyson Jesse, *Murder and Its Motives* (Pan Books, 1958), p. 166.

15 *Evening Telegraph*, October 27, 1890.

SELECT BIBLIOGRAPHY

Archives

LMA: Board of Guardian Records, 1834-1906 and
Church of England Parish Registers, 1754-1906
National Archives: HO 144/237/A52045
Old Bailey Proceedings Online, November 1890, trial of Mary Eleanor Pearcey (t18901124-43)
Queensland State Archives; Registers of Immigrant Ships' Arrivals; Series: Series ID 13086; Roll: M1700
Royal Commission on Capital Punishment (1864-66). Royal Commission on Capital Punishment together with the minutes of evidence and appendix. (Parliamentary Papers, Session 1866, vol. 21)

Newspapers and Magazines

Aberdeen Evening Express
Auckland Times
Belfast News-Letter
Birmingham Daily Post
Blackburn Standard & Weekly Express
Bristol Mercury
Bristol Mercury & Daily Post
British Medical Journal
Canterbury Journal, Kentish Times & Farmers' Gazette
Cornwall Gazette
Daily News
Derby Daily Telegraph
Devon & Exeter Gazette

El Motin
Evening News and Post
Evening Standard
Evening Telegraph
Freeman's Journal
Herts Advertiser
Hull Daily Mail
Illustrated Police News
Leeds Mercury
Liverpool Mercury
Lloyd's Weekly Newspaper
Manchester Guardian
Morning Post
North-Eastern Daily Gazette
Nottingham Evening Post
Oxford Dictionary of National Biography
Pall Mall Gazette
Portsmouth Evening News
Reynolds's Newspaper
Ripperologist
Sheffield Evening Telegraph
Singapore Free Press and Mercantile Advertiser
St James's Gazette
St. Pancras Guardian
The Echo
The Lancet
The News & Observer
The Scotsman
The Star
The Sunday Times
The Times
The World
Truth
Western Mail
Women's Penny Paper
Yorkshire Post and Leeds Intelligencer

Books

Abbott, Geoffrey, *The Book of Execution: An Encyclopedia of Methods of Judicial Execution* (1995)

Adam, H.L., *Old Days at the Old Bailey* (1935)

Adam, H.L., *Police Work from Within: With some reflections upon women, the law, and lawyers* (Ontario Legislative Library, Online version)

Barrow, Lauren, Ron Rufo and Saul Arambula, *Police and Profiling in the United States: Applying Theory to Criminal Investigations* (2014)

Begg, Paul, Martin Fido and Keith Skinner, *The Jack the Ripper A to Z* (1991)

Bell, Neil R.A., Trevor N. Bond, Kate Clarke and M.W. Oldridge, *The A-Z of Victorian Crime* (2016)

Bly, Nellie (aka Elizabeth Jane Cochrane Seaman), *Ten Days in a Mad-House* (1887)

Bronfen, Elisabeth, *Over Her Dead Body: Femininity, Death and the Aesthetic* (1992)

Browne, Douglas G., and E.V. Tullett, *The Scalpel of Scotland Yard* (1952)

Clarkson, Charles Tempest and J. Hall Richardson, *Police!* (1889)

Colquhoun, Kate, *Did She Kill Him? A Victorian Tale of Deception, Adultery and Arsenic* (2014)

Cullen, Tom, *When London Walked in Terror* (1965)

Denford, Steven, *Streets of Kentish Town* (Camden History Society, 2005)

Duff, Charles, *A Handbook on Hanging* (1928)

Ellis, Havelock, *Studies in the Psychology of Sex* (1927)

Evans, Stewart P., *Executioner: The Chronicles of James Berry, Victorian Hangman* (2004)

Flanders, Judith, *The Invention of Murder* (2011)

Gaute, J.H.H. and Robin Odell, *Lady Killers* (1983)

Gaute, J.H.H. and Robin Odell, *Murder 'Whatdunit'* (1982)

Graham,Clare, *Ordering Law: The Architectural and Social History of the English Law Courts* (2003)

Hopkins, R. Thurston, *Life and Death at the Old Bailey* (1935)

Howe, S.G., *On the Causes of Idiocy* (1858)

Jesse, F. Tennyson, *Murder and Its Motives* (1958)

Joseph, Keith, 'Introduction' in *Samuel Smiles, Self Help* (1859, 1986 edn)

Knelman, Judith, *Twisting in the Wind: The Murderess and the English Press* (1998)

LaPlante, Eva, *Seized: Temporal Lobe Epilepsy as Medical, Historical, and Artistic Phenomenon* (2000)

Laurence, John, *Extraordinary Crimes* (1931)

Lewis, R.H., *Victorian Murders* (1988)

Logan, Guy B., *Rope, Knife and Chair: Studies of English, French and American Crimes* (1928)

Macnaghten, Melville, *Days of My Years* (1914)

Mann, J. Dixon, *Forensic Medicine & Toxicology* (1893)

Mitchell, Sally, *Daily Life in Victorian England* (2008 edn)

Mitton, Lavinia, *The Victorian Hospital* (2008)

Newburn, Tim, Alan Wright and Tom Williamson, *Handbook of Criminal Investigation* (2007)

Odell, Robin, *Jack the Ripper in Fact and Fiction* (2008 edn)

Pilbeam, Pamela, *Mme Tussaud and the History of Waxworks* (2003)

Pinney, Lady Hester, *Thomas Hardy and the Birdsmoorgate Murder 1856* (1966)

Porter, Roy, *Madness: A Brief History* (2002)

Ramsland, Katherine, *Beating the Devil's Game: A History of Forensic Science and Criminal Investigation* (2007)

Reinarz, Jonathan and Leonard Schwarz (eds), *Medicine and the Workhouse* (2013)

Richardson, John, *Camden Town and Primrose Hill Past* (2002)

Robbins, Jane, *The Magnificent Spilsbury and the Case of the Brides in the Bath* (2010)

Roberts, Margaret and Michael Wink (eds), *Alkaloids: Biochemistry, Ecology, and Medicinal Applications* (1998)

Seymour-Smith, Martin, *Hardy* (1994)

Shorvon, Simon, *Handbook of Epilepsy Treatment* (2010 edn)

Taylor, Robert, *White Coat Tales: Medicine's Heroes, Heritage, and Misadventures* (2007)

Whittington-Egan, Molly, *Doctor Forbes Winslow: Defender of the Insane* (2000)

Williams, Montagu, *A Magazine of Record and Review,* (Vol. XI. September-December, 1892)

Winslow, L. Forbes, *Recollections of Forty Years* (1910)

Woodhead, G. Sims, *Practical Pathology* (3rd Edition, 1892)

INDEX

CPSIA information can be obtained
at www.ICGtesting.com
Printed in the USA
BVHW041217060620
580860BV00002B/232

9 780253 034625